TREACHEROUS PASSAGE

Treacherous Passage

*Germany's Secret Plot against
the United States in Mexico
during World War I*

BILL MILLS

POTOMAC BOOKS
An imprint of the University of Nebraska Press

Library of Congress Cataloging-in-Publication Data
Names: Mills, Bill, 1958– author.
Title: Treacherous passage: Germany's secret plot
against the United States in Mexico during World
War I / Bill Mills.
Description: Lincoln: Potomac Books, an imprint
of the University of Nebraska Press, 2016. | Includes
bibliographical references and index.
Identifiers: LCCN 2016010733 | ISBN 9781612348544
(cloth: alk. paper) | ISBN 9781612348735 (epub) |
ISBN 9781612348742 (mobi) | ISBN 9781612348759
(pdf)
Subjects: LCSH: World War, 1914–1918—Diplomatic
history. | Mexico—Foreign relations—Germany. |
Germany—Foreign relations—Mexico. | World
War, 1914–1918—United States.
Classification: LCC D619.3 .M56 2016 | DDC
940.4/87430972—dc23 LC record available at
https://lccn.loc.gov/2016010733

Set in Minion by Westchester Publishing Services.

For Michelle and Darcy

CONTENTS

ILLUSTRATIONS

ACKNOWLEDGMENTS

This book had an unusual inception. While researching my previous work, *The League*, a history of the American Protective League—the Justice Department's volunteer detective force during World War I, I came across a thrilling account about a German raider called the *Alexander Agassiz* that was captured by a U.S. Navy gunboat off the coast of Mexico. According to the writer, the *Agassiz* was seized as the result of a conversation overheard by an undercover operative in a San Diego restaurant.

Years later, while searching through the records of the U.S. National Archives, I discovered that this period account of the *Alexander Agassiz* affair was fiction, either invented by the author or the result of reliance on inaccurate records. Delving deeper into the background of the episode I found truth more amazing than fiction, a tale of soldiers of fortune training a German Mexican army to invade the United States, sunken warships reclaimed from the sea for battle, a formidable German trading house dedicated to profit and subversion, heroes and turncoats, drama on the high seas and in high court. The more that I learned about this forgotten true-life adventure, the more fascinated I became, and soon began writing the manuscript that developed into *Treacherous Passage*.

Many talented individuals assisted in gathering the material for this book. Researcher-translator Manuel Osuna was invaluable in tracking down records in Mazatlán, Mexico, and providing Spanish translation. Manuel is an uncompromising and determined researcher. When a key publication from the 1920s was discovered missing at a city archive, Manuel tracked down a college professor who had a photocopy of the document and sent me a copy of the photocopy! Heather Smedberg in Special Collections &

Archives at the UC San Diego Library located extensive documentation on the early history of the *Alexander Agassiz* and the Marine Biological Station in the Scripps Institution of Oceanography Archives. Annegret Wilke of Politisches Archiv des Auswärtigen Amts (Political Archive of the German Foreign Office in Berlin) gave generously of her time to locate German government records related to Fritz Unger's appointment as honorary consul in Mazatlán. Rebecca Livingston did an outstanding and exhaustive job combing through State Department and Military Intelligence records on Dr. Paul Bernardo Altendorf held in the National Archives at College Park Maryland. Archivist Jennifer Albin was extremely helpful in locating the complete court records of the *Alexander Agassiz* Prize Court Trial at the National Archives at Riverside, California.

I am also very thankful for the support and guidance of my exceptional agent, Anne Devlin, and for the enthusiasm and editorial skill of Tom Swanson and the aid of Emily Wendell at Potomac Books, University of Nebraska Press.

For the assistance provided by all of these individuals I remain deeply grateful.

Prologue

"The *Morelos* Will Be Ours"

The mutiny on board the federal gunboat *Tampico* began over love for a woman. It was said that twenty-four-year-old Lieutenant Hilario Malpica, the ship's executive officer, had fallen for a brown-eyed beauty whose family was devoted to the Constitutionalist cause. For weeks, Malpica had secretly plotted to take over the Mexican warship for the Constitutionalist rebel forces. His opportunity came on the night of February 22, 1914, when half the ship's company had been granted shore leave to celebrate the Carnival at Guaymas. Aided by Rabatet, the paymaster, and engineering officers Estrada and Johnson, Malpica took charge of the remaining crew members, then boldly informed Captain Castellanos and Chief Engineer Smith that their ship was under mutiny, and invited them to join the rebel forces. The invitation was rejected out of hand.

"If you make no resistance you will not be harmed," Malpica told them evenly, "and at the first opportunity you will be handed over to the federal government."

His former superiors acquiesced, and the rebels gained their first naval gunboat without a struggle. Now fully in command, Malpica gave orders to set course for Topolobampo on the Gulf of California in northwestern Mexico, a port that had recently been captured by the Constitutionalists.

As the *Tampico* steamed away from Guaymas, Malpica was presented with an incredible opportunity. The federal gunboat *Guerrero*, unaware of the mutiny on her sister ship, cruised directly across the *Tampico*'s bow. Standing at the helm, Malpica directed his crew to ram her at full speed. The *Tampico* was a modern steel-hulled gunboat equipped with a ram bow, and its impact on the unsuspecting *Guerrero* would have been truly devastating. Unfortunately for the mutineers, however, the *Tampico*'s steering gear broke down in the effort and she was forced to turn away, continuing on course to Topolobampo.

The mutiny on the gunboat *Tampico* was a minor act in a drama being played out across revolutionary Mexico in 1914. The year before, after a confused period of street fighting and artillery duels between loyalist and rebel army factions in Mexico City that would become known as *La Decena Trágica* (the Tragic Ten Days), General Victoriano Huerta had seized control of the government in a coup d'état. The democratically elected president, Francisco Madero, and his vice president, José María Pino Suárez, were driven to the outskirts of Mexico City at midnight and executed. Now established as "president," Huerta ruled the country with an iron fist. When a courageous senator from the state of Chiapas, Belisario Domínguez, gave a public speech denouncing Huerta as a tyrant, Domínguez was brutally murdered, his bullet-ridden body found weeks later in a roadside ditch. In the Mexican congress, Huerta was harshly castigated for the crime. In retaliation, Huerta dissolved the congress and ordered 110 congressmen to be arrested and hauled off to prison. Despite these repressive actions, Huerta's military dictatorship had the support of powerful factions in Mexico, including the hacendados, large landowners who wanted to retain their vast landholdings from populist confiscation, the Mexican Army, and initially, the church.

Outside Mexico City, opposition grew quickly against President Huerta, *El Usurpador*, "the usurper" who had murdered Madero. The governor of the state of Coahuila, tall and dignified former senator Venustiano Carranza, demanded the immediate ouster of Huerta and restoration of the Constitution of 1857, which had guaranteed Mexican citizens freedom of speech, freedom of the press, and freedom of assembly. Carranza proclaimed himself "Primer Jefe" (First Chief) of the Constitutionalists, and named Alvaro Obregón, a rancher from Sonora, as commander in chief of a Constitutionalist army in the northwest. Obregón proved an able organizer and military strategist, raising a powerful army that captured one federal town after another. Also allied with Carranza in the north was bandit-turned-revolutionary Pancho Villa, who transformed a ragtag group of disaffected workers from rural mining camps, haciendas, and villages into a sizable army that pursued Huerta's forces like a desert horde. In southern Mexico, Emiliano Zapata, who for years had been leading a campesino revolt against the hacendados who had stolen their land, similarly turned his followers against the Huerta government. By early 1914, less than a year after Huerta had assumed power, over 70 percent of Mexican territory was controlled by the Constitutionalist forces. Now with the mutiny on the *Tampico*, the revolution had advanced onto Mexican waters as well.

Steaming across the Sea of Cortez toward Topolobampo, Malpica knew that when word reached Mexico City that the *Tampico* had gone over to the Constitutionalists, the Huertistas would be hunting for him. He knew exactly who his pursuers would be—just as they knew *him*, for at the youthful age of twenty-four, Malpica had already served aboard most of the ships in the small Mexican navy. He understood the strengths and weaknesses of each gunboat just as he understood those of the officers who commanded them.

Hilario Malpica Rodríguez Saliva had entered the Heroica Escuela Naval Militar, the Mexican military naval school, as a cadet at the age of fifteen. After completing his studies, Naval Cadet Malpica was posted to the training boat *Yucatán* where he learned to maneuver a ship, and then to the gunboats *Bravo* and *Morelos* where he mastered the art of naval gunnery, before receiving his assignment on board the *Tampico*.

After Huerta seized power, the warships of the Mexican navy were dispersed to the regions of the western and gulf coasts, which were confronted with the greatest amount of rebel activity. The *Tampico* had been sent to northwestern Mexico where fighting was constant. Serving with distinction under fire, Malpica had been awarded the Medal of Naval Merit for valor, and was promoted to lieutenant. His superiors considered Malpica to be an intelligent and resourceful officer. He was particularly good at naval gunnery. They were qualities that would be sorely tested in the weeks ahead.

In February 1914, the Federal navy of Mexico had three warships patrolling the country's western coast: the gunboat *Guerrero*, at a displacement of 1,850 tons, almost a small cruiser, the 1,260-ton gunboat *Morelos*, and the smallest vessel of the lot at 980 tons, the *Tampico*. In addition to being larger than the *Tampico*, the *Guerrero* and *Morelos* were faster and better armed, carrying twice as many cannons. Operating in tandem, they would be a formidable, perhaps unbeatable opponent. The *Tampico*'s survival would depend heavily on Malpica's skill as a commander, and on his luck.

The *Tampico* steamed into Topolobampo harbor on the afternoon of February 24, 1914. While the crew took on coal and provisions, the former captain and chief engineer of the gunboat were placed on board the SS *Herrerias*, a steam-powered freighter headed south for Mazatlán, a coastal town still in federal hands. Malpica established contact with the governor of Sinaloa, Felipe Riveros, who relayed word of the *Tampico* mutiny to "Primer Jefe" himself, Venustiano Carranza. The rebel leader responded to the news of the ship's capture by promoting Malpica to Capitán de Navío, and announcing his official appointment as commander of the Constitutionalist gunboat.

As the days slowly passed in peaceful Topolobampo, the mutineers busied themselves preparing the *Tampico* for the inevitable battle to come.

They would not have long to wait.

Shortly after dawn on March 2, a large ship was spotted on the horizon. The federal gunboat *Guerrero* steamed into view and then anchored in a sheltered position just outside the harbor. The next morning, the gunboat *Morelos* appeared and moored next to the *Guerrero*.

The new arrivals brought a fleet of onlookers in their wake. In 1914, the west coast of Mexico teemed with warships from America, Britain, Germany, France and Japan, sent to protect their country's interests in Mexico from revolutionary unrest. The U.S. Navy alone had assigned sixteen ships to patrol the Mexican coast, and one of these, the cruiser USS *New Orleans*, was under orders to follow the gunboat *Guerrero* and report her every move to Naval Operations.

For three weeks, the *Tampico* remained sheltered within the safe confines of Topolobampo harbor, only venturing out of her secure anchorage for a few brief skirmishes with the two federal gunboats. The impasse continued until March 31, when the *Tampico* built up steam, raised anchor, and boldly proceeded down the channel. The *Guerrero* got under way at once and took up a position at the mouth of the harbor, with her broadside facing the *Tampico*. At a range of nine thousand yards the *Guerrero* opened fire and the *Tampico* instantly responded. It was the opening salvo of an intense, if erratic, artillery duel, in which each gunboat released volleys of 4-inch and 6-pounder rounds in the general direction of their adversary. For over two hours the roar of cannon fire echoed across the channel, with geysers of white water erupting from a seemingly endless succession of missed shots.

After three hundred shells had been expended, the firing suddenly ceased. With darkness fast approaching, the *Tampico* came about and headed back into the harbor, while the *Guerrero* returned to her anchorage outside the bar. Unknown to her adversaries, the *Tampico* had been struck seven times during the lengthy engagement—two 4-inch shells had passed through the officer's quarters, one 4-inch shell struck amidships, and four 4-inch shells hit her bow, one below the waterline. Incredibly, none of Malpica's mutineers had been injured. The *Guerrero*, in turn, had been struck three times, resulting in no significant damage.

A few days later, suspecting that the *Tampico* was aground, the gunboat *Morelos* made a cautious reconnaissance inside the channel to assess the smaller boat's condition. They discovered the *Tampico* sunk on the south side of the waterway near Shell Point, with waves rolling across the length of her deck. The gunboat had already been stripped of armament for the rebel forces—just two 4-inch cannon and one 6-pounder remained on their mounts.

With the *Tampico* no longer a threat, the *Morelos* departed for Mazatlán, a federal town that was under siege by the Constitutionalist armies, while the *Guerrero* steamed off to patrol the coast between Guaymas and Mazatlán and provide assistance to Huerta's troops where needed.

The fact that his command was now underwater did not weaken Malpica's resolve to defeat the enemy gunboats. The immediate problem was simple enough—the *Tampico* would have to be raised and restored to battle-ready condition. The warship remained submerged in the harbor until a deep-sea diving outfit could be located and men sent down to plug the holes in the gunboat's armored hull. When it was watertight, compressed air was pumped inside and the *Tampico* was brought to the surface. The gunboat was towed to the Topolobampo dock, where the ship's officers directed the repairs needed to return the salvaged vessel to serviceable condition. It would take months of hard work before she would be fit to sail again.

While Malpica's men struggled to make the *Tampico* seaworthy, the crew of the federal gunboat *Morelos* were having troubles of their own. The port city of Mazatlán had been under siege by the Constitutionalists for nine months when the *Morelos* steamed into its dangerous waters in May 1914. Over ten thousand rebel troops encircled the beleaguered city and terror gripped the population. Every inhabitant capable of leaving had fled to safer ground in the neighboring towns and villages. The city's water supply had been cut early in the siege, and now citizens and federal garrison troops alike relied on water from cisterns and public wells to survive. Food remained available only because federal gunboats kept the port open for supply from the sea; without the Federal navy, Mazatlán would have been starved into submission long ago.

The harbor was a hazardous anchorage at the best of times. From the south, it was exposed to the open ocean, while along the north and middle harbor, shifting currents formed hidden shoals and sandbars that made passage treacherous. As the *Morelos* steamed warily past the Faro Lighthouse into the inner harbor, suddenly, without warning, the unthinkable happened—the gunboat ran aground on a submerged shoal. To make matters infinitely worse, it grounded a few hundred yards from Isla de las Piedras "Stone Island," a towering mass of land near the mouth of the harbor, within easy rifle range of the Constitutionalist troops. Concern turned quickly to alarm. No matter what the federal sailors tried, the heavy gunboat remained hard and fast on the rocky shoal.

Observing the situation from a distant vantage point, General Obregón, the Constitutionalists' commander, released a message to the press: "The *Morelos* will be ours."

Shortly after five o'clock on the morning of May 5, Cinco de Mayo, a detachment of rebel riflemen took up positions among the rocks and cactus at the top of Manzanillo Point, the heights of Piedras, and opened fire on the stranded warship. A fusillade of bullets ricocheted off her armored superstructure and zinged through the air. "The *Morelos* answered with her six-pounders. The shots (being) fired by her could be seen to strike at various places along the face of the bluff, each kicking up a cloud of dust." The exchange between the rebel riflemen on the heights and the gunboat's artillery below continued throughout the day, as casualties began to mount on the motionless warship.

Frank Smith, a young Marine aboard the USS *California* watching the spectacle from a distance, observed: "As the firing continued after dark, the *Morelos*'s projectiles, in striking the rocky surface, would flash fire, and could be seen to dart in every direction. An occasional projectile would strike a granite shoulder and ricochet vertically into the air . . . The rebels made their share of the noise, although with smaller (field) guns than the Federals were using. Following each boom of the guns of the *Morelos* could be heard the cracking of hundreds of rifles . . . The *Morelos* ceased firing after a time, though an occasional rifle shot could be heard throughout the night."

The next morning, the duel between the Constitutionalist riflemen on the crest of the ridge and the gunners on the *Morelos* resumed. Artillery from the Federal fort Reynaldo Díaz on the opposite side of the harbor joined the fight, firing over the *Morelos* and driving the rebels from the crest of Piedras. But with each lull in the cannonade, the riflemen regained their positions and raked the *Morelos*'s decks with a shower of bullets.

On the morning of May 7, a new combatant joined the battle, when the federal gunboat *Guerrero* steamed into the east side of the harbor and trained her guns on the ridge. "After an hour or two of intermittent firing [from the *Guerrero*] without any apparent damage except for one shot which went high and demolished a building in the city, she then moved out of range of the rebel's field guns and anchored. There was considerable firing by the Federal fort, the *Morelos*, and the rebels during the day and evening, but [by] the following morning all was quiet."

Recognizing the hopelessness of their position on the stranded gunboat, with no chance of reinforcement or supply, the crew of the *Morelos* had lowered their flag under the cover of darkness and taken to the boats, abandoning their dead on the bullet-swept decks.

A team of rebel soldiers in canoes made their way to the grounded warship and set it afire with oil-soaked rags. After they departed, "the bridge and foremast became a pillar of flame. Quickly the flames crept aft along the decks of the *Morelos*. Intermittent reports and sharp gleams of light told that the fire had reached the ammunition. The sounds became more distinct, and presently combined in a furious din of cannonading, as if the dead gunners had arisen and were once more at the battery. For several hours the fire burned until the bridge and foremast fell in a great roar of flame and sparks. But for some strange reason, the fire reached no further aft than amidships. It halted at the funnels." The gunboat *Morelos*, once the pride of the Mexican navy, was a blackened hulk on the glistening blue waters of Mazatlán harbor.

Obregón's prophesy—"the *Morelos* will be ours"—had come true.

The destruction of the *Morelos* filled Malpica and his men with renewed energy to complete the repairs on the refloated *Tampico*. Only one federal warship now remained to challenge their control of the west coast of Mexico—the *Guerrero*.

To speed the *Tampico*'s return to service, the young captain decided to take the gunboat on a short voyage to Altata for an extensive overhaul. But despite weeks of expedient repair work, the ship was still far from seaworthy. Although the hull was watertight and the vessel remained solidly afloat, shell holes received during the last engagement had been plugged with makeshift leak-stoppers. Her 4-inch guns were in deplorable condition, with the breech blocks loose on their hinges, the barrel rifling dangerously eroded, and the sights, wobbly and out of alignment. The guns were now more dangerous to the crew than to any enemy. The boat's main engines, rusty and coated with grime, were only capable of operating at their slowest speed. Hundreds of holes in the boiler piping had been "corked" with wooden plugs. The generator had been ruined by saltwater while the ship sat submerged and there was no electric power on board; the compartments below were now illuminated by kerosene lanterns. The *Tampico*'s deck was littered with broken cases, bales of hay, damaged wooden fittings, and scattered rounds of ammunition. Three cows added to the disorder, wandering aimlessly through the debris, occasionally depositing manure onto the clutter.

On June 14, 1914, the *Tampico* departed Topolobampo harbor under the power of a single boiler for Altata, where Malpica planned to retube the ship's boilers, rebuild the machinery, and set out after the *Guerrero*. Once his nemesis had been destroyed, the *Tampico* could eliminate the merchant steamers trading with the federal strongholds of Guaymas and Mazatlán, cutting their supply of provisions and forcing them to surrender.

The gunboat had traveled only thirty miles from Topolobampo when disaster struck. A team of inexperienced firemen tending the only functioning boiler shoveled too much coal into the firebox and ruined it. With its boiler burned out, the *Tampico* was at the mercy of the elements, helplessly adrift on the rolling sea.

The next day a large ship was sighted to the east. It approached to within two miles of the idle gunboat and abruptly stopped. To the great relief of the men on board the *Tampico*, it was the destroyer USS *Preble*, one of the American warships that had been dispatched to observe naval activity along the waters of revolutionary Mexico. A launch was lowered from the *Tampico*, and Rabatet, the former paymaster, motored over to the *Preble* and presented Malpica's compliments to Lieutenant J. H. Klein Jr., the destroyer's commander. Rabatet optimistically described the current state of the *Tampico* for the American officer, telling him that repairs would be quickly completed and by sunset the gunboat would be on her way to Altata. Rabatet then saluted and returned to his ship.

A few hours later, a second boat from the *Tampico* visited the *Preble*, this time with chief engineer Johnson and his assistant Estrada aboard. They told Klein the sorry truth that the crew had been unable to repair the boilers. The *Tampico* was now at the mercy of the sea, and if assistance was not provided, the ship would gradually drift ashore.

"Can you tow us the eighty miles to Altata?" Johnson anxiously inquired.

"We cannot," Klein replied, "I have received orders to observe strict neutrality."

The Mexican officers begged Klein to send a radio message to the American admiral requesting approval for the *Preble* to tow their ship to Altata. Johnson also relayed an invitation from Captain Malpica, asking the American commander to come aboard the *Tampico* to meet with him. Klein sent the radiogram to the commander in chief of the U.S. Pacific Fleet as requested, and a few hours later departed on a launch for the *Tampico*.

In his official report, Lieutenant Klein described his visit to the Mexican gunboat:

> At about 5:30 p.m., I boarded the *Tampico*. Captain Malpica excused himself for not having called, pointing to bandages on his left foot. [Malpica's foot had been injured two weeks earlier, and as a result he could only hobble about.] During my conversation with him I gained a very favorable impression of his ability and determination. He spoke a little English, and, with my poor scraps of Spanish, we managed to piece out a very fair conversation. He seemed very grateful for my having forwarded his request for a tow to the commander-in-chief, and was anxious for me to inspect his ship thoroughly, to see for myself in what a pitiful condition she was. Accompanied by the executive and the chief engineer, I inspected the ship from truck to keel.
>
> I was most anxious to see her, but as the inspection progressed I grew more and more depressed. It was impossible to see such a helpless vessel, completely at the mercy of the wind and sea, totally unfit to steam or remain afloat, much less commence the unequal struggle with the *Guerrero* which was imminent and inevitable, without a feeling of pity for these poor fellows. Above all, I could not suppress a feeling of admiration for this brave man, which increased at the end of the inspection, when upon asking Malpica what he would do if the *Guerrero* appeared, he defiantly answered: "I'll fight her and sink her if she will only come within range of my guns." These words could only come from either a fanatic or a remarkably determined man.
>
> Before I left, he insisted that I have a drink with him . . . He seemed loath to have me go, and made me promise that I would come aboard at noon the next day to sample a cocktail for which he claimed exceptional virtues.

Lieutenant Klein returned to the *Preble* and watched the *Tampico* with deep apprehension, wondering whether Malpica would be alive the next day to keep their drinking engagement. Hours later, the destroyer's radioman intercepted a message from the USS *New Orleans* stating that the cruiser was now trailing the *Guerrero* on a southerly course. Based on the direction and speed that was given, Klein determined that the powerful *Guerrero* would pass the present location of the *Tampico* at 7 a.m. the next day.

Few of the men aboard the *Preble* slept soundly that night, knowing the surprise that lay in store for the helpless *Tampico*, but also aware that they could not warn her without violating the orders from the U.S. naval command to assist neither side.

At dawn two ships were seen rapidly approaching from the north, the Mexican gunboat *Guerrero*, followed by the *New Orleans*. The *Guerrero* soon spotted the smaller *Tampico* at anchor and cleared for action. The *Tampico*, in turn, hoisted an enormous Mexican national ensign to the gaff and also made ready for action. The *Guerrero* and *Tampico* would face each other flying the *same* national colors.

True to his vow, Malpica fired first, releasing a salvo at the *Guerrero* from his 4-inch guns that fell four hundred yards short at a range of eight thousand yards. The *Guerrero* responded with a single 4-inch shell that landed one thousand yards *over* the *Tampico*. For the next thirty minutes the two ships exchanged artillery fire with equally poor results. Some of the *Tampico's* shells dropped halfway to the *Guerrero*, likely the result of ammunition that was defective from having been underwater for several months. To the American observers, the *Guerrero's* point of aim, in turn, appeared to be "the Gulf of California," with the distance of its shell bursts from the *Tampico* sometimes measured in *miles* instead of *yards*. (After one particularly bad shot by the *Guerrero*, a quartermaster aboard the USS *Preble* was heard to say, "Those boobs on the *Tampico* will starve to death before the *Guerrero* hits her.")

Eventually the *Guerrero* closed in on the stationary *Tampico*, launching shrapnel shells that struck between the smoke stack and forward bridge. Flames instantly erupted from the quarterdeck and soon spread across the entire ship. With no pressure in the water mains, there was no hope of the crew extinguishing the fire, and preparations for abandoning ship began in earnest.

The *Tampico's* gas-powered launch and one "pulling boat" came around her bow to the starboard side where a number of crewmen leapt on board, then motored to the port side where other sailors did the same. The flames on the quarter deck had flared up and a large volume of smoke enveloped the 4-inch gun on the after deck. In spite of this, the gun crew defiantly released a few final rounds, while one of the gunners stood up on the burning poop deck and waved a large flag.

The gasoline launch and the pulling boat quickly came about and headed toward shore, hoping to reach the safety of shoal water. The *Guerrero* set off in pursuit at full speed to intercept them. After a chase that lasted half an hour, the *Guerrero* caught up with the two boatloads of men. With no chance of escape, the *Tampico*'s sailors pulled their boats alongside the *Guerrero* and a ladder was lowered for them to climb into captivity.

Captain Malpica stood at the bow of the lead boat in full view of the men on board. Malpica was a man of great honor and pride, unable to accept the dishonor of having failed in his mission to vanquish the federal navy for the Constitutionalists, and of failing the woman that he loved. He scanned the faces of the men lining the deck above him. Then with chin held high, Malpica removed his revolver from its holster, calmly raised it to his head, and pulled the trigger.

There was a sharp report and he crumpled to the deck.

The men aboard the *Guerrero* stared down at Malpica's lifeless form in stunned disbelief. The federal gunboat immediately half-masted her colors, and the two American warships followed suit. The commander of the *Guerrero* sent a radio message to the captain of the *New Orleans*, thanking the Americans for lowering their colors "in honor of Malpica." Captain Irwin of the *New Orleans* and Lieutenant Klein of the *Preble* called upon the commanding officer of the *Guerrero*. In a later account of the visit, Klein wrote:

We met the captain and the executive officer, and had a short talk with them. They showed us the two holes in the *Guerrero*, which had done no damage to either ship or personnel. There was no gayety or any feeling of exultation aboard that ship; to the contrary, a funereal air seemed to pervade everybody and everything. They were very sorry that the battle had had to be fought, and especially regretted the death of Malpica. As they said, Malpica had been respected and admired by all the officers of the *Guerrero*, many of whom had previously served with him. They were profuse in their praises of his courage and ability and mourned his loss as that of a true friend instead of a defeated enemy. The captain of the *Guerrero* stated that the prisoners would be treated kindly and I doubted very much if he would turn them over to the Federal authorities when he reached Mazatlán.

Across the water, the flaming wreck of the *Tampico* gradually listed to starboard. Clouds of steam soon rose from the stricken vessel as seawater reached her boilers. The gunboat rocked sharply to starboard, and the bow came up vertically, then she sank by the stern in 130 feet of water. When the *Guerrero* steamed off, trailed by the two American warships, all that remained of the *Tampico* were a few bits of floating debris bobbing on the dark blue waves.

Malpica's body was taken to Maztlan, where the captain of the *Guerrero*, Ignacio Arenas, and his crew purchased a plot in perpetuity in the city cemetery for their fallen comrade. Lumber was scarce, so the men cut up tables and used the wood to craft a fine coffin for Malpica, which they lined with black canvas. At the top of the casket they painted a poem to lost sailors of the sea, and at the foot they inscribed the legend "Armada Nacional—R.I.P."

In Mazatlán harbor, the blackened forecastle of the gunboat *Morelos* protruded from the water like a silent monument to the sea battles of the revolution, and the valiant odyssey of Hilario Malpica. It remained there for three years, until another group of men became determined to use a salvaged warship to challenge a powerful adversary.

For the story of the *Morelos* had not ended with her sinking, it had only begun . . .

1   A Simple Business Transaction

The harbor at Mazatlán was one of the busiest in the country in 1917. Even with a reduction in trade due to the war in Europe, Mazatlán remained the principal port of entry on the west coast of Mexico and business was still good enough to keep the dock workers busy from morning until dusk. The average depth in the harbor was only eighty feet, so arriving steamships were required to anchor offshore where they awaited an unusual offloading ritual.

When the tide was out, passengers disembarked from the steamers into gasoline-powered launches, which took them to rowboats that beached onshore. The first passengers from each rowboat that landed were carried on the backs of "boteros," or boatmen, until the rowboat could be fully dragged out of the water to enable the remainder to exit. Their luggage came onshore the same way. Meanwhile, a fleet of launches, rowboats, and lighters would descend upon the steamship. Stevedores climbed on board, followed by launch hands, who would bid against one another for the chance to carry the remaining trunks and baggage ashore.

Over $5 million worth of commercial goods were exported from Mazatlán each year, primarily hides, gold and silver ore, chickpeas, and sugar, and a somewhat lesser amount was imported. At high tide, freight was loaded and offloaded at a small wharf using lighters, but when the tide was low, every item that arrived or departed was carried on the back of a man. Outgoing crates were transported from the customs house by a "cargador," or porter, who carried it on his head and shoulders, wading across 100 to 200 feet of water before depositing it in a waiting lighter that transported it to the steamship. The boxes could weigh anywhere from

150 to 350 pounds. Imports were handled the same way. A seemingly endless line of cargadors fueled the system in each direction, carrying up to 1,000 tons of freight in the course of a ten-hour working day. At one point, gas-powered hoists had been mounted onto the wharf to allow the freight to be handled more expeditiously, but the hoists were not well-received by the cargadors, who responded by going on strike. They were quickly removed and man-powered transport was resumed.

The customs house was the focal point of the bustling activity in the harbor. It was a large, single-story structure built in the Spanish style, featuring a colonnade of arched columns in tropical white that formed a portico along one side, and was adjoined by an equally substantial warehouse where goods were held pending the payment of tariff charges. Whether import or export, each item of freight had to first pass through the customs house for appraisal and payment of duties.

It was here in August 1917, that Señor Miranda, the administrator of the Mazatlán dockyard, presided over a most unusual gathering. The revolution had drawn closer to an end that year with the approval of a new constitution and the election of Venustiano Carranza as president of Mexico. Although the country would remain a chaotic and troubled land for years, a level of stability had returned with the establishment of Carranza's government. One of the first orders of business for the new administration was to increase federal revenues, and in the shipwrecks of the recent revolution—such as that of the gunboat *Morelos* in Mazatlán harbor—the Ministry of Finance and Public Credit saw an immediate source of hard cash.

Before it was sunk by the Constitutionalists, the *Morelos* had been the finest warship in the Mexican navy. Launched at the Sestri Ponente shipyard near Genoa, Italy, in 1905, the *Morelos* was a classic example of modern naval design. Its armored hull was 250 feet long, with a beam 34 feet wide. Powered by two sets of three-cylinder engines of 2,600 horsepower, with steam supplied by two Blechynden water tube boilers, the gunboat had a top speed of 17 knots (19.6 mph). The capacity of its coal bunker was sufficient to provide a range of 5,000 miles at 10 knots. The ship had quarters for 26 officers and 90 crewmen, and could provide living space for an additional 260 troops. At the time it was built, it had been armed with two 4-inch rapid-fire guns and four 2¼-inch cannons. Although these armaments had been stripped from the wreck years before for the rebel army, the electric ammunition hoists remained on board. As scrap, the value of the *Morelos* was significant—likely measured in tens of thousands of pesos to the treasury. Its three-bladed propellers alone, made of manganese bronze and 8 feet in diameter, would be worth a tidy sum.

The Finance Ministry dutifully placed advertisements in the *Official Journal* and newspapers throughout the region, announcing that the wreck of the former navy gunboat *Morelos* would be sold at public auction at the customs house in Mazatlán on August 14, 1917. All parties interested in bidding at the auction would be required to deposit a 15,000 peso ($8,000) bond in advance at the customs house.

On the day of the auction, Señor Miranda, the dockyard administrator, surveyed the small group of bidders standing before him. There were no bankers in fancy suits in attendance—the men wore work pants, boots, and shirtsleeves. A few puffed on cigars. Most were scrap metal buyers from the Sinaloa area, or men like Blendes, the American who operated between San Francisco and Mazatlán in search of promising scrap opportunities. They were tough, hard-nosed businessmen who had already estimated the cost of refloating the wreck, towing it to one of the large west coast ship-breaking yards, and trucking the scrap to the nearest steelworks. With America's entry into the war in Europe, a manufacturing boom was under way that had sent the price for scrap iron and steel soaring. As a result, the bidding for the *Morelos* was expected to be intense.

Señor Miranda started the bidding at 1,000 pesos and it rose rapidly from there. 4,000–5,000–6,000 pesos . . . The bids came in quick succession, with hand signals flashing throughout the crowd—7,000–8,000–9,000 pesos . . . When the bidding reached the 12,000 peso mark, the speed of the offers slowed as the scrap men paused to tabulate the rising cost of the wreck against its fixed return. At 15,000 pesos, most of the bidders in the audience had become spectators. The final bid of 35,000 pesos ($18,550) released an undercurrent of murmurs throughout the crowd. That was a lot of money to pay for a sunken wreck—the scrap margin would be exceedingly thin. Heads turned to catch a glimpse of the winning bidder.

The victor was Cornelius Adolph Heintz—to those who knew him, probably the man least expected to win the auction. Heintz had a well-deserved reputation for unscrupulous business dealings and a propensity for passing worthless checks. Even more surprising to the authorities running the auction was the name of the party that had backed Heintz by putting up his $8,000 bond—the powerful German trading house of Melchers Sucesores.

Cornelius Heintz was a twenty-eight-year-old engineer from Los Angeles. The son of a German father and an American mother, he had departed the United States for Mexico on April 1, 1917, the day before President Woodrow Wilson asked a joint session of Congress to declare war on Germany. In the vernacular of the day, Heintz was a "slacker," a draft dodger who had deserted his country to sit out the war in Mexico. Considered traitors in the United States and unmanly cowards in Mexico, slackers were universally despised on either side of the border.

The *San Bernardino News* described the slacker community in Mazatlán in an article published in 1918 as "outcasts from home and country . . . half-starved and utterly hopeless . . . The Southern Pacific railroad refuses to give employment to a man who has fled his country to escape military service. The Mexicans despise the American slackers and have little or no work to give to them."

Heintz's stated purpose in traveling to Mexico was to fulfill the terms of an employment contract that he'd accepted to inspect a derelict gas schooner called the *Anvil* that was anchored in the harbor at Guaymas. He held a degree in mechanical engineering from the Throop Institute—later renamed CalTech—and had some experience in marine engineering. After assessing the schooner's condition and providing recommendations for its repair, Heintz was hired by the ship's owner, a German named Bernard Hilbing, to return the *Anvil* to seaworthy condition. Heintz's association with Hilbing would lead the young engineer into involvement in a succession of German intrigues.

At one time Hilbing had been the manager of the Foreign and Central American Department at Parrott and Company, a private banking firm, where he became highly knowledgeable regarding the import–export business and fluent in Spanish and English. Most of his time with Parrott had been spent trading in coffee with firms in Central America, including the mercantile trading houses of Mazatlán. Hilbing's professional career took a turn for the worse in 1914, when he had been caught embezzling $2,000 from his employer and was summarily dismissed. He then took a position with the Western Equipment Company, engaged in the import and export of steel products, from which he also departed under a cloud of suspicion, this time related to a heavily padded expense account. In 1916, Hilbing branched out into a new export field—supplying munitions to Mexican revolutionists. U.S. authorities suspected Hilbing of shipping arms and ammunition to Esteban Cantú, the governor-general of Lower California, via Pacific coastal steamer for transshipment to the army of Pancho Villa, by then, a sworn enemy of the United States.

Heintz worked at overhauling Hilbing's schooner throughout the summer of 1917, until it was ready for sea. He was then offered a six-month position as chief engineer of the *Anvil* at $240 per month, but this opportunity vanished when Heintz learned that his employer had been taken into custody by American immigration authorities.

Hilbing had sailed the reconditioned *Anvil* to Los Angeles (LA), where he planned to pick up a former employee of the Krupp munitions works named Place and proceed with an "unspecified cargo" to Salina Cruz, Mexico. Upon arrival in LA, however, he was seized by U.S. Immigration officials for falsely stating his nationality as "USA" on the crew manifest. In October 1917 Hilbing's detention became permanent when a presidential warrant was issued declaring him to be a German alien enemy "whose presence at large is a danger to the public peace and safety of the United States." Hilbing became War Prisoner No. 596, and was interned for the next two years at Fort Douglas, Utah.

With his employer in jail, Heintz had lingered in Guaymas for three weeks, and then departed for Mazatlán in search of new employment. Hilbing had been on a first-name basis with the senior managers of all the German mercantile houses in Mazatlán since his coffee trading days with Parrott and Company and had introduced many of these men to his associate, Cornelius Heintz. In Mazatlán, Heintz called on Herr Unger and Herr Haüs of the firm Melchers Sucesores, and in secret meetings proposed a plan to acquire the sunken gunboat *Morelos*.

The largest and most powerful of the foreign firms that controlled commercial trade in Mazatlán was Melchers Sucesores, or Melchers Sucs (pronounced Melchers *Soos*). From the company's headquarters and main warehouse on Arsenal Street, a fortress-like two-story cement structure with barred windows and heavy wooden doors, the managing partners of Melchers Sucs reigned over a trading empire.

Founded in 1846 by Heinrich Melchers of Bremen, Germany, Melchers Sucesores had been created to take advantage of the opportunity presented by Mazatlán's central geographic location, Mexico's substantial mineral and agricultural resources, and the local market's demand for manufactured goods from Europe. There were no railroads linking the cities of the Mexican interior with those of the west coast, and seaports like Mazatlán became key distribution points for the country. An endless flow of goods from Europe and America arrived in Mazatlán harbor to be transported to the warehouse of Melchers Sucesores, where they would then be purchased by area merchants and loaded onto mules for transport to inland shops. Melchers Sucs imported silks from France, linen from Ireland and Silesia, textiles from Austria and Germany, and wine from Spain, along with a wide variety of manufactured products, from firearms and ammunition, to plumbing supplies, sewing machines—and even Studebaker automobiles. In addition to retail goods, Melchers Sucs also distributed commercial machinery and supplies to satisfy the needs of domestic mining and industrial concerns.

The company's founders, and their descendants, had returned to Germany before the end of the nineteenth century, leaving operation of the firm in the hands of a succession of capable managing partners. In the succeeding years, Casa Melchers ("the house of Melchers") expanded beyond basic import/export activities into a variety of other business endeavors. The company became a broker of Brazilian rosewood, heavily in demand by European textile mills for color dye, and also established a plant to manufacture yarns and fabrics. They became shipping agents, and the primary exporter of gold and silver ores from over a dozen mines in western Mexico as well as agricultural produce from across the region. They acted as a manufacturer's representative for foreign companies seeking to penetrate the Mexican market, including the Santa Cruz Cement

Company, Krupp steel, and the California Vinogrit Powder Company, a large producer of dynamite.

To support its trading activities, Melchers provided commercial credit on a wide scale. Mining and farming interests throughout western Mexico placed orders for equipment exclusively through Melchers Sucesores due to the generous credit terms that the company provided—typically six months before payment was due. Casa Melchers financial operations expanded significantly during the Mexican Revolution. State and national banks in Mexico had traditionally issued their own currency, which was not backed by silver or gold. During the revolutionary period, Carranza suspended bank charters to eliminate the financial instability that was being caused by the issuance of essentially worthless currency. To enable business to continue, banking operations shifted to the trading houses themselves. Melchers Sucs became a private banker, buying and selling notes, holding cash reserves, financing commercial transactions, and transferring funds between companies and foreign banks around the world. Casa Melchers even sold fire insurance policies in Mexico that were underwritten by European insurance companies.

For more than seventy years Casa Melchers prospered, overcoming every business, political, and societal challenge encountered, from outbreaks of bubonic plague and yellow fever, to the upheavals and violence of the revolution and the threat to their port-based market domination posed by the expansion of the Southern Pacific Railroad of Mexico into the region. To the company's good fortune, in 1909 the railroad stopped laying rails at Tepic instead of Guadalajara (as had been planned), ensuring that inland merchants would continue to rely on Melchers' well-stocked warehouses for their goods, instead of sourcing products from distant Manzanillo.

By the second decade of the twentieth century, Melchers Sucesores future looked as promising as its past. Then an event occurred that sent business into a tailspin—World War I broke out in Europe. The firm's channels of communication with the home office in Germany were immediately cut, which also terminated their ability to conduct financial transactions with companies in the various capitals of Europe. The English naval blockade of Germany eliminated any possibility of the German-owned company receiving goods from the mother country, or even Germany's enemies.

To make up for the loss of European imports, Casa Melchers increased purchases from America, but a second blow fell in 1917 when the United States declared war against Germany. Melchers' funds in American banks were confiscated by the U.S. government, and all conduits to American business partners were severed as well. To restrict Germany's ability to finance the war and eliminate the chance for German-owned businesses in neutral countries to build up financial credits and goods for use in postwar trade (which would remove the pressure that they might bring on the German government to end the war), on October 6, 1917, the Trading with the Enemy Act was passed by the U.S. Congress. The new law made it illegal:

> for any person in the United States, except with license of the President granted to such person, or to the enemy, or ally of the enemy, as provided in this act, to trade or attempt to trade, either directly or indirectly, with, to, or from, or for, or on account of, or for the benefit of, any other person with knowledge or reasonable cause to believe that such other person is an enemy or ally of an enemy [of the United States], or is conducting or taking part in such trade, directly or indirectly, for, or on account of, or on behalf of, or for the benefit of, an enemy or ally of enemy.

Violation of the act was punishable by a fine of not more than $10,000 or by imprisonment for not more than ten years, or both. To make it easier for American companies to identify enemy firms, an "Enemy Trading List" was published that included the names of all known companies and individuals with whom trade was forbidden. Prominent among the enemy firms on the "Listas Negras" as the blacklist was called in Mexico, was Melchers Sucs and its senior managers Friedrich Unger and Gustav Burgmeister.

The two managing partners of Casa Melchers were fiercely competitive businessmen. Friedrich Heinrich "Fritz" Unger, a forty-one-year-old manager from Bremen, Germany, had arrived in Mazatlán in 1896 to take a position with the firm. Always immaculately attired in a fine suit with vest and gold watch chain, the 5-foot 10-inch Unger had short brown hair and a neatly trimmed mustache. Fluent in Spanish, German, and English, with piercing blue eyes and a serious demeanor, he had risen rapidly in the organization and by 1910 was elevated to managing partner. In addition to overseeing the operation of Melchers Sucs, in 1914 Friedrich Unger was named the honorary German consul of Mazatlán, the German government's official representative in the city. His associate, Gustav Burgmeister, also in his forties, stood slightly taller, and with hair closely cropped, a dark mustache, and wire-rimmed spectacles, looked every bit the Prussian aristocrat. Burgmeister had become a managing partner of Melchers Sucesores in 1913, and was the honorary German vice-consul of Mazatlán. Together, Unger and Burgmeister were resolute in their dedication to the firm of Melchers Sucs and their allegiance to Imperial Germany.

Now alone and abandoned, cut off from the firm's owners in Germany and its trading partners in Europe and the United States, the managers of Casa Melchers were forced to reorganize business operations to meet their precarious circumstances. The first order of business to survive as a trading house would be to find ways to circumvent the blacklist. Unger and Burgmeister created branch offices in Culiacán, Guamuchil, San Blas, and Navojoa, ostensibly to broaden the company's market reach, but that also made their business dealings less visible to American authorities. In San José del Cabo, where there was no U.S. representative to inspect ship manifests or trace the ultimate destination of imported goods, they assigned agents like Señor Amarillas to recruit Mexican merchants to act as "cloaks," buying products in the United States for reshipment to Melchers Sucs warehouse in Mazatlán. Vessels flying the American flag were forbidden to transport German goods or passengers under the Trading with the Enemy Act, so Melchers Sucs purchased three coastal steamers, the *Pinotepa*, *Josefina*, and *San Cosme*, to carry their products under the Mexican flag. U.S. postal authorities would not deliver mail addressed to German government representatives, so Unger and Burgmeister had their mail addressed to Mexican employees, and the products for the trading house similarly ordered under Mexican names. In some cases, local companies were forced to buy goods from German trading houses like Melchers Sucs because they owed money to the German firm, or the trading house withheld their funds and refused to pay out in any way other than merchandise.

Despite these subterfuges, the Listas Negras continued to have a devastating impact on Casa Melchers revenues. The *Report of the War Trade Board* published shortly after the war ended would state that: "the business of the most important German houses on the west coast of Mexico still able to transact business, namely Melchers Sucs, had apparently been reduced to about 30% of its normal volume [by the U.S. blacklist]."

To the managing partners of Melchers Sucesores, the United States, formerly a friendly trading nation, had become a bitter enemy. America was shipping millions of troops overseas to defeat their homeland. The goods that Casa Melchers was denied from importing were being diverted to the Allied Forces. The U.S. government had targeted Melchers Sucs as a blacklisted firm and imposed trade restrictions that were driving the company to ruin. As the war progressed, Consul Unger and Vice-Consul Burgmeister would respond in kind, and prove only too willing to back any undertaking directed against their arch enemy, the United States.

Not far from Melchers Sucesores, on the crest of a hill overlooking the saltwater estuary at the eastern edge of Mazatlán harbor was the Cervecería del Pacífico brewery. It was a three-story brick and wood structure with an unusual outer appearance caused by the oddly-projected towers and cupolas required to accommodate the specialized machinery, fermentation and storage tanks housed within. The brewery had been constructed in 1900 with the financial backing of a small group of local businessmen that included Carl Melchers, a shareholder in Melchers Sucs, to satisfy the local population's thirst for good German beer. Their first product was a pilsner lager called Cerveza Pacífico Clara ("beer of the clear Pacific") that proved to be a great success throughout the region. Horse-drawn wagons loaded with oak barrels labeled "Cervecería del Pacífico" distributed the golden beverage to the cities and villages of western Mexico, generating a handsome profit for the brewery's owners. Among those growing rich from the brewery's output was the firm of Arzak Brothers, the Mexican distributing agents for the beer maker.

The senior partner of the distribution company, Louis Arzak, was a speculator, who during the summer of 1917 saw the opportunity for a quick financial coup in the sale of the gunboat *Morelos*. The project began as a simple business transaction. Cornelius Heintz, the young German American engineer, learned that the *Morelos* was to be sold at auction and raised the prospect of making a bid for it with Fritz Unger, whom he had met sometime before through his employer, Bernard Hilbing. Unger, in turn, introduced Louis Arzak to the opportunity. Unger and Arzak were close friends after years of business dealings.

During secret meetings held at the German club in Mazatlán and the brewery, the three men formulated a plan to acquire the sunken gunboat. Arzak would provide the funds required to purchase the ship. Heintz would act as the "front man," bidding at the auction to conceal Arzak's interest and thereby hopefully achieve a lower sale price. Melchers Sucs would post the $8,000 bond needed for Heintz to register as a bidder and handle the transfer of Arzak's payment to the customs house. If Arzak was victorious, Heintz would be paid to raise the *Morelos* and return it to serviceable condition, while Arzak would arrange for the gunboat to be scrapped at a ship-breaking yard and receive the profits. Unger participated in the venture purely as a favor to his friend, Louis Arzak.

After Heintz's success at the customs house auction, a diver sent down to inspect the *Morelos* made a remarkable discovery. When the ship was sunk in 1914, eyewitness accounts had told a thrilling story of the *Morelos* being boarded and set aflame by the Constitutionalists, who then blew the bottom out of the stricken gunboat with dynamite. According to the *San Francisco Chronicle*:

> It was a thrilling spectacle. With the discharge of the dynamite, the forward deck yawned; the bridge and foremast became a pillar of flame. Long tongues of fire shot through the pall of smoke, illuminating the combers of the reef, which heaved against the hull as if seeking to soothe the gaping wounds in the sides of the ill-fated ship.

After examining the wreck, however, Arzak's diver reported that the hull appeared to be in fine shape. There had been no dynamiting; the rebels who captured the gunboat had simply opened the sea valves to send the *Morelos* to the bottom. An even greater surprise came when the safe on board the *Morelos* was opened and found to contain 40,000 Mexican gold pesos, a handsome windfall for Louis Arzak who had paid only 35,000 pesos for the gunboat at auction.

A ship that sinks in the sheltered waters of a harbor typically does not encounter the same destructive forces as a vessel that goes down in deepwater. The deterioration caused by marine life and weather is far less, and unless the ship is subjected to strong currents or heavy waves it will often remain in good condition for salvage. This proved to be the case with the *Morelos*.

The gunboat was soon raised and moored in the estuary near the brewery, where Heintz gave it a thorough inspection. The wooden decking of the ship had been severely burned by fire forward of the funnels, but the machinery, including engines and boilers, were serviceable and in fine condition. Several deck beams were rusted and there was considerable surface corrosion on the hull, which had remained solid and seaworthy. For a ship that had been underwater for three years, the *Morelos* was in remarkably good condition.

Based on the positive appraisal, Arzak reconsidered his plan to break up the gunboat. As scrap metal, the *Morelos* would return a profit of tens of thousands of pesos, but as a fully restored warship or merchant steamer, it could well be worth *hundreds* of thousands of pesos. Considered together, the *Morelos* and the 40,000 pesos in gold found on board was the same as a "free" gunboat + 5,000 pesos when the purchase price was taken into account, and the beer distributor's total expense to repair the salvaged ship had been significantly reduced. Arzak decided to rebuild the *Morelos* from stem to stern and then hunt for a buyer for the restored warship.

At the right price, it shouldn't be too difficult to find someone interested in owning it.

As Arzak worked to locate materials and assemble a team to overhaul his prize, he was unaware that others had been watching the gunboat from the shadows for some time. Months before the customs house auction, German agents in Mexico and the United States became aware that the stricken warship would soon be available for sale, and saw it as a cut-rate means to acquire a commerce raider for intercepting Allied freighters off the Pacific coast. Frederick Hinsch, a former sea captain of the North

German Lloyd shipping line, and an organizer of German sabotage operations in America, had formulated a scheme to buy the *Morelos* from the Mexican government and arm the ship for offensive operations.

Hinsch's plan to obtain the gunboat was revealed in information gathered by American investigators after the war. In the spring of 1917, a courier named Raoul Gerdts Pochet was dispatched to the United States by Fred Herrmann, a German agent in Mexico City, with a coded message for Hinsch: "Tell 2584 [Hinsch] his plan OK. Am in close touch with major and influential Mexicans can obtain old 3175 [cruiser] for 50,000 West Coast."

Pochet would later tell investigators that in reply, Hinsch "asked me to tell Herrmann that he [Hinsch] was busily engaged in getting guns of 70.5 millimeters across the border into Mexico where they would be used to equip a destroyer in Mazatlán, for intercepting ships carrying cargoes from San Francisco." Nothing would come of Hinsch's plan to buy the *Morelos*, however, after German officials in Mexico devised a better scheme to make use of the idle warship.

The German navy's High Seas Fleet of battleships and cruisers, constructed at a cost of billions of marks before the war, remained sheltered in home waters for most of the conflict. Except for an occasional foray into the North Sea, the German surface fleet remained safely anchored behind defensive minefields at their bases in Wilhelmshaven and Kiel. The Royal Navy enjoyed a 2 to 1 advantage in capital ships, and a direct engagement might have resulted in the destruction of the German fleet. As a result, the German Admiralty was left with two alternatives for bringing the war to the Allied nations: submarines and commerce raiders. Germany's U-boats had proven to be an effective weapon against the merchant vessels supplying Great Britain, but their use in sinking unarmed ships without warning was considered a violation of the rules of war and had heightened the risk that neutral countries like the United States would declare war against Germany. Therefore, the commerce raider became the principal means for the German navy to strike at enemy merchant vessels without constraint, particularly during the early years of the war.

The first commerce raiders were navy cruisers that had been stationed overseas to protect German colonial possessions. When the war began in August 1914, warships like the *Königsberg* in German East Africa, the *Karlsruhe* in the Caribbean, and the *Emden* in the Indian Ocean were dispatched on solo raiding missions to destroy or capture Allied merchantmen. The most successful of these was the light cruiser SMS *Emden*. The *Emden* had been guarding Germany's prized colony in China, the port city of Tsingtao, when she was directed to link up with the East Asia Squadron of Rear Admiral Graf von Spee. As Spee's squadron prepared to sail off to battle the Royal Navy, the captain of the *Emden* received orders to set off as a lone corsair.

"You are hereby . . . detached with the task of entering the Indian Ocean and waging cruiser warfare as best you can."

During the next three months, the *Emden* raised havoc across the Indian Ocean. In a voyage that covered over 30,000 miles, the commerce raider sank sixteen British merchantmen, captured three colliers and a Russian mail steamer (that was returned to Tsingtao for conversion into a German auxiliary cruiser), commandeered the supplies from two captured merchant ships, sank a Russian cruiser and a French destroyer, and shelled British oil tank installations in the city of Madras on the east coast of India. The losses inflicted by the *Emden* totaled approximately $6 million, or fifteen times the original cost of building the cruiser itself. Aside from the swath of destruction that she left in her wake, the *Emden* also caused the Allies to delay freight shipments, suspend troop convoys, and divert substantial naval resources to hunt her down. At one point during her cruise, seven Allied warships were combing the Indian Ocean for the elusive German warship. The *Emden*'s luck finally ran out on November 6, 1914, when the cruiser was caught by surprise after landing a contingent of seamen to raid one of the Cocos Islands, and was destroyed by the guns of the Australian light cruiser HMAS *Sydney*.

The landing party from the *Emden*—three officers and forty-six men sent to destroy a British wireless and telegraph station on Direction Island—were left stranded at the desolate outpost. Spotting a 97-ton schooner, the *Ayesha*, riding at anchor offshore, the leader of the German force, Kapitanleutnant Hellmuth von Mucke, seized the vessel for a fast getaway. The *Ayesha* was loaded with water and provisions from the British station, four Maxim machineguns and twenty-nine Mauser rifles brought from the *Emden*, along with nautical charts and a German naval battle flag. Then von Mucke and his men set a course for Padang in the Dutch East Indies. After a 1,700-mile journey through the Indies, with warships from the Royal Navy frantically searching for them, the sailors on the *Ayesha* sighted the German collier *Choising*, which they boarded to continue their passage back to Germany. Accorded a hero's welcome upon his return, Kapitanleutnant von Mucke wrote a book about the adventure titled *The Ayesha*, which was published in Berlin (in German) in 1915, in the United States (in English) in 1917, and saw worldwide distribution.

As the war progressed, the Kaiserliche Marine expanded its fleet of auxiliaries by pressing merchant freighters into service as commerce raiders. Although not as heavily armed as an auxiliary cruiser, a freighter had the advantage of tremendous cruising range and provided an element of surprise when Allied merchant ships were encountered. The first of these disguised attack craft was a freighter called the *Pungo*. Launched as a raider in 1916, it was fitted with four guns hidden behind drop-down doors in the deck walls and two concealed torpedo tubes. "Her masts had been rebuilt with telescopic mechanisms so they could be lowered and raised, and sheet iron panels were carried on board to alter the appearance of her funnel and superstructure." Recommissioned as the SMS *Moewe*, the covert warship prowled the Atlantic for four months laying minefields that sank three merchantmen (and the Royal Navy battleship *King Edward VI*), and captured a further fifteen freighters, two of which were taken as prizes and thirteen sunk, before retiring safely to port in Kiel.

Another disguised merchant freighter, the SMS *Wolf*, took an even greater toll on Allied shipping. The *Wolf* was armed with seven 5.9-inch guns, three 2-inch guns, and four torpedo tubes, all hidden behind special drop-down steel doors on the deck walls. The raider also carried a large complement of naval mines in modified storage holds, and was even equipped with a seaplane for aerial reconnaissance. During a voyage that lasted fifteen months, the *Wolf* laid over 450 mines in underwater fields off South Africa, Ceylon, India, Singapore, New Zealand, and Australia that sank sixteen ships. She captured a further fourteen merchant vessels—from a 508-ton three-masted American trading bark to a 6,500-ton Japanese mail steamer, and returned to Kiel with her cargo holds bulging with scarce commodities taken from the plundered ships.

Whether auxiliary cruiser or disguised freighter (some German passenger liners were also pressed into service), the commerce raiders all shared a common weakness: the ever-present need for coal. A raider could carry enough water and provisions to remain at sea for months, and cleaning the hull or rebuilding the engine could be delayed even longer, but having enough coal to fire the boilers was an immediate necessity. Once a commerce raider's coal bunkers had reached the minimum level for the ship to return to port, it *had* to replenish its coal supply or consider breaking off operations. Unlike the Royal Navy, which maintained naval bases around the world for refueling its ships, there were only three possible sources of coal for a German commerce raider at sea: a coaling station in a neutral port—no longer an option after the war began—a German collier dispatched to rendezvous with the raider at a prearranged location, or an enemy collier seized to plunder *its* coal.

The German navy had anticipated the problem of coaling surface ships overseas before the war began and responded by creating an organization called the Naval Etappe. The Etappe was a clandestine network of land-based naval supply hubs, each located in a major port around the globe and commanded by a mid-rank officer. The Etappe supply officer handled the coaling, provisioning, intelligence, and communication for all German warships within an assigned geographic area. The Etappe stations based in neutral countries operated throughout the war, becoming in effect, secret supply bases of the German empire.

The man in charge of the German naval supply organization in New York City was naval attaché Captain Karl Boy-Ed. He had originally been dispatched to America to study the U.S. Navy—its ships, personnel, coastal defenses, and plans for expansion, a task well-suited for the intelligent and suave German naval officer. Heavily built, with a bull neck and strong jaw, Boy-Ed was highly charismatic, had a good sense of humor, and became very popular in the diplomatic and naval circles of Washington. After the war began, Boy-Ed's official duties were superseded by a secret role assigned to him by the German Admiralty: Etappe supply officer for all surface raiders operating in the Atlantic. Working under the code name

"Nordmann" by day from his private office at Room 801, 11 Broadway, New York City, and from a suite at the German Club by night, Boy-Ed's Etappe station operated closely with German steamship companies like Hansa, the Hamburg-Amerika Line, and the North German Lloyd to supply German surface ships at sea. In the years before the war, the Kaiserliche Marine had contracted with a number of German steamship lines for provisioning German surface raiders from American ports after hostilities had commenced. The arrangements included use of the Admiralty's code for communication between the supply ships and German warships at sea.

In August 1914 a cable sent from Berlin transformed the German merchant marine in the United States into a virtual division of the War Office, and established New York as the main base for supplying surface ships in the Atlantic. Over $2 million was immediately cabled from the Deutsche Bank in Berlin to American banks for Boy-Ed to disburse to Hamburg-Amerika and the North German Lloyd for chartering freighters, and to buy coal and provisions to supply the patrolling commerce raiders. The steamship companies attempted to keep their participation in the supply operations secret by contracting intermediaries to front as the ostensible shippers of the cargo and to provide American customs officials with false manifests and destinations in order to obtain harbor clearance. A score of freighters were chartered by German steamship companies during the first months of the war and dispatched with coal, provisions, and naval stores for warships in the Atlantic:

> *Thor*—sailed from Newport News and cleared for Fray Bentos
> *Berwind*—sailed from New York and cleared for Buenos Aires
> *Lorenzo*—sailed from New York and cleared for Buenos Aires
> *Heina*—sailed from Philadelphia and cleared for La Guaira
> *Nepos*—sailed from Philadelphia and cleared for Monrovia
> *Mowincle*—sailed from Philadelphia and cleared for Monrovia
> *Unita*—cleared from Philadelphia and cleared for Cadiz
> *Graecia*—sailed from New York and cleared for Cadiz
> *Macedonia*—sailed from New Orleans and cleared for Cadiz
> *Navarra*—sailed from Pensacola and cleared for Pernambuco

"Supercargoes" were assigned to each chartered vessel—company representatives who had the authority to issue revised sailing instructions to the ship captains once they were outside the three-mile limit, redirecting them to a lonely spot on the high seas where they would lie in wait for the German raider. Over a dozen chartered ships sailed before American authorities became aware of this violation of neutrality and clamped down on Boy-Ed's secret supply operation.

The German naval attaché channeled money for the supply of commerce raiders operating on the Pacific Ocean as well. In August 1914, when the world war unexpectedly broke out, the German cruiser *Leipzig* was patrolling the Mexican coast and desperately low on coal. Boy-Ed arranged for the Deutsche Bank to transfer $350,000 to the banking house of Speyer and Company in Manhattan, which a confederate then telegraphed to the Nevada National Bank in San Francisco to purchase coal for the cruiser.

Shortly before dawn on the morning of August 17, the *Leipzig* boldly steamed into San Francisco harbor and moored at "Man-of-War" row to take on coal and supplies. When the collector of the port learned that coaling of the warship had begun without his authority, he ordered it to be stopped at once, and dispatched an inspector to ensure that only enough coal was taken aboard the *Leipzig* to reach the nearest German port, Apia, Samoa, in accordance with American neutrality regulations. The German cruiser departed San Francisco with only a partial load of coal on a southerly course toward Mexico.

Within days, the freighter *Mazatlán* arrived in San Francisco flying a Mexican flag of registry, and took on the 900 tons of coal that had originally been consigned to the *Leipzig*. Although flying the Mexican flag, the Mazatlán was owned by Captain Frederick Jebsen, a reservist in the German navy. After discussing the situation with government officials in Washington, the San Francisco harbor authorities allowed the *Mazatlán* to clear the port under a $20,000 bond to deliver the coal to a company in Guaymas, Mexico, as consigned. North of Magdalena Bay, the *Mazatlán* picked up the *Leipzig* and transferred mail and supplies to the cruiser, before continuing on to Guaymas, where the 900 tons of coal was lightered ashore and delivered to the firm of Iberri and Company. The German steamship *Marie* soon appeared in Guaymas, purchased the coal from Iberri, and then rendezvoused with the *Leipzig* on the open ocean to coal the German cruiser.

When the subterfuge was discovered, U.S. officials were outraged and newspaper headlines decried this flagrant violation of American neutrality. To help calm the situation, Consul Fritz Unger of Mazatlán provided a response to the *San Francisco Chronicle*, explaining that the transaction was perfectly regular and fully in accordance with the neutrality provisions:

> In loading a cargo of coal at Guaymas, which eventually was delivered to the German cruiser *Leipzig* . . . the Mexican steamer *Mazatlán* of the Jebsen service committed no breach of neutrality.
>
> Iberri and Company of Guaymas were the consignees of the *Mazatlán's* coal cargo, which aroused comment here prior to the departure of the vessel for the lower coast, and they received it in good faith . . . A day after the fuel was lightered at Guaymas the *Leipzig* came in and purchased it.

In December 1915, the U.S. government put an end to naval attaché Karl Boy-Ed's clandestine operations by demanding that he be recalled to Germany for violating American neutrality laws. Meanwhile other Etappe stations at key strategic points around the world continued to disburse money, obtain coal and provisions, and arrange supply vessels for German raiders at sea.

In the estuary near the Cervecería del Pacífico brewery, Consul Unger watched work progress on board the gunboat *Morelos*. Cornelius Heintz, the German American engineer had left the project to repair another boat in Mazatlán harbor, and Arzak had replaced him with an Italian engineer named Lorenzo. There was now a considerable amount of wood planking lying about the deck, and already the poop break bulkhead had been entirely rebuilt with lumber. Many of the rusted deck beams were also reinforced with wood. The stringers and frame appeared in good shape. One of the chain cables of her ground tackle had been laid out in bights for repair. Some of the double-bottom manhole plates were open, allowing onlookers to peer inside where men were busy scaling and repainting the forward holds. The wreck of the fallen foremast still lay across the deck, but the mainmast was now standing and appeared good as new. The entire hull had been repainted a deep gray war color, and from a distance of fifteen feet, the *Morelos* presented a very seaworthy appearance.

It was clear that Arzak's workmen were doing an excellent job of bringing the gunboat back to life. Altogether, Unger counted fifty men hard at work, and observed that five of them were fellow Germans.

After the overhaul had been completed, the *Morelos* would make a fine warship. Aside from the battleships and cruisers of the powerful American Pacific fleet, the *Morelos* probably represented the only remaining warship available for duty on the entire west coast of the Americas. This was the factor that had prompted German agents Frederick Hinsch and Fred Herrmann to consider buying the *Morelos* from senior officials in the Carranza government and arm her with smuggled cannons for use as a commerce raider.

As Unger quietly watched the progress of the workmen restoring the *Morelos* and congratulated Louis Arzak on his good fortune, his face masked a secret that he shared with only his closest confidants. The authorities in Berlin had an end in mind for the gunboat *Morelos*, something of critical strategic importance—a plan that could alter the balance of naval power in the Pacific as long as the Americans didn't learn of it.

2 "I Will Shoot You Down like a Dog!"

The streets of old Mazatlán were paved with cobble stones, and as level as the waves of an ocean storm. There was no planning as the city expanded; it had grown a block at a time as the need arose. Streets could be wide at one end and narrow at the other, and when the end was reached, a half-block turn might be required before continuing. As a result, the visibility down many city streets was limited to a single block. The absence of street signs throughout the rabbit warren of roads and back alleys made travel all the more confusing.

Dr. Paul Altendorf had no trouble finding his way through Mazatlán or any other city in Mexico. He spoke Spanish like a native, and during his three years in the country had grown accustomed to the sight of donkey carts bumping along dusty roads, street sellers calling out their wares at all hours of the day, barking dogs, and the smell of charcoal cooking fire permeating the air.

On this morning of December 23, 1917, Dr. Altendorf had an important meeting to attend on Arsenal Street. As he strode purposefully on his way, passing strangers gave him the respect accorded to a man wearing the uniform of a colonel in the Mexican army, and to a man wearing a holstered Colt .45 revolver at his side. When Altendorf arrived at the headquarters of Melchers Sucesores, he was escorted through the cavernous central administration hall filled with young German men sitting stiffly at their desks, poring through shipping invoices and accounting ledgers, and led to the well-appointed private office of Fritz Unger.

The German consul greeted him with a hearty welcome. Altendorf had been spoken of most highly by the German officials in Mexico City and his reputation preceded him. Dr. Paul Altendorf was a secret agent who worked for the head of the German Secret Service in Mexico, Kurt Jahnke. With the approval of the German Minister to Mexico von Eckhardt, Altendorf had received a commission as a captain in the German Army. He had also been made a colonel in the Mexican Army with the consent of President Carranza himself. An Austrian by birth and a trained medical doctor, Altendorf was fluent in English, Spanish, and German. He had an average build and height, a nondescript face with thinning black hair, and a black mustache. Dr. Altendorf could readily pass as a Mexican when speaking to Mexicans, and moments later, transform his persona to that of his native Austria and brief an audience of Germans with the cultured articulation of a Prussian nobleman. He was highly intelligent and resourceful, the ideal man for intelligence work.

Altendorf opened the meeting by bringing Unger up to speed on the status of the most crucial secret service operation in Mexico to date—the army training camp for German reservists at El Claro in Sonora. Despite the interruption caused by the elimination of the traitor Schwiertz, planning was now under way for the joint German Mexican invasion of the United States. To support the effort, the secret service had been clandestinely importing ammunition and material from America, but additional items would be needed.

Unger walked to his desk and removed a folded document from a stack of similar items and spread it open, revealing a detailed map of the United States. These maps, he informed Altendorf, had been ordered from a company in New York on the express instruction of the German resident minister, von Eckhardt. To mislead American customs inspectors, the order had been placed by Melchers Sucesores with Martínez and Company, a printing concern in northern Mexico.

There were about two hundred fifty maps in all, highly detailed economic and production maps of excellent quality. Most were of Mexico, but approximately fifty of the maps covered the United States. Wheat, corn, cotton, lumber, and other production centers of each country were designated by shaded areas; manufacturing cities and towns were precisely identified and keyed. Altendorf could see that the copper-producing areas of Michigan and Arizona were ringed in orange, whereas the Dakotas were given a different color that signified wheat production. There was a key to each map located in the lower left corner. The maps were about thirty inches square, mounted on muslin, and folded to pocket size, with no labels indicating where they had been printed.

Altendorf congratulated Unger on his accomplishment—the maps would be most useful to German agents and saboteurs. Unger informed the doctor that he had already distributed a number of the maps to agents in Mexico and had been instructed to forward the balance, with the exception of six, to the firm of Muller and Company in Mexico City. The six maps that had been retained were for the use of German agents who would soon be sent to the United States.

Their conversation was interrupted by a Spaniard who arrived to talk business with Unger. The managing partner of Casa Melchers gave him orders for seven thousand pairs of shoes and other merchandise totaling $80,000 for shipment to a Spanish company in Mazatlán on behalf of blacklisted German business houses. As Unger's dealings with the Spaniard grew more involved, he suggested to Altendorf that they continue their discussion later that night at a club in Mazatlán.

That evening, the pair met at the Casino Allemand, a popular German club, where Unger introduced Altendorf to Vice Consul Gustav Burgmeister. A round of beer was ordered, and Burgmeister raised the topic of the situation in Tepic. Altendorf listened with polite interest while Burgmeister outlined his activities in Tepic, the capital city of the Mexican state of Nayarit. Burgmeister's duties as vice consul included collecting and forwarding German subjects to Tepic where they would ostensibly give their services to the German Red Cross, which operated a plantation there, and then forward the funds to the Fatherland for use in Red Cross work. But in fact, Burgmeister confided, there was no Red Cross facility anywhere near Tepic. It was actually a German reservist training camp of the type that Altendorf was involved with at El Claro. Graduates of the Tepic camp were to be utilized in the same German Mexican enterprise—the invasion of the United States.

After several hours of camaraderie and Cerveza Pacífico Clara beer, Dr. Altendorf bade the pair goodnight, explaining that he would be taking a steamer to Manzanillo the next day on another assignment. Unger and Burgmeister wished him a safe journey and watched the doctor depart.

Altendorf was a capable man. Someone they could trust.

Paul Bernardo Altendorf was the most important American spy in Mexico during World War 1. As "Agent A-1," Altendorf reported to Byron S. Butcher of the U.S. Army Military Intelligence section in Nogales, Arizona. Altendorf had a remarkable ability to meet people and quickly gain their confidence. After winning acceptance from a key individual, he would use that person's support to curry favor with others, broadening his influence and raising his stature within the group. Altendorf had nerves of steel and a force of personality that made people *believe* what he told them without question.

Dr. Altendorf made a strong impression on those he met. William Neunhoffer, an agent of the U.S. Justice Department in Mexico observed: "Altendorf states that he is 43 years old, but has the appearance of being about 35. He is approximately 5 feet 8 or 9 inches tall, weighs about 160–170 pounds, has black hair streaked with gray, thin on top, gray eyes, black moustache, skin smooth and white, full face, and carries himself very erect. He is a man of handsome appearance and talks rather rapidly. It seems he has been in every country in the world . . . The doctor is highly educated and speaks English and Spanish well although with a pronounced German accent."

Altendorf had been born in Cracow on June 1, 1875, the son of Joseph Altendorf, a prominent banker. He was educated at Jaczka College in Cracow, where he studied design and foreign language, and then completed coursework in medicine at the University of Cracow, specializing in chiropody. Altendorf not only spoke English and Spanish well, he was also fluent in German, French, Polish, Yiddish, and Italian. Following an uprising in 1846, the Polish city of Cracow had been annexed by Austria-Hungary to become the Grand Duchy of Cracow, an Austrian territory. As a Pole from occupied Cracow, Altendorf harbored an intense hatred of Austria and Germany. After receiving his medical degree, he fled Poland to avoid serving in the Austro-Hungarian army.

The young doctor went to Paris in 1894, and then relocated to Egypt two years later. In 1900, he served as a corporal in an English cavalry unit, Brabant's Horse, during the Boer War in South Africa. After the conflict ended, he traveled to South America, and from 1904 to 1914, worked as a physician in a number of South American countries, including Argentina, Brazil, Uruguay, Paraguay, Bolivia, Chile, Peru, Ecuador, and Colombia, after which he journeyed to Cuba, before finally landing in Mexico.

When the world war began, Altendorf was practicing medicine in Mérida, the capital of the Mexican state of Yucatán. At the time, the sympathy of Carranza and many other Mexicans lay with Germany in the conflict "if only because of the fact that they (the Germans) were now in active opposition to the detested Colossus of the North," the United States. The German government shared a very close relationship with the Carranza administration, and more than eighty German officers were actively serving in the Mexican army as advisers.

The governor of Yucatán, General Salvador Alvarado, was a member of the pro-German camp. When he learned that Altendorf had been making public statements favoring the Allied cause, the governor sent a messenger to Altendorf advising him that he would live longer if he went elsewhere—he had twenty-four hours to leave Mérida. Altendorf attempted to travel to America from the Mexican port of Progreso by steamship, but because he was considered an Austrian subject, the steamers of the U.S. Ward Line refused to allow him passage.

Altendorf moved to Frontera, a more distant city in Yucatán, but again ran into trouble. Alvarado had announced that all citizens were to turn in their gold and silver to the government in exchange for "bilimiques," paper pesos backed by nothing but the Constitutionalist government's promise to redeem them. One of Governor Alvarado's officers, a man named Domínguez, discovered that Altendorf was holding $5,000 in specie that he had not traded in for paper pesos, which resulted in Altendorf's making another hasty departure, this time by boat for Puerto México (Veracruz state).

From Veracruz, Altendorf set out on a 175-mile journey by train to Mexico City. The first leg of the trip was made by railroad push car, the only immediate transport that he could obtain. The doctor loaded his baggage and a quantity of tinned provisions on board the push car and hired three Mexicans to assist with the pushing. For days they proceeded slowly along the track, pushing away from morning to night. One evening around nine o'clock, Altendorf saw seven men riding toward them in the tropical moonlight. He later recounted:

> I handed one of my forty-fives to a peon I thought the bravest and prepared to use the other myself. We stopped the car until the men came quite close. When two of them dismounted and were preparing to shoot, I opened fire. My first shot hit one of the two in the shoulder. A second shot struck the other in the right leg near the knee. At this, the other men turned tail and fled. I shot one of the horses lest the wounded men might get away; then we went up to the wounded men. They said they were Zapatistas and that because we had a push car they thought we were federal troops trying to repair the line.

After attending to the men, they continued on their way. The next morning, ten miles from Achotal, their push cart was stopped by bandits. Altendorf was able to bluff his way past by claiming that he was a doctor bringing medicines to men wounded in a train ambush farther down the line. Altendorf and his three companions pressed on, covering another forty exhausting miles by push car, until they reached a train junction called El Burro where Altendorf was able to board a train heading toward Mexico City.

The train had traveled for only two and a half hours, when the passenger cars were raked by a volley of rifle fire. It quickly came to a stop and a gun battle erupted between rebels hidden in brush beyond the tracks and thirty-five of Carranza's soldiers on the train. When the firing died down, a rail that had been lifted by the rebels to stop the locomotive was replaced, allowing the train to continue on its journey.

The next day Altendorf boarded a different train for Córdova. This second train had covered less than two miles when it was fired on by Zapatistas, forcing Altendorf to jump outside into the bush along the tracks. As he described it:

I sprang to the ground at once with my revolver in hand. A youth some 50 yards away raised his rifle and fired at me. I courteously returned the shot, whereupon the youth remembered an engagement elsewhere.

There was an escort train with about 150 soldiers on board ahead of us. In addition to this, nearly every passenger was heavily armed. After a fusillade lasting a few minutes the train proceeded.

Four times more in a distance of ten miles this performance was repeated without any casualties so far as I could discover.

Twenty miles outside of Mexico City, the army escort train rolled onto a siding, and Altendorf's train proceeded alone into the capital. Forty-two days had passed since he had departed from Mérida, but Altendorf had at last reached his destination.

As the train drew slowly to the platform, a hotel runner came aboard soliciting business for the Hotel Juárez, which he represented to be the finest German hotel in the city.

"Who is the proprietor?" Altendorf asked.

"Mr. Otto Paglasch," the runner replied, "a German."

With no other plans, Altendorf checked into the Juárez, and the next morning asked to see Herr Paglasch. The instant the hotel proprietor appeared, Altendorf identified him as a Prussian and adjusted his dialect accordingly. Speaking to Paglasch in high German, he told the hotelier that he was a doctor from Yucatán who had just arrived in the city to buy medicines and, if business conditions were right, to relocate there. Since he was a total stranger in Mexico City, could Herr Paglasch perhaps render him some assistance? Paglasch beamed and told Altendorf that he would be delighted to do all that he could for him.

In the days that followed, Altendorf observed that Paglasch was well-connected in Mexico City's sizable German community. He also noted that the hotel overflowed with priceless artifacts—expensive paintings, Gobelin tapestries, vintage Persian rugs, rare antiquities and the like, treasures stolen from the national museum and the homes of wealthy citizens, which Paglasch had been able to acquire at nominal prices on the black market. The valuable collection made it obvious to Altendorf what motivated

Otto Paglasch, and seeing an opportunity to cement his own relationship with the influential hotel proprietor, the doctor presented him with a set of ancient Mayan statuettes. Paglasch was overwhelmed by the gift and invited Altendorf to take coffee with him at the Café Europa, where the new resident made the acquaintance of a number of prominent Germans.

Four days after Altendorf moved into the Juárez, Paglasch introduced him to two young Germans, Kurt Jahnke and Lothar Witzke. Jahnke, the senior of the pair, was in his mid-thirties with a swarthy complexion, dark hair, and a hard-eyed gaze. His companion Witzke, who went under the name Pablo Waberski, was a twenty-two-year-old from Posen, East Prussia, who had blond hair and blue eyes, and moved with the agility of a trained athlete. Although Altendorf had no idea at the time, the two men were one of the most deadly teams of saboteurs in history. Jahnke had been the director of all sabotage activities conducted in neutral America for the German consul general in San Francisco, Franz von Bopp. Witzke, a lieutenant in the German Navy, had served aboard the cruiser *Dresden* until it was sunk in South American waters, and then made his way to San Francisco where he was enlisted in sabotage activities. While working for Captain Frederick Hinsch (the German agent who planned to smuggle cannons from the United States into Mexico to arm the gunboat *Morelos*), the pair had clandestinely rowed a boat across New York Harbor in the dead of night to trigger the explosion that destroyed the munitions depot on Black Tom Island in the harbor, causing $20 million in damage.

Following a genial conversation, Jahnke invited Altendorf to join him for dinner that evening, and Altendorf, unaware of who he was, accepted. During the meal Jahnke ate sparingly and appeared quite ill, informing Altendorf that he feared he was a very sick man.

"I am a physician," Altendorf responded, "and I should deem it a privilege, as a good German, to place my services at your disposal."

Jahnke gladly accepted Altendorf's invitation and made an appointment to visit the doctor the next morning. When Jahnke appeared for his examination, Altendorf went out of his way to make a strong impression. The patient was ordered to strip to the waist, while Altendorf used a stethoscope and thumped his patient's chest a good deal more than was necessary.

"You are a sick man, Herr Jahnke," the doctor told him solemnly, "but I hope to straighten you out in a few days, if you follow my instructions implicitly."

Altendorf prescribed an elaborate course of electrical treatments and told Jahnke that he must eliminate all beer consumption until further notice. Despite Jahnke's insistence that he was seriously ill, Altendorf had diagnosed the problem as a simple acid stomach from drinking too much beer. The electrical treatment was "mental medicine" for a man who thought himself sicker than he was.

After Jahnke's "miraculous" recovery, he invited Altendorf to dine with him once again. By this time, the doctor had a good idea what Jahnke wanted to discuss.

He evidently wanted to size me up, so I allowed him to discover that I was consumed with a desire to do some noble thing for the Fatherland; for by that time I had learned that Herr Jahnke was none other than the head of the German secret service operating in the United States from his headquarters in Mexico City, and that Witzke was one of his most trusted agents of destruction.

Satisfied at last, Jahnke came to the point.

"Have you ever done any secret service work?" he asked.

"No, I am afraid I am too nervous for that sort of thing. Besides, one must have special training for everything."

This was merely to throw him off guard and make him more desirous of employing me. Inwardly I could have danced the cancan, or have done anything real devilish to express my joy. Still I hesitated, the interview ending with an appointment for the next morning, when I was to decide.

"I'll tell you what, doctor," said he. "My friend Major Schwiertz who is operating in Sonora is now here in the city recruiting Germans, and Mexicans too, to be drilled as soldiers. For we are getting ready to give those American swine something to do that will keep them so busy they will not have time to ship troops and support to France."

"I shall be most happy to accept anything that will give me an opportunity to do something for the Fatherland," I replied.

I was ready to begin my career as a German secret service agent.

Shortly after accepting Jahnke's offer, Altendorf was able to open a channel of communication with the U.S. Army Military Intelligence section in Nogales, Arizona. He suspected that a trader doing business with the Germans was an American agent. The man's English was too correct, and he seemed to take undue interest in any secret information that was revealed in his presence. Altendorf approached the man in private and asked whether he would be willing to contact the American military in Nogales on his behalf. Fortunately for Altendorf—if he had been wrong it would have cost him his life—the trader *was* in the employ of American intelligence and agreed to deliver a sealed parcel of papers for him. They were his first report as a volunteer operative.

The doctor from Cracow was in an ideal position to provide the army with valuable information on German intentions in Mexico. While serving as an agent, Altendorf promised never to reveal any American intelligence methods or procedures, and in his later memoirs, described passing his information to go-betweens with aliases like "Smith" or "Jones," who either hand-delivered them to Lieutenant Daugherty, the MI officer in San Antonio who reviewed and compiled the information that Altendorf provided, or conveyed them to one of the U.S. consulates in Mexico for transmission to Military Intelligence.

After his dinner meeting with Jahnke, Altendorf was introduced by Paglasch to Major R. W. Schwiertz, who hired him as an instructor at the German Mexican training camp at El Claro, Sonora. Altendorf was placed on Minister von Eckhardt's payroll and given a railroad pass issued by the Carranza government that allowed him to ride free of charge on Mexican railroads. To the doctor's puzzlement, Schwiertz also took Altendorf to a tailor and ordered two uniforms for him to wear; one as a captain in the German infantry, and the other as a colonel in the Forty-Fifth Mexican Regiment. To Altendorf "it looked like there had been a merger of the German and Mexican governments."

At the Hotel Cosmos where they now resided, Lieutenant Auch, Schwiertz's aide-de-camp, "a typical rough German soldier lacking the education and polish of Schwiertz," briefed Altendorf on the plans for the German Mexican training camp. It had been established at El Claro, approximately fifty miles from the U.S. border where a colony of 1,400 men was now based. The camp was supported by General Calles, Carranza's governor in Sonora, on the condition that the men trained there serve in the proposed army of invasion that would strike the United States in concert with the final German drive in France that was expected to end the war in victory for the Fatherland. It was believed that a force of 45,000 men—mostly Mexicans, but with enough German reservists interspersed to maintain military order—would be sufficient to achieve their objective because the United States was viewed as near defenseless after sending the bulk of its army overseas. The German's theory held that once a beachhead had been established by the invaders on American soil, the invasion force would be augmented in short order by German immigrants, labor agitators, anarchists, and disaffected southern blacks who would sweep the country from coast to coast. Even if the scheme achieved only limited success, the consequences could be significant. The year before, a raid on Columbus, New Mexico, led by Pancho Villa, had resulted in a punitive force of American army regulars being dispatched to Mexico and the entire U.S. National Guard being massed at the border.

Their current task in Mexico City, Auch explained, was to purchase supplies for the proposed army of invasion. Major Schwiertz had received a letter of credit from General Calles that had been endorsed by von Eckhardt for this purpose.

Over the next several days, Altendorf accompanied Schwiertz on his purchasing mission around the Mexican capital. The doctor provided his superior with a long list of medicines and drugs that would be needed by the force. When they had obtained about $15,000 worth of material, Altendorf was told to prepare for departure to Hermosillo, the capital of the state of Sonora, where they would personally meet with General Calles.

The baggage that the German team packed for the train ride to Hermosillo could have supported a military expedition by itself. In addition to clothing, food, and supplies, their hand luggage included twenty-six rifles and three thousand rounds of ammunition.

"It may come in handy," said Schwiertz. "We may have some trouble along the road."

After their train departed from Mexico City, progress along the line proved very slow, with frequent stops. They reached Irapuato late in the afternoon of the first day, and decided to stay for the night because it wasn't safe to run trains in Mexico after dark. The arrival of a group of men in German uniforms created a sensation at the station. Major Schwiertz publicly announced that they were traveling to Sonora as military instructors to train an army of Germans and Mexicans for an invasion of the United States.

"We will drive the American swine out of Texas, Arizona, and California, and then the Mexican flag will float once more over the vast territory of which you were robbed by the gringos years ago," Schwiertz proclaimed.

On the third day of their journey, the trip was livened up when a volley of bullets came crashing through the woodwork and glass of their coach. Altendorf noted:

> It was the bandit attack without which a railroad journey in Mexico would be considered incomplete. As soon as the firing began all the passengers threw themselves on the floor. When the train stopped, Schwiertz, Auch and myself seized our rifles and sprang to the ground, as did the 20 soldiers comprising our escort and a few of the passengers.
>
> Altogether the fight lasted about 15 minutes. It was impossible to ascertain exactly what happened to the bandetti who had the advantage of concealment in the thick jungle, but a dozen of them were seen to drop, of which five, I think, fell to my rifle, for I learned to be a crack shot as a youth while hunting in Poland. On our side, one woman was killed and three women badly wounded. We proceeded after a delay of two hours and a quarter.

The journey to Hermosillo was broken up with frequent stops along the route, where the group detrained for discussions with middlemen brokering supplies for the German Mexican force. Schwiertz haggled with a Turk in Mazatlán for khaki uniforms from San Francisco, Colt automatic pistols, and ammunition, to be paid for with cash, hides, and ores taken from American mines in Mexico. With the assistance of a renegade American named Dalcowicz, Schwiertz was also working a deal to sell thousands of tons of structural steel and eighteen miles of standard gauge railroad ties from a disused American-owned copper mine to the Mexican government for conversion into guns and shells for the proposed invasion of the United States. As part of the deal, Schwiertz would receive a payment of $2,000 "under the table" for his services.

It was becoming apparent to Altendorf that Schwiertz was not entirely driven by his allegiance to the Fatherland . . .

When they reached Hermosillo, Schwiertz, Auch, and Altendorf cleaned the dust from their German uniforms and set out for "el palacio," the government palace, to pay their respects to their benefactor, governor, general (and future president of Mexico), Plutarco Elías Calles. "The palace" turned out to be a worn, two-story barnlike structure made of brick, from which Calles ruled his state with an iron fist. After receiving a welcoming salute from a thirty-man honor guard, the German secret service men ascended a broad flight of stairs and met Calles in his office, where they found him standing beside a cheap rolltop desk. Governor Calles was six feet tall, solidly built, with steel-gray hair, a trim mustache, and piercing brown eyes. He greeted them with enthusiasm, and Schwiertz introduced the governor to the newest member of his staff.

"General, let me introduce Capt. Dr. Altendorf, whom I wired to you about."

I acknowledged the introduction with a military salute, which pleased Calles greatly. After a brief conversation about nothing, such as is usual under the circumstance, Calles remarked on my perfect Spanish, whereupon Schwiertz remarked:

"Yes, and he almost looks like a Spaniard, although he is a German Austrian. He will be a very valuable man here."

Since it was approaching midday and Calles had other business to attend to, the meeting ended with an appointment for Altendorf to meet Calles again later in the afternoon. When the doctor returned at the appointed hour, he was received by the governor alone and they discussed the coming drive against the United States. Altendorf inquired whether Calles thought enough men could be assembled for a successful invasion of America.

"Oh yes, we have enough men," he replied. "With the assistance of experienced German officers we can put the men in the field. We Mexicans are not afraid of the United States. We have very brave men, but we need good leaders. We have some German officers here and we are promised more from South America. We are not short of money, as Germany is supplying us . . . Above all we know positively that the Mexicans and Germans in the United States will join us and that is enough to ensure victory."

The interview ended with Governor Calles conferring upon me the rank of colonel in the Mexican army. He personally handed me the insignia for cap and coat. When I told Schwiertz of my appointment he was delighted.

"I told you that we Germans and the Mexicans are one," he exclaimed.

The third day after our arrival at Hermosillo, Schwiertz, Auch, and myself left for El Claro.

When they reached the training camp, Schwiertz learned that there had been trouble in his absence. An American deserter named O'Connor had been left in charge, and while running the operation, had discovered the lengths of Schwiertz's graft and underhanded dealings. Schwiertz had sold a Ford car stolen from El Claro, pilfered $1,100 worth of ore, appropriated copper plate from a mine that was supposed to be shipped to Mexico City, and sold drugs that had been imported for the use of the Mexican government to Johansen and Felix of Mexico City, pocketing the cash. O'Connor had deserted El Claro in disgust and was now headed straight to Governor Calles with evidence of Schwiertz's thievery.

Altendorf took aside Ostermann, the training camp quartermaster, and questioned him about O'Connor's allegations. Ostermann told Altendorf that things were indeed bad and more trouble was likely on the way. The books for El Claro were in terrible shape. Schwiertz had taken a lot of camp money with him to Mexico City, and a lot of hides were missing as well. The men had not been paid and would soon be asking for their money. Schwiertz had been in charge of handling all funds, the worried quartermaster told him.

Schwiertz found Altendorf and asked to see him alone. His future in Mexico would be in serious doubt once O'Connor reported to the governor, and the German secret service man was deeply concerned.

"You must help me out of this trouble," Schwiertz told him. "You can speak Spanish much better than I, and besides, Calles thinks very highly of you, first because von Eckhardt has recommended you very strongly, and I added a great deal more in your favor, and finally because you personally impressed the governor. So I want you to go to him as fast as you can get there and talk in my favor. Assure him that everything that O'Connor tells him is a lie, and paint the fellow as black as you can . . .

To say that I was delighted with the turn affairs had taken would hardly do justice to my feelings. Developments thus far seemed to warrant the assurance that the attempted mobilization of a force to invade the United States might be thwarted before it assumed serious proportions, while at the same time I should be able to dispose finally of an annoying troublemaker. But I drew a long face and was all sympathy with Schwiertz.

The camp commander assigned Altendorf a Ford automobile and a German Mexican chauffeur—a tough-looking hombre—for the sixty-mile trip to Hermosillo. The car was loaded with extra gas cans, several containers of drinking water, and as a precaution, hand tools in case they broke down. Altendorf carried a Winchester rifle and a Colt .45 revolver, while the chauffeur was armed with an army carbine, since they would be traveling through dangerous Yaqui country for the length of the trip.

It was late afternoon by the time the two men departed from El Claro. After they had covered twelve miles of rough terrain, near Santa Ana, the road faded out entirely. They proceeded blindly through unbroken brush and rocky sand to the railroad, where for the greater part of the way, the road ran parallel to the tracks. At one point, Altendorf discovered that they were twenty-five miles off course, but at three thirty in the morning, they once again reached the railroad and followed it toward Hermosillo. They were delayed by a succession of gullies, one of which took a full hour to cross, and had to repair a flat tire, but finally reached their destination at four o'clock in the afternoon. The last thirty miles of the journey had required ten hours of motoring, and their average speed for the entire twenty-five-hour trip had been less than two and a half miles an hour, but they were grateful to have passed through the hostile territory unharmed.

Altendorf immediately called on the governor. Calles was surprised at the doctor's appearance and expressed admiration for his nerve in making such a dangerous journey without escort. Altendorf informed Calles that he had come to discuss Schwiertz's troubles at El Claro, but the governor cut him off, advising Altendorf that he was already aware of the situation at the training camp. He had dispatched a personal representative to investigate. Altendorf was told to keep quiet about the subject and say nothing about their discussion after his return to El Claro.

When the doctor-spy arrived back at the training camp, Schwiertz was waiting for him. How had the meeting gone with Calles, he anxiously inquired? Altendorf warned Schwiertz to be careful or he would have some trouble, revealing that the governor was now fully aware of the allegations.

The next day, a telegram from Calles arrived ordering Schwiertz to report to the capital as soon as possible. Full of misgivings, Schwiertz asked Altendorf to accompany him to Hermosillo. They found Calles waiting for them in his office. After a frigid reception, Calles launched into a verbal attack on the corrupt secret service man. The report from his personal representative had been received and now Calles had the full details of Major Schwiertz's crooked financial dealings. The governor angrily demoted Schwiertz to "jefe de policía de la frontera," a commander of border police in charge of twenty-one men.

For the next week, Altendorf worked behind the scenes to get rid of Schwiertz entirely. He arranged for a U.S. military intelligence agent to organize a phony deal to smuggle drugs across the border that would produce evidence showing that border police leader Schwiertz had received a payoff, then he called on Governor Calles and supplied him with the "evidence," including additional information that suggested Schwiertz was in reality an American spy.

Major Schwiertz was once again called to the governor's palace. Calles received him alone, and following another verbal tirade, called for an aide to bring in "the colonel." Altendorf later recounted:

Schwiertz was evidently surprised at my appearance. He was still more surprised by what followed, for I opened up on him at once. As soon as we had all three taken seats at a small table, at Calles request, I asked, "Schwiertz, when are you going to pay me the money you owe me? General Calles gave you $400 for me, but you denied to me that you ever received it. You are a thief."

Schwiertz gasped in astonishment. He had lost his tongue, so astounding to him was the turn events were taking.

I gave him no chance to recover. Pointing my finger at him I continued, "You are a traitor! This man, general, is an American spy. He has sold the secrets from your office, secrets from the office of the German ambassador [Minister]. He has sold the German codes and the Mexican codes to an American agent named Page. If von Eckhardt knew what happened here he would have this man killed."

Being still speechless, Schwiertz responded in the only manner he could think of. He sprang up and aimed a blow at my face which I dodged. Calles was on his feet almost at the same instant, with revolver drawn.

Covering the enraged Schwiertz, he exclaimed, "If you make another move I will shoot you down like a dog. Leave the room immediately."

Schwiertz now found his tongue and tried to offer some explanation, but Calles cut him short, saying, "I will not hear a word. You are a scoundrel. Leave the country in 24 hours."

My first big scheme had succeeded. One dangerous German had been rendered harmless.

In short order, Calles filled Schwiertz's position with a colonel from the Mexican Army. Altendorf would later learn that Schwiertz went to great lengths attempting to even the score. He organized a plot to lure Altendorf from his room at the Hotel Cohn in Hermosillo and murder him in the street, and a second scheme to waylay him after an arranged fishing trip with a German sea captain. Altendorf was informed by French vice consul Pardo that he had actually seen Schwiertz and his gang digging the doctor's grave. But in the end, the two would part ways without further incident. Recognizing that his game was up, Schwiertz eventually escaped in a launch with five other Germans to Lower California.

In late 1917 a courier from the Military Intelligence Department at Nogales brought Altendorf instructions to investigate blacklisted German firms in Mexico. His job was soon made easier when Herr Marks, the proprietor of his hotel, introduced him as a "good doctor" and a "good German" to two well-dressed women, Maria Haas and Maria Wilkinson. Altendorf became friendly with the pair, who it transpired earned their livelihood smuggling goods across the border for German firms. By calculated design, he romanced Maria Wilkinson ("truly a handsome woman") for use as a source of information, plying her with expensive perfume, a wristwatch, and other gifts before eventually being invited to her bed. Following several days of "fishing," Altendorf learned that Melchers Sucesores had been able to accumulate thirty tons of lard from the United States, buying it in small quantities in the name of various Mexican "cloak" companies. The lard was to be shipped to Mexico City for the manufacture of glycerin and converted into explosives. He also discovered that Melchers Sucs was attempting to corner all available supplies of dye woods in Mexico (used in coloring textiles, such as army uniforms) to prevent their being acquired by the United States and its allies.

To obtain additional information, Altendorf went "shopping" through-out the city, ostensibly in search of common items like shirt collars but, in reality, searching for evidence of transactions that violated the American blacklist. In the course of each store visit he would stop to talk with the proprietor, steering the conversation to the source of the products on the retailer's shelves. He was repeatedly told, "We have no trouble in obtaining goods, we buy from Melchers Sucesores who have agents in the United States where they can get all they want." It seemed to Altendorf that, with regard to enemy companies circumventing the blacklist, all roads led to Melchers Sucesores, Señores Unger and Burgmeister managing partners.

Altendorf informed Governor Calles that he had been watching a myste-rious stranger in the city for some time. The man might be an American agent—or a good German, he couldn't be sure—but he wanted to trail him to the border to find out. Calles thought it was a good idea, so on December 13, 1917, Altendorf departed for Nogales, Sonora.

Upon arrival, he arranged contact with Byron S. Butcher, a thirty-one-year-old civilian employee of the Military Intelligence section at Nogales, Arizona, just over the border. They met at a safe house the following night, and the Polish doctor ended his days as a volunteer operative, being officially sworn in as an agent of the U.S. Army Military Intelligence Department. Butcher earnestly reminded him that he would be held responsible for Altendorf's conduct. In response, the doctor assured him that nothing would ever be found on him if he had the misfortune of being discovered, and that he was determined to kill himself before being captured. Altendorf carried a hidden .32 pistol for that purpose, in addition to a .45 revolver that he carried in plain sight, as was the custom in Mexico.

At the military intelligence headquarters in Nogales, Major S. W. Anding sent a message regarding Altendorf to the department intelligence officer at Fort Sam Houston:

> This man has been continuously investigated since his arrival in Sonora October 20th with R. W. Schwiertz . . . To A-1 alone is due the credit that General Calles dropped Schwiertz from his payroll. A-1 made a full report to Calles on the activities of Schwiertz and demonstrated beyond a question that the German agent was a rogue.
>
> This office is convinced of his ability and reliability, considers him one of the most important finds, and predicts that he will prove an invaluable asset to the American government. He has already provided more information of real value than any other dozen informants. His information has been checked and rechecked and found to be correct.

On his return to Mexico City, Altendorf was summoned by Kurt Jahnke. The spymaster informed him that he was leaving for Veracruz to meet a Spanish steamship bringing important papers and a large sum of money that had been forwarded from Germany to Spain by submarine. Since he would be gone for over a week, Jahnke suggested that Altendorf stay at his home during his absence, as he wanted someone he could trust watching the house while he was away.

With tremendous self-control, Altendorf restrained himself from appearing overeager in responding—Janhke's home residence also served as the head office of the German secret service in Mexico. He thanked Jahnke for his kind offer and assured him that he was the best man that he had ever met, but he could not impose on his generous nature to such an extent. Jahnke was insistent, and after a brief period of arm-twisting, Altendorf yielded and agreed to stay at Jahnke's home. The servants were instructed that the doctor was to be the temporary master of the house, and everything was placed in his charge. Jahnke told Altendorf that upon his return he would discuss details of a most important assignment—a trip to the U.S. border with Lothar Witzke. The following day Jahnke left for Veracruz in the company of a German agent named Gaebel.

Altendorf could not believe his good fortune!

Alone in the house for thirteen days, and free from interruption except for the occasional visitor, Agent A-1 made the most of this opportunity to pry into the secrets of the German espionage establishment in Mexico. He opened letters addressed to Jahnke as soon as they were delivered and then carefully resealed them, eliminating any sign of tampering. He searched through Jahnke's files and examined the contents of his private desk. One letter that he found disclosed a plot to blow up oil wells and tank farms in the Tampico oil fields. Another from a German consul in Ecuador described a plan to sabotage nitrate plants in Chile. With each passing day, a stream of correspondence arrived outlining schemes along similar lines, all of which Altendorf dutifully copied for American military intelligence.

He also had the opportunity to meet an assortment of visitors that appeared looking for Jahnke, including a clergyman named Francisco Durán who was being paid $300 a month by the German spymaster to visit Cuba and meet neutral steamers in order to expedite important communiqués from Berlin, and a female courier named Beatrice Martínez Peña who traveled between Mexico and the United States to convey instructions and obtain reports from German agents. Peña even left a copy of her passport with Altendorf, who conscientiously forwarded its details to military intelligence.

The train carrying Jahnke on his return to Mexico City arrived on the morning of January 14, 1918. Altendorf and Witzke met Jahnke at the train station, and together they walked to his home, located nearby. The three men were followed by Gaebel, the agent who had accompanied Jahnke to Veracruz. Gaebel carried two heavy leather bags that Altendorf later learned contained a huge sum of money, part of which was in gold coin, for use in funding secret operations.

Jahnke was in high spirits, and after returning home, jubilantly briefed them on their upcoming assignment.

"Well, Witzke," the spymaster began, "you and the doctor will leave for the border on the 16th. I have received everything I wanted. I have the plans for the invasion of the United States, all complete from Berlin, and the funds to finance the preliminaries."

In the discussion that followed, Altendorf learned for the first time that the scheme to invade America from Mexico had not been dreamed up by local officials, but was planned by the General Staff in Berlin to coincide with the final German drive in France during the spring of 1918. The U.S. invasion would be supported by the Kaiserliche Marine with submarines that were to pass through the Strait of Magellan and proceed around the west coast to San Francisco, where they were to destroy shipping, shell the city, and generally terrorize its citizens.

"Is that the reason Witzke took soundings in the harbors of Manzanillo and Mazatlán?" Altendorf asked.

"Yes. We will have submarines on both the Atlantic and Pacific coasts," Jahnke happily responded.

Witzke's assignment was to slip into the United States on a secret operation that would pave the way for the invasion. He was to arrange for the destruction of munitions plants, food supplies, and any other material that would be useful to the American defenders, as well as instigate an uprising of disaffected southern blacks against the white population "and subvert the Black 9th and 10th Cavalry stationed in Arizona, inducing the troopers to mutiny." Some of these actions he would carry out on his own, others with the assistance of radicals from the Industrial Workers of the World trade union and an unmentioned "third party." Lastly, Witzke was tasked by Jahnke with the assassination of an American intelligence officer who had been interfering with German secret service activities in the United States and Mexico.

"Doctor, listen very carefully to what I have to say," Jahnke said to Altendorf. He continued:

> You will accompany Witzke to Hermosillo where you will introduce him to General Calles and tell him that Witzke is traveling on a Russian passport into the United States, but that he is a German agent. Rademacher, our consul at Guaymas, will know all about this and will have informed General Calles before you get to Hermosillo. You will go and see Carranza tomorrow. Carranza will also advise General Calles fully. Everything has been arranged by Herr von Eckhardt. When you have explained everything to Calles after introducing Witzke, I want you to ask Calles to procure a revolver for Witzke. Never mind what it costs. We will pay whatever price is necessary.

In January 1918, crime was running rampant in Mexico City and anyone who could afford to buy a firearm carried one. The gun shops of the city had been stripped bare, and pistols were in particularly short supply, so obtaining a handgun for Witzke became a key part of Altendorf's assignment. It would be the weapon used to kill the American intelligence man.

"You must do away with that special agent Butcher at Nogales—he is in our way," Jahnke told Witzke. "You will send your messages to the doctor and he will forward your communications to me. If everything works out right, I shall come over with someone else. The first thing for you to do is to see the I.W.W. delegates on the border and let the third party who is going with you operate with his own class of people. Give him all the money he wants. He is all right."

The conference ended when Jahnke departed to meet with Minister von Eckhardt.

The agents gathered later at Jahnke's residence for dinner. During the meal, Altendorf tried to glean additional information by showering Witzke with flattery. The ace saboteur responded with a boastful account of his achievements in the German secret service to date, describing how he had ignited the explosion at the munitions depot on Black Tom Island in New York Harbor, destroyed a ship carrying war supplies, started fires in the Oregon logging camps, and ruined the boilers of the U.S. troop transport

Minnesota, among other acts of sabotage. For his accomplishments, he had been awarded two decorations, the Iron Cross First and Second Class.

Turning to face Altendorf, Witzke concluded his summation by indifferently adding, "I have laid many people in the cemetery. If you are not straightforward with me I will put you there."

Altendorf responded with a genial smile, considering the comment an idle boast. Later he was to learn that Witzke was deadly serious, when the young agent described in detail how he had murdered several individuals with his own hand. One was a woman whom he had lived with while operating as an agent in New York City; another, a woman in Mexico City.

On January 16, 1918, Altendorf and Witzke left Mexico City for the border. It would be an arduous journey—they were to travel by train to Manzanillo, catch a steamer to Mazatlán, and then continue by train to Nogales, Sonora, where the agents would cross into the United States on foot. The mysterious "third man," a black named William Gleaves, traveled with them, although to maintain secrecy, Witzke avoided all conversation with him in Altendorf's presence.

They reached Irapuato on the first day of their trip, and remained there for the next several days waiting for a train to Colima. Restless from the unplanned delay, and looking for something to do on their second night in the city, Witzke proposed that they go out on the town. Altendorf agreed, but to remain on top of his game, confided that he wouldn't be able to drink much, offering as an excuse that he suffered from Bright's disease (today known as acute nephritis, a kidney ailment).

Throughout the evening as they toured Irapuato's night spots, Altendorf refrained from alcohol, while happily plying Witzke with liquor, until the young agent became a stumbling drunk. Altendorf escorted him back to their hotel, where Witzke promptly passed out, giving Altendorf the opportunity to go through the papers in his pockets and write a report on their contents for military intelligence.

On January 19, they caught a train to Colima and resumed their journey north. Upon reaching their destination, the agents learned that the connecting train to Manzanillo would be delayed for at least two days due to a bandit attack that had disrupted service on the line. To ensure that they wouldn't miss their steamer, Witzke paid $80 to hire a locomotive and tender—which they boarded outside of town to avoid being seen, and the trio continued on to Manzanillo, arriving in time to book passage on the SS *Josefina*.

The steamship docked at Mazatlán without incident and the men temporarily parted company. Witzke called on Consul Unger at Melchers Sucesores to discuss matters related to their mission, and then retired to a local bordello. This provided Altendorf with the opportunity to visit the U.S. consul in Mazatlán, William Edgar Chapman, with a message for him to code and telegraph to Byron S. Butcher in Nogales:

> January 26th, 10 a.m. to Butcher from A-1: I arrived Mazatlán from Mexico City last Thursday, leaving for Hermosillo on Saturday 26th with two German spies [Witzke and Gleaves] . . . plotting assassination in Nogales where they are to arrive next Monday. [Altendorf provided detailed descriptions of the "third man" Gleaves and of Witzke.] Use care as he [Witzke] is dangerous. I will be in Hermosillo one day. Would you not have Joe Bru meet me at the Cohen Hotel there at once. Got news for you . . .

From Mazatlán, the three men traveled by rail to Hermosillo, where Altendorf accompanied Witzke to meet the governor. Calles received them cordially and, after giving orders to his staff that no one else was to be admitted to his office, discussed the plans for the secret campaign of destruction and murder that Witzke was to set in motion in the United States as a preliminary to the invasion. When Altendorf told the governor that he had been instructed to procure a revolver for Witzke, Calles touched a button summoning his chief of staff, Colonel García, who obtained a .45 caliber revolver for which Witzke paid $60.

A few days later, Witzke and Gleaves left Hermosillo on a passenger train for Nogales, Sonora, where they would cross the border into the United States. Altendorf had been instructed to stay behind in Hermosillo and remain under cover, but the instant the German agents' train left the station, he rushed back to his hotel, donned a chauffer's uniform, shaved off his mustache, and disguised himself as a Mexican. Then he returned to the station unrecognizable in his new persona and caught a passing freight train to the border.

When he reached Nogales, U.S. Consul Ezra Lawton arranged for him to pass to the American side under cover of darkness. Altendorf was taken in secrecy to Butcher's quarters, where he was debriefed regarding his trip to Sonora and Witzke's mission in the United States. Learning that Witzke was now in Nogales, Sonora, a military intelligence informant code-named M-2 was dispatched to the Central Hotel in Nogales, where Witzke was staying. The informant was able to locate Witzke, and a message was shortly received that the German agent was planning to enter the United States the following day to conduct some banking business.

As soon as Witzke passed through American immigration, he found himself confronted by two determined men, Butcher and Harry Sharp, another intelligence agent, who shoved revolvers into his ribs and placed him under arrest. Byron S. Butcher, the military intelligence officer that Witzke had come to kill, clamped handcuffs on Witzke's wrists.

Paul Bernardo Altendorf had arranged the capture of the most important German secret service agent to be apprehended in the United States during World War 1, and the only German spy who was sentenced to death. Unbeknownst to Altendorf, William Gleaves, the man who Jahnke and Witzke believed would initiate an uprising of disaffected blacks in the south and coordinate the destruction of American mines and industrial plants, was actually an agent of British Naval Intelligence who, like Altendorf, had infiltrated the German secret service to report on enemy intentions in Mexico.

Now safe in America, Altendorf felt "as if a great weight had been lifted from my heart." In the coming weeks, he prepared a typewritten report on the workings of the German espionage establishment in Mexico, acted as an interpreter for military intelligence, and unwound from the tension of working months under cover. His peaceful respite ended when a wire arrived from military intelligence headquarters in Washington: Agent A-1 was to cross the border and return to duty in Mexico.

Butcher called Altendorf to a briefing on his next assignment. Although every effort had been made to keep Witzke's arrest a secret, there was no way of knowing whether word of it had reached Mexico. If the news of Witzke's capture *had* leaked out, both the Germans and their Mexican counterparts would assume that Altendorf was the one that had betrayed him and his life expectancy would be significantly reduced.

"The mission is exceedingly dangerous," Butcher advised. "I would not take the risk myself."

Altendorf dismissed the warning, and provided Butcher with the name of his family in Cracow so they could be informed of his fate if the worst should happen.

Butcher outlined the objectives of Altendorf's new assignment. He was to learn whether the Germans were aware that Witzke had been arrested, find out why a certain German agent had recently appeared at Nogales, obtain information on individuals supplying blacklisted German companies, find out if the Germans had any radio stations in Mexico, and lastly, learn whether there was any truth to the rumor that the German navy had established a submarine base in Lower California, Mexico.

In order to share at least some of the risk that Altendorf would be facing, Butcher informed Altendorf that he would accompany him below the border as far as Guaymas. Departing on a Southern Pacific express train while traveling in separate coaches, they proceeded uneventfully through Nogales, Santa Ana, and Hermosillo. Late on the evening of the second day of the trip, Butcher rose to leave the train at Empalme, seven miles from Guaymas. Before disembarking, he took advantage of the darkness of the railway platform to speak to Altendorf without being seen.

"Doctor, I might as well bid you goodbye now," Butcher told Agent A-1 in a hushed tone, "because in my opinion, you'll never come back."

Unfazed, Altendorf proceeded to Culiacán where he arranged a meeting with General Iturbe to discuss business transactions with blacklisted companies. Then he went on to Mazatlán where he knew that he would face serious questions concerning the fate of Witzke. His first stop in the city was Melchers Sucesores where he called on Fritz Unger.

From the moment that he entered Unger's office it was apparent that things were not as they should be.

"Where is Witzke?" Unger inquired, staring at him with intensity.

"I don't know. That's what I came to find out," Altendorf replied.

Without pausing, the consul shot back, "Have you seen the n–gger [Gleaves]?"

"Was he one of us?" Altendorf asked in surprise.

"Yes," Unger responded. "He was an I.W.W. agent."

Altendorf removed a wrinkled telegram from his pocket and handed it to Unger. It was signed "Ruiz," Witzke's code name, and read simply:

Los Angeles, February 8, 1918.

I am in Los Angeles arranging my business. Will be in Nogales in eight days.

Ruiz

The telegram was a fake that Altendorf had sent to himself in Nogales, but it seemed to satisfy Unger for the moment. Reassured, he asked Altendorf what his plans were in Mazatlán. The doctor told him that he was in need of money and was planning to set up a practice there. Unger responded that there were few physicians in the city, and that he should be able to make a good living in Mazatlán.

"Come and see me often," the consul told him.

With a straight face, Altendorf assured Unger that he would, aware that much of the information that he was seeking was likely to be found in the consul's office.

During the week that followed, Altendorf worked to establish a medical practice in Mazatlán. It would provide an ideal cover for his work as a spy and open new opportunities for gathering information for military intelligence. He rented an office at the Hotel Francia, hung out his "shingle," and had cards printed for distribution in the street to advertise his services.

A short time later he received a visit from Pedro, the cargador who had transferred his baggage to shore at Mazatlán harbor during his previous visit to the city. The laborer stopped by, hoping to obtain future luggage-handling business from Altendorf, and during the casual conversation that followed, mentioned that some Germans were working day and night to get the salvaged Mexican gunboat *Morelos* ready for sea. Pedro's remark jogged Altendorf's memory, and he recalled a fragment of a conversation he had overheard between Witzke and Unger during the trip to the border that the *Morelos* would be useful when German submarines appeared in the Pacific.

Altendorf made a note to look into this effort by Germans to restore an old Mexican warship—this gunboat *Morelos*.

He was not alone. Consul Unger continued to monitor the progress of Arzak's team with great interest. When the U-boats arrived on the Pacific coast, they would need a submarine tender to operate. Just as German commerce raiders relied on supply ships contracted by Karl Boy-Ed and other Naval Etappe officers for coal and naval stores, the Kaiserliche Marine's Pacific U-boats would need a sub tender to shuttle them the diesel fuel and provisions needed to operate while at sea. After it was fully overhauled and ready for service, the *Morelos* would fill that role, allowing German submarines to be brought to bear against Allied merchant ships plying the western coast of the United States.

Unger understood the part that he would play in supporting the plan quite clearly. The Carranza government would confiscate the *Morelos* as soon as Arzak had completed fitting her out for sea and then turn the gunboat over to the German Navy for use as a submarine tender, at no cost to either government. The fuel and supplies that the *Morelos* would convey to the U-boats were to be obtained through the offices of Melchers Sucesores, which in effect, would become the Etappe for the scheme.

The only potential difficulty was the time required before the *Morelos* would be seaworthy. From his discussions with Arzak, Unger knew that the salvaged gunboat would not be ready to sail before May 1918, yet the final German offensive in France was expected to commence at the end of March, according to Ambassador von Eckhardt. A way *must* be found for diverting the attention of the American navy away from Europe. If not a major warship, perhaps an armed vessel like the schooner *Ayesha* of the *Emden* adventure could be located to sail off into the Pacific drawing American warships in pursuit.

Staring out across Mazatlán harbor, a plan began to form in Unger's mind, and he knew just the ship and exactly the person to carry it out.

3   The *Alexander Agassiz*

The white schooner struggled into Mazatlán harbor and dropped anchor. Listing heavily to starboard from an unbalanced load, her mainsail tossed across the decking like a worn rag, the latest voyage of the *Alexander Agassiz* had ended in ignominious failure. The 85-foot vessel was the sole asset of the Pacific Coast Trading and Shipping Company, a coastal trader that operated at the bottom of the pyramid in comparison to the powerful trading houses like Melchers Sucesores. Since being organized the year before, through lack of knowledge of local conditions and local agents, total ignorance of the shipping business, and above all, its boat having to fly the American flag in Mexican waters, Pacific Coast Trading had fallen deeply into debt.

The contract signed with Señor Meistiero had been expected to reverse the downward spiral. Santos Meistiero, a wealthy Spaniard from Tepic, had agreed to pay $500 per month in American gold to charter the *Alexander Agassiz* to carry his cargo and trade goods, and was to pay an additional $100 per month in American gold for the owner's services in running the boat. At last profitability had seemed within reach. The first assignment from Meistiero was to carry a consignment of corn from San Blas to Manzanillo—an easy trip of 285 nautical miles. The schooner's hold was loaded with sixty-five tons of corn and off she headed down the coast.

Their troubles began at once.

The *Alexander Agassiz* was rated to carry a maximum of fifty tons of cargo and was now dangerously overloaded. Before the schooner had traveled far, seawater began to wash over her deck, filling the hold. To save the boat, the crew threw two hundred bags of corn overboard, and about four hundred gallons of distillate (the kerosene-like fuel that powered the engines) was washed away as well. The schooner's captain took down the sails and ropes and used them to lash the corn in place; when the corn was thrown over the side, the ropes went over at the same time. With its unevenly distributed load, the *Alexander Agassiz* was close to capsizing. As a final blow, the engineer hired for the trip had proved incapable of handling the engines and both went dead on the high sea.

Through an act of Providence, another boat soon arrived on the scene. Its engineer came aboard the *Agassiz* and restarted the engines, allowing the schooner to limp into Mazatlán, where the crew was ordered to offload the remaining corn. Since the corn was now wet, the schooner's owner didn't want to take the chance of the grain swelling up and bursting the sides of the boat.

It was a major setback. Without Señor Meistiero's business, the "Pacific Coast Trading and Shipping Company" would sink even further in red ink. At this point, most men would have accepted defeat and quit the business altogether. But if anyone expected that to happen, they had never met the woman who owned the *Alexander Agassiz*—Maude M. Lochrane.

The role of a woman in society was narrowly defined in 1917, in both public and private life. Women did not have the right to vote. If a woman was married, she was expected to stay at home, manage the household, and care for the children. If she was single, she could obtain a clerical or secretarial position, or work as a teacher; the thought that a woman could lead a corporation was inconceivable. A woman was considered "proper" if she was demure, self-effacing, and attentive. When appearing in public, she was expected to wear a dress of appropriate length, with a hat that ensured that the sun never colored her fair skin. A woman who was openly engaging toward male counterparts, or drew attention by dying her hair, ran the risk of being scorned as an "adventuress."

Maude Lochrane was ahead of her time. Forty years old, she could easily pass for ten years younger. She had strong Irish features, light blue eyes, and a full head of bright auburn hair that gave her the nickname "the geranium." Maude's red hair complemented her complexion—a perpetual sunburn highlighted by freckles. Although she stood just five feet four inches tall and weighed a mere 110 pounds, Maude Lochrane exuded an energy, alertness, and fiery temperament that far outweighed her diminutive stature. Upon learning that business partners had pulled a shady deal, her response to an associate was "many has been the time when I would have liked to have them by the throat." She could captain her schooner from morning 'til night and then discuss business over a beer at the cantina (saloon) in Mazatlán. One man who knew her at the time described her as "Miss Maude Lochrane with a head of auburn hair, yes, decidedly auburn. Her complexion was tanned to a—well I shall call it—red. Once seen she was never to be forgotten."

Maude Lochrane's childhood had been marred by tragedy and hardship, and the experiences of those early years helped to create the burning desire for success that would characterize much of her life. She was born in Michigan on April 16, 1878. Adopted as an orphan at the age of six by a family named Wheeler, her formal education had ended in eighth grade, when she "had to go out to work and earn a living." From that point forward, Maude would battle her way through life on her own, learning as she went. Along the way she developed a considerable capacity as a businesswoman.

In 1903, at the age of twenty-five, Maude took a position as a stenographer with the A. C. Varney Company, an architectural firm in Detroit, and was able to gain some experience in architectural drawing on the side. Two years later, becoming restless, she entered service to an elderly woman named Mrs. Gilson whom she cared for and accompanied on a transcontinental trip to California. Maude was "quite an entertaining talker," and in her next job as sales agent for an electric vibrator company, she traveled throughout Texas, Arizona, and New Mexico hawking the firm's products. In 1906, she returned to California and was employed as a bookkeeper by the Southwest Electrical Company, a manufacturer of electrical wiring and fixtures. She advanced quickly in the Southwest organization, and within a year was promoted to manager of the company's San Bernardino branch office. It seemed that Maude's early years of hardship were now behind her and a bright financial future lay ahead. Her rising stature became apparent to all in a front page story that was published in the November 14, 1907, edition of the *San Bernardino Daily Sun*:

SYNDICATE IS FORMED

Local Men Get Together to Put under
Cultivation Kern County Lands

A meeting was held yesterday of the members of the syndicate which recently acquired 485 acres of choice land in the Kern County foothill district for taking steps to perfect an incorporation, it being determined to adopt the name "Foothill Citrus Farms Company." The incorporation papers will be forwarded to Sacramento at once. The capital stock of the corporation has been placed at $24,000 with $9,600 actually paid in.

The stockholders and their holdings are: A.A. Cox $400, Miss Maude M. Lochrane, $800, C. Meyer $400, Ralph L. Haven $800, A.A. Neff and F.L. Henry $2000 . . . As soon as the corporation is perfected officers will be chosen. The company controls three-quarters of a section of land located in the Kern County foothill district that is especially adapted to the culture of both the orange and apple, as well as many other fruit crops and vines. Apples and oranges grown in this vicinity are as fine as any produced in the State.

Readers of the *Daily Sun* were likely impressed that a young woman, a recent arrival to the city, had acquired the means to participate in a real estate investment with a prominent group of local businessmen. One reader took particular interest in the story—Hiram S. Roach, the president and general manager of the Southwest Electrical Company. Ten months later, another story appeared in the *San Bernardino Daily Sun*:

IS ANXIOUS TO FIND A GIRL

Electrical Supply Man Says He Has
Been Buncoed by a Fair Lady
Who Is Now among the Missing

Where is Miss Maude Lochrane? H.S. Roach of the Southwest Electrical Company is seeking her, and says that he will have a warrant for her, charging her with embezzlement.

It is alleged that while Miss Lochrane was managing the local store of the company Roach became suspicious that her accounts were not straight. She was transferred to Riverside, and the company put experts on her books. The allegation is made that they discovered a shortage of something like $1,600.

Roach took the matter up with the District Attorney's office, and says that when he returned from the mountains he was informed that there was no way that a case could be made against the young woman. She, in the meantime, had left the locality, and though it is now two months since she left, Roach proposes to commence prosecution.

In justice to the absent woman, it should be said that at the time she was threatened with arrest she retained an attorney here, being determined to lift the cloud from her name if Roach pressed his proposed prosecution.

Whether Maude Lochrane—initially hired as a bookkeeper by the electrical products company despite having only an eighth-grade education—was guilty of honest accounting errors or grand larceny will forever remain a mystery. For whichever reason, Maude quickly relocated to El Paso, Texas, where in the coming years she took a variety of jobs, from "canvasser" (opinion taker) to the proprietor of the Raymond Hotel. In 1915, after the seven-year statute of limitations had expired, eliminating any chance of Hiram Roach prosecuting her to recover the alleged shortage, Maude resurfaced in California and settled in Los Angeles. There she pursued a new career as a reporter, while devoting her free time to civic causes in greater Los Angeles.

At this point she met a man named Guillermo Taliferro, better known as "William Taylor," who proposed the idea of forming a coastal shipping company to carry freight and passengers between Mexican ports. William Taylor had a number of personal shortcomings; he was a somewhat lazy and indifferent individual, he lived off money sent to him by his wife in Massachusetts, which he spent on beer and other women, and the U.S. government had outstanding charges against him for handling counterfeit Mexican currency. But Taylor had one attribute that made him invaluable to Maude Lochrane—a male name to use in corresponding with businessmen on shipping matters. Although William Taylor would be listed as "General Manager" of the Pacific Coast Trading and Shipping Company and Maude Lochrane as "Secretary," it was Maude who would organize the company, arrange financial backing, and be the driving force behind it. She began by leasing a small office in the prestigious Merchants Trust Building in downtown Los Angeles, had a telephone installed, and arranged for impressive stationary to be printed. Then Maude and William Taylor went searching for a boat to charter and discovered the *Alexander Agassiz*.

In 1903 a Harvard-educated zoologist, Dr. William E. Ritter, and a group of like-minded colleagues founded a research station for the study of marine biology on San Diego Bay, which they named the Marine Biological Association. They began operations in a converted boathouse next to the exclusive Hotel del Coronado, and collected specimens with a rented schooner piloted by a Portuguese fisherman. From these humble beginnings, the marine station grew rapidly and, with patronage from a group of wealthy San Diego citizens led by newspaperman E. W. Scripps and his sister Ellen, produced significant oceanographic findings. Scripps even donated his personal yacht, the *Loma*, to the association to help further its work. In 1906, when the *Loma* ran aground and was wrecked near the Point Loma lighthouse, the directors of the association decided to commission a boat specifically designed for use in marine zoological research. A contract was signed with San Diego boat builder Lawrence Jensen, and six months later, the research vessel *Alexander Agassiz* was launched.

Named after an eminent Swiss marine biologist, the *Alexander Agassiz* was a schooner-rigged "ketch" with a large deck area in front of the main mast and the wheel placed behind the rear mast. A flat-bottomed boat designed to operate in shallow water as well as on the open ocean, the schooner was eighty-five feet in length and had a beam twenty-six feet wide, yet only drew five feet of water and could house nine people comfortably. To augment its sail power, the *Alexander Agassiz* was equipped with two 30-horsepower Western Standard engines that could deliver a maximum speed of 9 knots. Its fuel tanks had a combined storage capacity of 650 gallons of distillate, providing a range (powered by engines alone) of 850 miles. The combined cost of the boat, engines, sails, instruments, and accessory hardware totaled $16,000, a significant sum in 1907, but the *Alexander Agassiz* would prove to be a fine vessel for conducting marine research and well worth the original investment. After her trial cruise to the Coronado Islands off the coast of northwestern Mexico, Dr. Fred Baker, who ran the schooner for the association, noted approvingly, "the boat is above criticism except in very minor matters," and the schooner was soon employed in a series of nautical excursions in support of the station's scientific studies.

Within a decade of its founding, the Marine Biological Association was recognized as one of the most significant marine research institutions in North America. On February 13, 1912, it gained even greater prominence when it became a department of the University of California—the Scripps Institution for Biological Research—by assigning "all properties, privileges, and rights" to the university. One of the assets transferred was the schooner *Alexander Agassiz*, which was described in the official record of the University of California as "a two-masted schooner . . . fitted out with the standard equipment of the International Commission for Investigation of the Sea, including apparatus for sounding, for dredging to a depth of 6,000 feet, for trawling, for hydrographic work, and for plankton work. The boat is thoroughly seaworthy and available for collecting expeditions not only along the California shores but for deep sea voyages as well."

Now part of the state university system, the research plans of the Scripps Institution began to change in scope and the *Alexander Agassiz* was found to be unsuitable for the marine exploration being contemplated. It had also become expensive for the school to operate. In July 1914, the *Agassiz* was taken into dry dock for repairs; its log would show that the schooner had only been in commission for seven days during the previous year. While the vessel sat moored at its anchorage, budgetary pressure was being brought to bear on the Scripps Institution by the Regents of the University of California, and questions were raised concerning the research vessel *Alexander Agassiz*, now viewed as something of a white elephant.

Then in late 1916, without any advance notice, the Scripps Institution received an offer to rent the dormant schooner. It arrived in the form of a letter that landed on the desk of W. C. Crandall, the institution's business manager, from William Taylor, the general manager of the Pacific Coast Trading and Shipping Company, who inquired, "Will you kindly advise me by return mail as to whether the boat *Alexander Agassiz* is for charter?

If she is, will you please write full particulars. We want the boat for work on the West Coast."

After conferring with university officials, Crandall responded, "The Alexander Agassiz is not for charter, but she is for sale. With some alterations she can carry easily 60 tons and be a very comfortable boat. Sale price is $6,000. The *Agassiz* is probably the best built boat of her type in these waters and her engines are in excellent shape."

The two aspiring entrepreneurs, Maude Lochrane and William Taylor, were thrilled at the opportunity presented to them. The only problem was that Maude had a total of $500 in her bank account. It would take some creative financing to account for the remaining $5,500 of the purchase price. Maude contacted her brother Frank Wheeler and his wife Minnie and invited them into the partnership. Minnie and Frank owned real estate in Los Angeles and Venice, California, that could be used as security against a loan. Then she wired an offer to the Scripps Institution: the company would pay $6,000 for the *Alexander Agassiz*, with $500 in cash, and the remainder in installment payments of $300 per month at 7 percent interest until the purchase price was paid in full. As security collateral they offered a property located in Boylston Heights, Los Angeles, valued at $13,000 that carried a $3,000 mortgage.

Crandall brought the proposal to E. W. Scripps and Dr. Ritter, who responded that although the school was experiencing serious budgetary pressure and the schooner was unsuited to their present work, Pacific Coast Trading would have to provide ironclad security for the deal to be approved.

Crandall wired Taylor that "his" offer was unacceptable unless it was backed by a $5,000 bond covering the unpaid balance of the purchase price.

It was a formidable obstacle, but Maude remained undaunted, and turned to the one man she knew who had the financial resources to back her with a $5,000 note—Joseph Mesmer of Los Angeles.

Joseph Mesmer was the president and owner of the St. Louis Fire Brick Company, a major manufacturing enterprise, but more than that, he was an institution in the city of Los Angeles. Among his accomplishments, he had been a member of the Board of Freeholders that wrote a new charter for the city in 1887. He had worked to secure $280,000 in subscriptions to pay for the land used for the Los Angeles post office and federal building, and another $32,000 in subscriptions to obtain the building site for the Chamber of Commerce. He single-handedly brought about the demise of the Alcatraz Paving Trust, a group of businessmen trying to monopolize the supply of paving materials for public roads, an action that significantly reduced the cost of the city's thoroughfares. The *Los Angeles Herald* described Mesmer in 1905 as "one of the best known men in Los Angeles. Everybody knows him and everybody knows he is honest. He is a man of wide business experience who has held positions of trust and gained the confidence of the people." Mesmer was the kind of man rarely encountered today. Not motivated by money, power or ego, his greatest satisfaction came from improving the general welfare of society.

Maude became acquainted with the city leader through her volunteer civic work in Los Angeles. Mesmer had been a member of the Board of Public Works during the reconstruction of the important Broadway Tunnel when they first met, and had been impressed by Maude's capable work in "making appraisals of property in connection with the opening of the tunnel." He was also impressed by Maude herself, a woman who began at the lowest station in life and had overcome tremendous obstacles to better her position.

Maude, Frank Wheeler, and William Taylor met with Mesmer and outlined their plan to buy the *Alexander Agassiz* and use the boat to carry freight between Mexican ports. After listening to their proposal, Mesmer agreed to back them with a $5,000 performance bond. He would make no money on the deal, and provided the bond purely as a favor to his friend Maude Lochrane. To secure the businessman from any future loss, Frank and Minnie Wheeler took out a second mortgage on the California real estate that they owned.

With a $5,000 surety bond from the renowned Joseph Mesmer as guarantee in case of default, the university's acceptance of their offer was a certainty. On January 12, 1917, the finance committee of the Regents of the University of California approved the sale of the *Alexander Agassiz* to the Pacific Coast Trading and Shipping Company for $6,000. The agreement that was executed by the parties called for a down payment of $600 in cash, and individual payments of $300 per month for eighteen consecutive months, with the $5,000 bond from Mesmer held as security.

The *Alexander Agassiz* was immediately moved to a new anchorage in San Diego, and work began on converting the schooner from a research vessel into a freight carrier. The private stateroom was torn out and the main cabin gutted, creating enough space for fifty tons of cargo. On deck, a small galley was constructed aft of the scientists cabin for use in preparing food for crew and passengers. The engine room, which had been well laid out by boat builder Jensen was in pristine condition, and left unchanged.

On January 27, 1917, Wheeler and Taylor sailed out of San Diego harbor with the American flag flying proudly from a staff at the schooner's stern, bound for Mazatlán, Mexico, in search of their first paying customers. For this initial trip, Maude would stay behind and manage affairs at the office. It was an exciting moment for the shipping company partners and they were in high spirits, believing that they were on their way to making a fortune.

But in business, as in life, timing is everything, and they could not have chosen a worse moment to launch a coastal shipping company in Mexico. While the *Alexander Agassiz* was on the open ocean cruising toward its destination, events were unfolding in Washington that would have a disastrous impact on the success of their venture. In response to the Kaiser's resumption of unrestricted submarine warfare, the United States formally severed diplomatic relations with Germany and the smell of war was in the air. To preserve U.S. merchant shipping for a conflict that now appeared inevitable, on February 5, President Wilson issued a proclamation that "no vessel registered or enrolled and licensed under the laws of the United States shall, without the approval of the Shipping Board, be sold, leased, or chartered to any person not a citizen of the United States or transferred to a foreign registry or flag. The penalty for violation . . . is forfeiture of the vessel to the United States and a fine of not more than $5,000, or imprisonment for not more than five years, or both."

In the months that followed the *Agassiz*'s departure from San Diego, Maude received no word from her partners. She was not overly concerned, since bandit attacks on the railroad often disrupted mail service south of the border, and letters were sometimes delayed or lost after being diverted for examination by censors in Mexico and the United States. Maude filled the empty time studying nautical navigation until she thoroughly mastered the subject, even receiving a navigator's license in the process. When news from her two business partners in Mexico finally arrived, it landed like a bombshell. To improve their ability to attract customers, they had transferred the registry of the *Alexander Agassiz* from the American flag to the Mexican flag, a flagrant violation of the recent presidential proclamation.

In a panic, Maude sent telegrams to Guaymas, San José del Cabo, La Paz, Manzanillo, and a handful of other ports along the Mexican west coast, trying to locate the schooner, without success. She anxiously discussed the situation with Joseph Mesmer and John Elliot, the collector of customs in Los Angeles. Elliot immediately dispatched several telegrams to Mexico, with equally poor results. Maude and Mesmer began to wonder whether Taylor might have run away with the *Agassiz* or sold it. After talking it over with Elliot, they decided that the best course to follow would be for Maude to leave for Mazatlán at once and try to locate the missing boat.

"Change that flag back again as soon as possible!" were Elliot's final words before she departed.

Maude booked passage on the Pacific Mail steamer *San Juan*, arriving in Mazatlán on June 4. The most exciting part of the voyage occurred when a passenger named Frederick Wilhelm Fay was taken off the boat by authorities in San Pedro, suspected of being a German spy. After hours spent wandering through a "Chinese puzzle" of Mazatlán streets, she finally located Taylor, who recounted the dismal story of the Pacific Coast Trading and Shipping Company's activities in Mexico to date.

After they had arrived in Mazatlán, he and Wheeler began making the rounds of the harbor soliciting customers. They landed a few jobs carrying freight and transporting Mexican soldiers between various ports, but were never paid enough to meet expenses. The problem was that the *Alexander Agassiz* flew an American flag of registry. In Mexico, as in the United States, domestic boats always received first preference for cargo. Only in those circumstances where a Mexican boat was unobtainable could the *Agassiz* win a job, and when the partners did find a paying customer, as a foreign vessel the *Agassiz* was assessed extra port charges, pilotage charges, and a variety of lesser fees to operate. Every time that they won business, they lost money. The two men quickly came to the conclusion that to survive in Mexico as a shipping company they would have to transfer the ship's registry to the Mexican flag. They contacted the French consul, Henri Claisse, who was acting in lieu of the American Consul at the time, and obtained the correct procedure to follow to have the flag changed. The leading lawyer in the port was consulted and permission was granted by the government in Mexico City for the *Alexander Agassiz* to operate under the Mexican flag. Although none of the officials in Mazatlán knew about President Wilson's decree forbidding the transfer of American ship registration, the men they were dealing with in Mexico City were fully aware of it, and demanded as a precondition that Wheeler and Taylor bond the boat to the Mexican government for 9,000 pesos ($4,500) for the illegal use of their flag. The end result would be that the *Agassiz* could carry cargo under Mexican registry, but Pacific Coast Trading would owe the Mexican government $4,500 for being allowed to do so. With no alternative, they had readily agreed.

Now flying the Mexican flag, the schooner at last began to win business—but continued to lose money. As a result of hiring extravagant and unreliable captains, combined with total ignorance of the shipping business, the company went deeper and deeper into debt. Following months of continuous losses, they reached rock bottom in early April when they landed in La Paz with $7 in cash, their fuel tanks empty, and no provisions.

At this moment of desperation, Providence appeared to shine on them when they made the acquaintance of H. A. Macintosh, an American trader with over fifteen years of experience working in Mexico. Macintosh was employed by the Los Angeles firm of Myers, Darling and Hinton to buy Mexican tomatoes and arrange their shipment to the United States. In need of a boat that would allow him to ship tomatoes between Mexican ports and inspect other agricultural products being offered for sale, Macintosh advanced Wheeler and Taylor money to buy fuel and supplies. The trader then accompanied them on a cruise to Mazatlán where the pair hoped to locate a paying freight customer. During the voyage, Macintosh gained a better understanding of the capabilities of the *Agassiz*, and by the time they arrived in Mazatlán, had advanced additional funds that brought the total owed him to $1,600, which the partners agreed to repay from their future earnings. The only condition to the loan was that Macintosh would receive first rights to the *Alexander Agassiz* whenever he had perishable goods to ship.

For the next six weeks Macintosh traveled aboard the schooner as "supercargo," supervising the handling and transfer of his produce as it was shipped between Magdalena Bay, Todos Santos, San José, La Paz, and Guaymas. Observing the haphazard manner in which Wheeler and Taylor conducted business, and seeing the shipping company sliding deeper into debt, Macintosh became increasingly concerned about the money that he had advanced the pair. When he learned that there was a $5,000 mortgage on the *Agassiz* owed to the University of California and further debts to the Mexican government, he took immediate action to protect his loan by requiring the partners to sign a *hipoteca* (mortgage) for $1,600 on the schooner. The terms of the *hipoteca* allowed Wheeler and Taylor to operate the boat only within specific limits, provided they employed a captain of whom Macintosh or his agent approved, and each month that the *Agassiz* was in operation Macintosh would receive $200 of the money owed to him. If they did not operate the vessel for any three consecutive months, foreclosure could be made.

At this juncture, Frank Wheeler decided that he had had enough of the shipping business. He walked away from the impending financial disaster and returned to Los Angeles, leaving his partner to run the business.

As Taylor brought the painful story to a close, Maude was dumbfounded at the level to which their promising venture had declined. In five short months, the company had amassed an accumulated debt of over $11,000, their ship was operating illegally under the Mexican flag, placing it under the threat of seizure by the U.S. government and making its owners subject to arrest and imprisonment, there was little prospect of the schooner operating "in the black" any time soon, yet if the *Agassiz* did not continue to haul cargo, Macintosh would foreclose on his mortgage. Abandoning the effort and fleeing to the United States as her stepbrother Frank had done must have seemed a tempting alternative to Maude, but owning the shipping company was her life's dream.

"Wheeler and Taylor had made a mess of things," she would later reflect, "but the life appealed to me, I confess, with all of its danger and worries, and troubles . . . Perhaps I have adventurous blood in my veins—and I don't like to give up."

Maude and her partner discussed what to do next. Taylor informed her that he was planning to take the boat south in search of freight jobs that would help pay down their debt and "show good faith in his works." The *Agassiz* was loaded with fuel and provisions for Taylor and an interpreter to make a trip down the coast to Manzanillo in search of customers. But half an hour before their departure, the interpreter came to Maude's hotel and informed her that "Mr. Taylor told me to say goodbye to my friends because we are going on a long trip." Taylor had also advised him that he was going to take the *Agassiz* as far south as he could, and when things became too hot, would either sell the boat or ditch it, and "Miss Lochrane can whistle." The interpreter told Maude that he refused to go on such a trip, and suggested that she travel in his place.

When Taylor boarded the schooner he was surprised to find Maude already there, with bags packed, waiting for him. The double-crossing partner argued that she wasn't needed on the voyage, and accused her of checking up on him—which was entirely true. Eventually, he was forced to accept the fact that his scheme had been foiled, and the pair departed for Manzanillo together.

When Maude returned to Mazatlán, trouble was waiting. While she was gone, the Mexican captain of the port had informed government officials that she was planning to take down the Mexican flag on the *Agassiz* and replace it with American colors. From a friendly Mexican who was able to speak broken English, she learned that the port authorities were now at work trying to have her arrested. Maude hurried to the telegraph office and wired John Elliott, the collector of customs in Los Angeles, asking him to send a telegram to the U.S. consul in Mazatlán advising him that the *Alexander Agassiz* was American-owned, and directing that he assist her in restoring the American flag on the vessel. Consul W. E. Chapman filed paperwork naming Maude Lochrane as the master of the *Agassiz* (so that the boat would have an American flag captain) and the U.S. flag was raised on the schooner. Maude's quick action ended the attempt by the Mexican authorities to have her imprisoned.

Another problem that Maude faced was the shared ownership of the *Alexander Agassiz*, which was restricting her ability to make legally binding business decisions. Gaining full ownership of Pacific Coast Trading would not prove a difficult task, since by now her partners had long given up any hope of success. She first contacted her stepbrother Frank Wheeler, who offered to sign over his interest in the company after all outstanding debts had been paid. She agreed, and secured a power of attorney signed by Frank and Minnie Wheeler to dispose of their interest in the *Agassiz* under that stipulation. After nearly being arrested with Maude by the Mexican port officials, and as deep in debt as his partners, William Taylor also agreed to leave the partnership, selling his interest in the schooner to Maude for $110 with the proviso that she would assume all outstanding debts against the boat and the company. Under these terms she acquired Taylor's stake in the firm as well.

Maude was now the sole owner of the Pacific Coast Trading and Shipping Company—and fully responsible for its obligations. Her first order of business was to legally transfer the ship to *Mexican* registry so that it could operate within Mexican coastal waters at a profit or be sold to a buyer in Mexico. She visited Consul W. E. Chapman to seek his support in changing the schooner's registry, but Chapman refused.

"The *Alexander Agassiz* is an American boat and shall not sail under any other flag than American," he told her firmly.

She appealed by wire to the U.S. Shipping Board, requesting that she be allowed to either change the registry to the Mexican flag or sell the boat. A month later the response came from Washington: "Do not change the flag or sell boat." Chapman advised her not to expect the shipping board to reverse their opinion; after government bureaucrats made a decision, they would not take the time to go over the matter again or reverse their decision.

With no alternative, Maude continued to pursue freight business between Mexican coastal ports under the crippling handicap of American registry. She managed to secure a contract to carry a cargo of Pierce Coal Oil to Topolobampo and was able to return with a load of alfalfa, but freight rates had fallen again and margins were slim. Then came the contract with Señor Meistiero in which the *Agassiz* was overloaded with corn and nearly capsized on the way to Manzanillo, a disastrous setback.

Adding to her woes, after months of hard use, the schooner's engines were now running poorly and the boat was in need of general repair. She inquired around Mazatlán harbor, searching for someone capable of operating and repairing marine engines. In the American store she met a mining man named Osborn who had a good understanding of oil and gasoline engines, but he declined her offer to work on the *Agassiz*. The shaky financial position of Pacific Coast Trading was widely known in the port, and with her forward manner, Maude struck him as an adventuress.

At this dark moment, she had the good fortune to locate an experienced marine engineer, a man with a reputation for overhauling gas-powered engines and repairing boats. When he was not engaged in a repair project, he ran a boardinghouse in Mazatlán to make ends meet. She had met him the previous July at the American Consulate. When he came to look the *Agassiz* over, she noticed that he had a revolver in his pocket, but there was nothing unusual in that; a lot of men in Mexico carried guns for personal protection. She was worn out and glad to find somebody to look after things, and it was clear the engineer knew what he was doing. She hired him on the spot—an American slacker named Cornelius Heintz.

Heintz took the helm and piloted the *Alexander Agassiz* into the estuary, then waited for high tide, and skillfully ran the schooner up onto the beach as far as possible. Mazatlán had no dry dock at the time, and beaching was the only way to service a boat out of water. He started working on the *Agassiz* even while the tide was still running out, almost as if he had an important deadline to meet. Heintz produced a work crew to assist him in his labors, an unusually industrious group of foreigners—two Norwegians and a Dutchman—who came aboard at different times and were similarly skilled at boat repair. They were clearly men who knew the sea, their rolled sleeves revealing an assortment of colorful nautical tattoos.

Working under Heintz's supervision, the men added a new keel, recaulked the hull, mended the sails, and set to work overhauling the engines, which had become fouled with seawater. Maude marveled at the speed and efficiency with which they carried out their tasks, achieving more in two or three days than the local laborers did in two to three weeks.

Perhaps her good fortune in locating Heintz was an omen that her luck was about to change?

Maude placed great confidence in fortune-tellers, spiritualists, and clairvoyants. Before she organized the Pacific Coast Trading and Shipping Company, a clairvoyant had told her that she would go off on a long voyage and make her fortune. It was this prediction that had sustained her through the months of disappointment and hardship. A few days before Heintz appeared, Maude had received an overture from a sea captain named Fritz Bauman for a voyage to the South Seas, and she knew at last the clairvoyant's prophesy would soon come true.

4   For Honor and Fatherland

In September 1917, six months before Cornelius Heintz began overhauling the tired schooner, an eminent person booked passage on the *Alexander Agassiz* for a trip from Mazatlán to Manzanillo—Fritz Unger, managing partner of Melchers Sucs and German consul. Although it would later be prohibited for American vessels to carry German passengers between foreign ports under the revised statutes of the Trading with the Enemy Act, at the time, there was no law regarding who could travel as a passenger aboard an American boat. It is unclear why Unger made the journey on the *Agassiz* rather than on one of Melchers' own coastal steamers. He said nothing about the war during the trip, but passed the time in small talk with Maude about common topics of the day, observing how the schooner handled on the open ocean and enjoying the cruise.

In the months that followed, Melchers Sucesores began to discreetly gather information about the *Agassiz*. The American trader H. A. Macintosh recalled, "Melchers Sucs, during my presence in Mazatlán, were repeatedly making inquiries of me as to the speed of the *Alexander Agassiz*, her seaworthiness, etc. I had very little use for them however, and avoided the matter wherever possible."

The reason for the consul's interest in the American schooner became clear to Cornelius Heintz one day in early February 1918, when he received word that Unger wanted to see him. He would later recall the meeting with Unger in exacting detail.

Heintz arrived promptly at the consul's office and found him seated comfortably in his leather-backed office chair, deep in conversation with a man bearing the unmistakable look of a seafarer. Unger ushered Heintz into his office and closed the door behind them, then introduced him to Fritz Bauman, a captain of one of the interned German merchant ships at Santa Rosalía, and a reserve officer in the German navy. Bauman had spent much of his life at sea, including service aboard ships of the Matson Navigation Company, running passengers and freight between San Francisco and Honolulu. When America joined the war, Bauman was briefly interned as an enemy alien at Angel Island, an Ellis Island–like immigration station located in San Francisco Bay, before being deported to Mexico.

The three men shared a common heritage and the atmosphere at the meeting was cordial. Although Heintz was not a native German, he was the son of a German father and had deserted America rather than fight his German cousins. He was accepted as a true German, and even held membership in the German club. The war overseas was going well for Germany and the men's hearts were high. Russia had been defeated, and even now German divisions from the Eastern Front were being transferred to France for the final drive that would end the conflict in victory for the Fatherland.

Unger earnestly advised the men that he had called them together to discuss a most important matter, and swore them to secrecy, before revealing the reason for their summons. A German commerce raider was going to be launched from Mazatlán to prey on Allied shipping in the Pacific; a small boat capable of capturing an unsuspecting steamer for use in seizing and sinking additional Allied ships. The vessel that was going to be appropriated for this purpose was the American schooner *Alexander Agassiz*.

The plan was quite simple.

It was common knowledge that Miss Lochrane's shipping business was on the verge of collapse; her fortunes had declined to the extent that she was now living on the boat. Captain Bauman was to induce Miss Lochrane to take the *Agassiz* to sea by telling her enchanting stories of how the schooner could earn a huge profit trading between islands in the South Seas. He would then offer his services to navigate the boat to that destination at no expense, proposing that once there, she could make whatever arrangements she cared to in pursuing the riches of the South Seas trade. Unger had learned that the *Agassiz* was in disrepair after months of continuous operation without maintenance. As part of the scheme, Heintz would offer his services as a marine engineer to Miss Lochrane and return the schooner to a level of seaworthiness that would allow it to make an extended voyage at sea.

The German consul paused, and looked at the men gravely.

Shortly before departure, Bauman would board the vessel with a hand-picked crew of German sailors. When they reached the open ocean, well clear of the mainland, Bauman's men would seize the *Alexander Agassiz* and embark on the raiding expedition. Captain Bauman would be in overall command of the vessel, which would carry a commission issued on the authority of the German government validating its use as a raider. They were to seize all ships and cargos that Bauman deemed advisable, destroy what Allied commerce they could, and then proceed on to Germany.

The crew would "get rid of Miss Lochrane at the earliest opportunity."

The *Alexander Agassiz* would be suitably equipped for the expedition. Bauman was to travel to the port of Santa Rosalía in Baja California, and obtain the necessary charts and navigational instruments from the German square-rigged schooners interned there. They would also provide him with the heavy machine guns and ammunition needed to arm the *Agassiz*. The German crew would carry Winchester rifles from Melchers' firearms inventory and their own personal side arms. The schooner would have a Kaiserliche Marine battle flag to be deployed after reaching the high seas.

In addition to the honor that they would gain from their service to the Fatherland, Bauman and Heintz would be partners in the venture, awarded a percentage of the value of all ships sunk, destroyed, or captured. The monetary reward would be paid to them when they reached Germany. As a sign of good faith (and likely to provide deniability for Melchers Sucs in the event of capture), Heintz was expected to put $300 in American gold into the project for supplies and materials to repair the schooner. In return, he would receive 5 percent of the value of the vessels destroyed or captured as his share. Unger advised Bauman that he would speak to him privately with regard to the prize percentage he would be paid.

When he had completed his briefing, Unger leaned forward expectantly. Would they agree to participate in the historic mission? Both men responded with enthusiasm and immediately agreed to their part in the operation. It was an excellent plan, certain to succeed by its very unlikelihood—no one would conceive of an American schooner turning German commerce raider. After discussing a few final details, the course of action was settled, and they agreed to meet again in four weeks' time.

The proposal from the two Norwegians, Mr. Bauman and Mr. Madden, almost sounded too good to be true. Maude had met them in the German *biergarten* (beer garden). After a few drinks, the swarthy Mr. Bauman, a navigator with the Matson Line, told her of a tremendous opportunity that existed for coastal trading vessels like the *Alexander Agassiz* in the tropical waters of the South Seas. He explained that at present, there was no competition for the interisland trading business, and unlike the situation in Mexico, no government regulations or port charges. Bauman was eager to get to the islands himself, and so certain of the prospects for easy money in the South Seas that he offered to navigate the *Agassiz* there at no charge, leaving Maude to cash in on the plentiful trading opportunities. His associate, Mr. Madden, a ruddy-faced merchant seaman with light brown hair, solemnly confirmed Bauman's story, advising Maude that he knew the South Seas well and had seen the riches to be made with his own eyes.

Madden was, in fact, a German national named Arthur Martens. Born in the port city of Lübeck, the thirty-six-year-old Martens had been schooled in the German merchant marine, and served on both German and English merchant vessels. A qualified ordinary seaman, Martens could "reef off the gear," handle rigging, and perform any other tasks required on a sailing ship. In 1914, Martens had found himself stranded in the United States, with no means of returning to Germany through the British blockade. At the time, he was a mate on board an oil tanker called the *Maverick* that was being detained in San Francisco Bay by U.S. authorities, and which would later be used in a German plot to smuggle arms for a Hindu uprising in British-ruled India. In 1916, Martens left for Mexico, and was reported to have offered his services to General Calles in the event of war between the United States and Mexico, but the offer was not accepted. Bauman recruited the itinerant seaman in Hermosillo to serve as first mate on the *Agassiz* expedition.

By the time their discussion in the biergarten had ended, Maude was convinced that the two Norwegians knew what they were talking about.

Running the *Alexander Agassiz* between islands in the South Seas could be the answer to all her problems. The boat's American registry would cease to be an issue, and with port charges eliminated and profit margins increased, she would be able to pay off the University of California and Macintosh in no time. It was a good thing that Bauman and Madden held neutral Norwegian passports. The blacklist had forced her to reject a score of business offers from Germans and pro-Germans whose names appeared on the list. At the insistence of the American consul, she had just turned down the opportunity to carry a boatload of Japanese to a port near the Mexican border because it would have violated U.S. immigration laws. Now everyone who booked passage on an American boat between foreign ports had to show their passports—even Mexicans. This latest operating handicap would also be removed in the distant South Seas.

Maude happily accepted Mr. Bauman's offer and sealed the deal with a handshake. As soon as the *Alexander Agassiz* was properly overhauled for the trip, she agreed to set sail with them for the South Seas.

The port city of Santa Rosalía is located on the eastern side of the arid Baja California peninsula. It was founded as a copper mining community in 1884 by Compañía del Boleo, a French mining concern, to support efforts to exploit the rich copper deposits found in the area. Processing the ore extracted from the mines required an ample supply of coke for smelting, and in the prewar days, this was delivered to Santa Rosalía on a regular basis from Germany by a fleet of four-masted, square-rigged schooners. The ships had been built in British shipyards at the end of the nineteenth century, and sold to German shipping companies when the opening of the Panama Canal made their use in the tramping trade unprofitable for their English owners. Fourteen of these relics from the bygone age of sail continued to travel a circuitous route from Hamburg to Santa Rosalía and back, delivering coke for the Boleo smelter and returning with a cargo of copper for the continent, until the world war broke out in Europe.

The German-registered schooners were immediately interned in the port of Santa Rosalía. It was a temporary measure, since the war was only expected to last a few months, but as months turned to years, the hulls of the sailing ships rocking at anchor gradually became covered with barnacles until it was impossible to sail them. Their restless German crews passed the time touching up peeling paint, unfurling and sunning the sails, and scraping what barnacles they could from the ships' bottoms, while dreaming of the day when they would return to Germany.

Having served as the captain of one of the square-riggers at Santa Rosalía, Bauman knew the officers and men of the small fleet very well. Some would have extra navigational instruments of the type needed to traverse the Pacific and, as auxiliaries of the German navy in time of war, he also knew that some of the ships carried a machine gun in their holds.

The German merchant captain left for Santa Rosalía in mid-February 1918 and returned to Mazatlán three weeks later with a trove of items for the raiding expedition, including a sextant, a chronograph, a compass, and nautical charts covering both the Pacific and Atlantic Oceans. Of even greater significance, Bauman was able to pry loose a German heavy machine gun together with its mount and a single box of belted ammunition. These items were discreetly, transported to the German consular office at Melchers Sucesores, where they were hidden away for use in the coming operation.

In the saltwater estuary near Mazatlán harbor, repair work was nearing completion on the *Alexander Agassiz*. Heintz had been able to obtain replacement parts for the engines, which were now running reliably, and had gone over the boat in exacting detail, even rebuilding the boat's lavatory. The final task, repairing the damage that had been inflicted on the boat's sails during the failed attempt to carry corn to Manzanillo for Señor Meistiero was now proceeding well under the experienced hands of seaman Madden. For four straight days Madden "bent," or retied, the lines to the schooner's two foresails and its large main sail with the assistance of two Mexican laborers. The *Agassiz* had a respectable amount of rigging and it was slow and painstaking work, with Madden tying lengths of braided cord to the eyelets in each sail and threading or "reeving" the halyard lines through block and tackle. When he was finished, the sails were ready to be run, and the schooner was capable of going to sea once again.

Word soon arrived that Unger wanted to see them.

On the evening of March 12, 1918, after the Melchers Sucesores building had closed for the day and the last remaining workers had trudged wearily home, seven men entered and made their way to the office of managing partner Fritz Unger.

The crewmen that had been recruited to serve aboard the commerce raider *Alexander Agassiz* were similar in appearance and convictions. In addition to Captain Fritz Bauman, First Mate Arthur Martens aka "Madden," and Chief Engineer Cornelius Heintz, the ship's company would include Frank Volpert, Hendrik Koppalla, Richard Brandt, and Charles Boston. They were men who had been toughened by years on the road or on the sea, and with only a few pesos to their names, were awed by the rich furnishings surrounding them.

Frank Volpert was a thirty-one-year-old bricklayer from Hoppeke, Germany. He had been visiting relatives in Cedar Rapids, Iowa, when the outbreak of war stranded him in America. The lanky tradesman had traveled south to Monterrey, Mexico, and then made his way to Mazatlán, where his outspoken support for Germany in the conflict brought him to the attention of Bauman. Volpert was known to carry a revolver at all times.

Hendrik Koppalla was twenty-three years old, and a sailor by profession. In public he claimed to be a Dutchman from Amsterdam, but in private confided his true nationality to fellow Germans. Koppalla had been at sea since his mid-teens, much of the time spent serving on two-masted fishing boats in the North Sea. In October 1917, Koppalla was deported from Angel Island to Mexico as an "undesirable alien." He had been recruited to look after the engines aboard the *Alexander Agassiz*.

Richard Brandt was a thirty-three-year-old lumber inspector from Mecklenberg, Germany, who was working as a rancher in California when America joined the war. A reservist in the German military, he had immediately fled to Mexico. Strongly pro-German in his sympathies, Brandt was approached in the German biergarten in Mazatlán to serve aboard the *Agassiz*.

Charles Boston was a twenty-seven-year-old general laborer from Mountain View, Missouri. An American citizen by birth, Boston registered for the draft at Bisbee, Arizona, in June 1917, and then left for Mexicali, Mexico, on a prospecting tour four months later. He was called to report for duty on March 1, 1918, but failed to return to the United States, and became, like Heintz, a draft "slacker." He was hired by Heintz to do general work on the *Alexander Agassiz* in February 1918, and was later chosen to join the raiding expedition.

Unger rose from his desk and surveyed the men assembled before him. As they were now aware, he solemnly told them, in a few days' time the *Alexander Agassiz* would sail from Mazatlán under the command of Captain Bauman on a mission of great importance to the Fatherland. Assisting him as second-in-command would be the ship's first mate, Mr. Madden. Removing a sheet of paper from his desk, Unger read them the orders to Captain Bauman that he had signed as German consul in Mazatlán: "Captain Bauman is to go to sea as master of the schooner *Alexander Agassiz*. He is to commandeer the first ship that crosses his path that he deems suitable for use as an ocean-going commerce raider. After taking possession of this vessel, he is to destroy all commerce that he can, and then do everything in his power to return to Germany with his prize. Further, Captain Bauman has been entrusted with significant letters in cipher code that he is to hand-deliver to a representative of the German government."

Unger instructed those in the group to raise their hands and swear an oath before him, as the German government's official delegate in Mazatlán, of their allegiance to the German flag and their commitment to obey the commands of Captain Bauman in carrying out the orders that he had been issued. All the men complied and swore an oath of allegiance, except Charles Boston, the American slacker from Missouri, who would not swear allegiance to Germany, but agreed to participate in the mission.

Unger handed a packet of coded letters to Bauman, along with a commission letter authorizing the *Alexander Agassiz* to go to sea as a German commerce raider. No specific nationality was mentioned in the letter with regard to the ships that were to be captured and destroyed; every ship on the high seas was to be looked upon as an enemy ship under the orders issued.

Unger next handed Bauman a secret code written in the German language through which he would be able to decipher any messages or letters sent to him. Unger once again instructed the merchant captain to deliver the letters as soon as he reached port in Germany.

The consul informed the raider crew that the *Alexander Agassiz* would sail within the week. The overhaul of the schooner was now complete and she was ready for sea duty. Provisions would shortly be brought aboard the *Agassiz* from Melcher Sucs' warehouse, along with enough fuel for five hundred miles of the journey—the sails would be the primary motive power for most of the voyage. Armaments would also be transferred to the ship at that time. Heintz saw a box of belted machine-gun ammunition in the office and casually examined the gleaming brass cartridges contained within. Behind the box of ammunition was a sealed crate that housed the heavy machine gun.

As the meeting drew to a close, Unger commended the men for their dedication to the German cause in the present war, and shook each of the crewmen's hands as they exited the building and disappeared into the night.

A few miles from the German consul's office, Maude Lochrane sat alone in her quarters on the *Alexander Agassiz*, still beached in the *esterro* (estuary), and composed a letter to Joseph Mesmer, her friend and mentor. The Los Angeles businessman had backed the purchase of the schooner with a $5,000 bond and then stood by her despite the overwhelming obstacles encountered, even lobbying congressmen on her behalf while trying to have the *Agassiz*'s registry legally changed to the Mexican flag. Now with a brighter outlook seemingly on the horizon, she penned Mesmer a quick note with the happy news that their troubles would soon be over.

Mazatlán, Mexico
Mr. Joseph Mesmer
Los Angeles, Cal.

Dear Mr. Mesmer,

Am writing both you and Mr. Sproule [assistant to the comptroller of the University of California] a line to tell you that I am getting things fixed up here . . . I know things will be satisfactory to all, and the U of C entirely satisfied and paid up entirely in the length of time they gave us from the first. I am fixing things so all debts can be satisfied. Two parties who were interested (in chartering the Alexander Agassiz) in December are now on the "Black List" & one is reputed to be "pro-G" [pro-German]. You can't imagine what the "List" & restrictions mean to the people here as there are so many foreigners here especially Germans. Would have written 3 days ago but couldn't tell you as many things were not quite certain yet.

> Best wishes to you all,
> Yours truly,
> Maude Lochrane

By now, Maude's financial situation had become the subject of common gossip throughout Mazatlán. Even visiting American businessmen were aware of her plight. She was pointed out to Gustaf Danielson, secretary and treasurer of the Cooper, Coate and Casey Wholesale Dry Goods Company of Los Angeles as "a destitute woman and a sad victim of circumstance." Out of sympathy for her impoverished state, the businessman proposed to W. E. Chapman, the American consul at Mazatlán, that they start a fund for her to subsist on. Danielson told Chapman that he would agree to put in $10 if the consul would do likewise.

But Maude's situation was not news to Chapman.

He had already been watching Maude Lochrane and the *Alexander Agassiz* for quite some time.

5   "She Is an Outlaw and a Dangerous Enemy"

Prominent among the buildings that lined the Olas Altas, the broad roadway that fronted Mazatlán harbor, was the American consulate, a two-story structure built in the Spanish style of old Mazatlán, with smooth sides of white cement, barred windows at street level, and ornate casement windows on the second story that opened outward like glass doors to overlook the sea below. The American consul in Mazatlán, W. E. Chapman, could often be seen standing at one of the windows, scanning the harbor with powerful binoculars like a military commander reconnoitering terrain, as he watched crates and boxes from visiting steamers being manhandled ashore by an unending procession of cargadors. "Military commander" was a fitting description for Chapman, who was the U.S. State Department's senior officer in the secret war being waged against the German empire in neutral Mazatlán.

In normal times, the duties of a consular official are to assist a country's citizens during their residence in a foreign nation, to process government travel documents, and above all, to help in promoting trade with the nation to which they have been assigned. But Consul Chapman's mission in Mazatlán was to *deny* trade between American companies and German-owned firms in Mexico, through enforcement of the blacklist, while maintaining a vigilant watch over German activities south of the border. In W. E. Chapman, the State Department could not have found a man better suited for the job.

William Edgar Chapman was born in the rural farming community of Mount Pisgah, Arkansas, in February 1877. Like most Americans of the time, after receiving a public school education, Chapman found work on a local farm. The Arkansas farm boy's quiet, secluded existence took a dramatic turn in 1898, with the outbreak of the Spanish–American War. The twenty-one-year-old enlisted in the U.S. Army and became a member of Company B, Thirty-Third Regiment United States Volunteers. Arriving too late for the conflict in Cuba, Chapman was sent to the Philippines, where he served from 1899 to 1901. After his release from the army, he remained in the Philippines for eight years, where he worked as a teacher, a school superintendent, the terminal agent for a railroad company, and as the general manager and editor of a Philippine newspaper. Returning to the United States in 1909 a capable manager with a strong command of the Spanish language, Chapman went to Washington DC where he obtained employment as a clerk in the War Department, while attending a business college at night. In 1910, Chapman was appointed the assistant superintendent of the State, War and Navy building, one of the largest and most significant buildings in the capital. Recognizing that he would need to further his education to achieve the higher position in government that he desired, Chapman attended law school and received a bachelor's degree in law (LLB) from the Washington School of Law in 1914, and a master's (LLM) from the National University Law School in 1915. He was admitted to the District of Columbia Bar in 1915, and after passing the U.S. consular examination was appointed a Consul of Class Eight and assigned to Mazatlán.

Through dedication and hard work, the Arkansas farmhand had transformed himself into a worldly, highly educated government official. Chapman was a "no-nonsense" bureaucrat; intelligent, resourceful, and driven by a desire to serve his country. He would prove a ready adversary for anyone attempting to circumvent American law or aid the enemies of the United States.

Chapman maintained watch over American companies trading with suspect firms in Mazatlán under the direction of the secretary of state. On a regular basis, cablegrams listing the names of businesses that were under suspicion arrived at the office of "William E. Chapman, Esquire, American Consul" for investigation. Chapman was instructed to obtain the correct company name and address, provide detailed information on current activities and business connections, the nature and size of the entity, and the length of time it had been in operation. He was to consult with representatives of the British, French, and Italian governments to determine which firms were to be indexed on the "Enemy Trading List" ("the blacklist"), the "white list" of businesses that had no affiliation with any enemy-owned companies, or the "cloak list" of "front" companies that allowed their names to be used by enemy-owned businesses in order to obtain American goods.

Chapman worked closely with the French Consul, Henri Claisse, and the British vice-consul, Theodore E. S. Watson to identify German firms and their surrogates operating in Mazatlán. This information was sent by Chapman to the State Department, who then forwarded it to the War Trade Board for use in restricting German businesses and their "cloaks" from obtaining merchandise from the United States.

On July 31, 1917, Chapman received a typical report from Henri Claisse, agent consulaire de France. "I have the honor to remit to you herewith a list, as complete as I could make it, according to my knowledge, of the firms established in the States of Sinaloa and Nayarit which are antagonistic to the policy of the government of the United States. I have for each firm given the reasons which form the basis for my criterion." Listed at the top of Claisse's enclosure, "Firms Considered As Unfriendly to the United States of America," was "Melchers Sucs, Mazatlán," of whom Claisse commented, "The head of the firm here is the German Consul, and of course the firm is the center of the propaganda in favor of German interests and against the enemies of Germany . . . [They] make use of other firms in their efforts to thwart the effects of blacklisting."

A communiqué with similar information was sent to Chapman by Theodore Watson, the British vice-consul, on August 4:

> With regard to D. G. Aguirre of Tepic (a suspect firm), I have ascertained that since the commencement of the war they have transferred their agency in Mazatlán from V. Patron, a Spanish firm, to Melchers . . . You will have noticed a circular in the local press announcing the formation of the "Compania de Transportes Maritimos, S.S." for lightering goods and passenger traffic, also to act as Shipping Agents. The President

thereof is F. Gregoire, an employee of the House of Wohler, Bartning Sucs. I have no doubt that this is the German-controlled shipping concern that I previously mentioned to you.

After receiving information from his fellow consuls, Chapman took immediate action. He initiated an investigation of the lightering company identified by Watson and sent a cable to the U.S. secretary of state the following month, advising, "M. Miranda, Director General, Company Transportes Maritimos, leaves today for San Francisco aboard the steamer 'City of Para' with articles of incorporation. Said company is trying to arrange business connections there, capital is almost entirely that of Germans in Mazatlán under names of Mexicans connected with them . . . If United States objects to American connections I have to suggest secret service San Francisco prevent them."

As Chapman gained experience in ferreting out information on companies violating the Trading with the Enemy Act, he became knowledgeable about the various subterfuges and deceptive practices that were being employed to evade the U.S. trade authorities. He was soon recognized as an expert on the operations of blacklisted firms in Mexico; a resource for the government to rely on not only for identifying enemy firms violating the law, but for devising methods to thwart them.

In an October 1917 report to the State Department, Chapman advised:

I am told by an American that at the time he learned of the arrangements of the Germans with José Sanchez y Cia [a suspected cloak firm] to get goods for them in the United States, he learned also that these Germans were laughingly boasting that Americans were too inefficient to effect an organization such as would seriously stand in the way of their getting all the goods from the United States which they desire.

I realize that it will take some time and a good deal of vigilance on my part and on the part of my colleagues and trustworthy associates to put a stop to this sort of thing, if it is the wish of the Government of the United States that it be stopped (I have no official information that it really is) but I am anxious to see it done and am confident that I can furnish the Department with information by which it can at least be very materially reduced.

I would strongly urge that all American authorities having anything to do with the granting of export licenses or the granting of shipments of goods where no license is required be given specific orders not to permit any bag, box, case, sack, package, bundle, or other form of shipment to leave any United States port for Mexico without first having clearly written thereon the full name of the firm whose name appears in the papers upon which the goods are invoiced and manifested for shipment.

Such a requirement would greatly facilitate observations by government agents in Mexico. For example, it would at this point make it easier for me, the several loyal Americans, the British Vice Consul, and the French Consular Agent to watch the handling of shipments by local carting companies to ascertain whether these shipments were being carted to the places of business of those whose names appeared thereon or to German houses, and if to the former, then whether they were later transferred to the latter.

In response, Chapman's superiors forwarded him a letter from Herman Oliphant, the assistant director of War Trade Intelligence, that stated reassuringly, "I hope you will take the occasion to assure Mr. Chapman that the War Trade Board is extremely anxious to stop the practices (he) referred to. I am recommending to the War Trade Board that Mr. Chapman's suggestion concerning the marking of packages be adopted, as I consider this an important and very practical means of enabling our Consular Representatives to acquire information such as we desire."

During the summer of 1917, Chapman was notified by the State Department that the U.S. Navy planned to assign sub chasers to Mexican ports on the Pacific coast to maintain surveillance of the area. The ships were to enter Mexican territorial waters only to obtain fuel, water, and supplies, as their limited range demanded that they operate from a fixed base, but would otherwise cruise offshore. Although the navy sub chasers would not be subject to the orders of consular officials, they were to be used by the consuls as conduits for communicating information about German activities, and to "keep a close watch in Mexican waters" and protect U.S. interests.

American naval officers were soon calling at the consulate in Mazatlán on a regular basis, with Chapman's observations and commentary being included in the weekly dispatches from the commanding officer of the USS *Brutus*, a collier stationed off the Mexican coast, to the commander of the U.S. Pacific Fleet:

> Mr. Chapman, the American Consul, stated that large quantities of merchandise are going into San Blas from the United States and continually finding their way into the hands of Germans. As the large German firm of Delius & Co. own or control most of that section, some means should be adopted to offset this steady supply, is Mr. Chapman's opinion . . .

> Mr. Chapman informed me that the "Enemy Trading List" is having the effect of causing many Mexicans, and some foreigners . . . to pretend to be pro-American and pro-Ally very strongly, but this sentiment is not genuine, but rather evidence that they have felt the pinch of the "black list" and a means to further their business interests . . .

> In talking over the "Trading With the Enemy Act" and its operation, Mr. Chapman stated that he has been embarrassed at times by lack of cooperation with his office on the part of the San Francisco officials by reason of their having cleared shipments consigned to firms that appear on the list.

By late 1917, the American blacklist was having a significant impact on the earnings of German-owned companies and the daily life of German nationals in Mexico. Intended as a means to induce German firms in neutral countries to bring pressure on the German government to end the war, the blacklist often had the opposite effect, bringing otherwise passive German businessmen into open hostility against the U.S. government.

On December 15, Chapman wired a warning coded "Red" to the secretary of state: "Germans embittered by black list make threats. German Consul said today Americans should no longer consider them responsible for what they do, also that one or more German officers (were now) with every Mexican Army general. Suggest advisability keeping naval vessel at Mazatlán for present for protection of Americans and interests." Chapman's warning was another indication of the extent to which the blacklist had transformed German sentiment from resigned submission into readiness for action.

To assist him in investigating the activities of German-owned firms in Mazatlán, Chapman relied on a network of spies and confidential informants. The web of intelligence gatherers that he cultivated included government agents, expatriate Americans, visiting U.S. businessmen, and a variety of friendly tipsters in the harbor area. One of his best sources of information, referred to in reports as "the special secret service agent assigned to the coast," was Paul Bernardo Altendorf. The intrepid doctor-spy made numerous visits to Mazatlán before establishing his medical practice there as a cover, and provided Chapman with a stream of confidential information regarding German intentions—everything from important diplomatic and military initiatives, to common gossip, such as "the consul [Unger] is furious at the U.S. government for establishing a base on the Gulf of Fonseca."

Chapman also gained valuable intelligence from American traders and merchants passing through Mazatlán on legitimate business. In March 1918, G. Danielson, the treasurer of a dry goods company in Los Angeles, arrived with a license from the War Trade Board that granted him permission to collect a sum of money owed to his company by Melchers Sucesores in payment for a prewar transaction. While waiting in the office of a Melchers Sucs manager, Danielson was able to read a "bill of goods" sitting on the man's desk, which revealed that a San Francisco-based company was taking orders from brokers that were acting as "cloaks" for German firms on the blacklist. After the meeting, Danielson visited the consulate and signed a sworn affidavit to what he had seen, which Chapman immediately wired to the State Department for relay to the War Trade Board.

On the opposite side of the scale from the Americans conducting lawful business in Mazatlán were the slackers—draft dodgers who had deserted the United States for Mexico in order to avoid military service overseas—men like Charles Boston and Cornelius Heintz. On the rare occasion when Chapman encountered Heintz in public, he would dismiss him with an unmistakable look of contempt.

But in private, their interaction was markedly different.

For Cornelius Adolph Heintz, the loathsome draft dodger, was also Chapman's most trusted informant within the German community of Mazatlán. Heintz began reporting to Chapman shortly after winning the gunboat *Morelos* at auction for Louis Arzak in the summer of 1917. Uneasy about his partners' purpose in acquiring the formidable warship—and the consequences of his own involvement in the project—Heintz had discreetly visited the American consulate to learn whether the U.S. government would have any objection to his employing Germans from Santa Rosalía to assist in refloating the vessel. Chapman contacted the State Department for guidance on the matter, but their reply was noncommittal. Taking the matter into his own hands, Chapman cautioned Heintz that he would be wise to have no further business dealings with German nationals, and in October 1917, Heintz terminated his partnership with Arzak on the *Morelos* project.

Although the marine engineer severed his business connections with the Germans on the advice of the American consul, he continued to maintain his social contacts, and remained in good standing within the German community. Heintz socialized with Arzak, Unger, and Burgmeister at the German club, and visited the Cervecería del Pacífico brewery on a regular basis to meet with his German "comrades" to discuss recent happenings and future plans. All knew that Heintz had come to Mexico at the invitation of Bernard Hilbing, now imprisoned in the United States as a dangerous enemy alien, and that he had refused to return to America so as to avoid being drafted to fight against Germany. In their eyes, Heintz remained a true German who could be safely confided in regarding important and confidential matters.

Through secret meetings at the consulate, Heintz kept Chapman aware of everything that occurred in the enemy camp. When the Mexican agent for an American shipping company booked two Germans on a U.S.-registered steamer for a voyage to Manzanillo, Heintz exposed this violation of the Trading with the Enemy Act to Chapman, who instructed the shipping company to refuse them passage, and arranged for the Mexican interme-diary to be added to the blacklist. If a rumor harmful to the United States was being circulated by Germans in Mazatlán, Chapman was immediately informed by Heintz. He also kept the consul updated on the progress of Arzak's workmen in rebuilding the gunboat *Morelos*.

Heintz received nothing in return for providing Chapman with confidential information. He would later recall, "I kept the American consul fully advised of everything that went on . . . but never received any pay for this, nor asked for any."

In early February 1918, Heintz paid a surprise visit to the U.S. consulate to report an astounding development to Chapman: Consul Unger planned to send the *Alexander Agassiz* to sea as a raider with a German crew.

Chapman was stunned by the news, and fired a score of questions at Heintz. Who was involved? When would the boat sail? What was their destination?

Heintz provided Chapman with a detailed account of the German scheme, describing how Bauman was to convince Maude Lochrane to set sail for the South Seas islands, the direction that he had been given to return the worn schooner to seaworthy condition, and the means by which the *Agassiz* would be armed and equipped for the raiding expedition.

Startled by Heintz's revelations, Chapman decided to sit tight and monitor new developments as they unfolded. It would be weeks before the *Agassiz* could be made ready for sea and equipped with arms and navigational instruments from Santa Rosalía. At present, the scheme was nothing more than idle talk. He would not alarm Washington by sending a wire about a German plot that might not get off the ground, or be drawn into premature action that would only serve to warn off the conspirators. Those responsible must be caught in the act with indisputable evidence for a case to be made.

Chapman directed Heintz to carry on as if he were a willing participant in the venture, "but keep both of your eyes open—and keep me posted on everything that happens."

The consul ruminated that after the *Alexander Agassiz* returned to port at the conclusion of her last voyage, Miss Lochrane had failed to deliver the ship's papers to him, as required by law. If she was not in possession of the documents, she would not be able to legally clear the port.

Chapman instructed Heintz to tell Maude to bring the ship's papers to the consulate.

"She does not intend to surrender them," Heintz informed him. "The Germans want to get away with them on board. They have coached her on what to say when you ask for them. She is to state that the papers got wet and damaged on the last trip to sea, and that they are in a drawer on the ship which is also wet and has swelled up so badly that it cannot be opened without forcing it."

Bristling with anger at the thought of such an open act of defiance, Chapman told Heintz to deliver Miss Lochrane the message that he expected to receive the *Agassiz's* papers at once.

That afternoon, Maude Lochrane called at the consulate to discuss some matters related to the schooner, and Chapman immediately asked her for the ship's papers. Her response was exactly as Heintz had predicted—the papers were in a drawer on the boat that had swollen shut and could not be opened without damaging it. If she could manage to get the drawer open, she would gladly deliver them.

She left a short time later, and the afternoon passed without the ship's papers being brought to the consulate.

The following day, when Maude returned to the consulate to meet with Vice-Consul Brown, Chapman entered the room and handed her a typewritten letter on consular letterhead that instructed "Miss Maude Lochrane" to deliver the ship's papers of the *Alexander Agassiz* to the American consulate.

Maude read the note, then carefully folded it and turned to Chapman.

"I see you want the papers," she stated calmly, "but as I told you, they all got wet and are in a drawer which is all swelled up so that it will have to be forced open."

"I cannot and will not accept excuses," Chapman sternly warned. "I must have the papers and I want them *today*."

"Well, I think I can get them for you," Maude replied. "I'll see what I can do about it."

Then she rose and walked out of the consulate.

The following morning, while working to repair the schooner alongside Madden and Brandt, Heintz watched Maude take the ship's papers from the wheelhouse and carefully douse them with water from the estuary. Now if the papers came into Chapman's possession, the story that she had not delivered them because they had become wet would appear to be true, he reflected.

Shortly before noon on March 9, Heintz called on the American consul to report a significant development in the German scheme. Bauman had returned from Santa Rosalía with charts, a sextant, a chronograph, and a compass. He had also brought a machine gun of the latest make, and one box of ammunition. Heintz did not know the caliber of the gun, but it "shot a shell that was about the size of a rifle cartridge." He informed Chapman that the *Agassiz* was almost ready to return to the sea, and that Bauman expected to depart Mazatlán within the next seven days.

For W. E. Chapman, the *Agassiz* plot had reached a critical juncture. With the latest revelations from Heintz, it could not be dismissed as the delusion of a few discontented German nationals stranded in the backwater of rural Mexico. The conspirators now had the means at hand to carry out their devious scheme. Chapman responded by sending a priority telegram to Washington, warning of the imminent danger.

Secretary of State
Washington, D.C.

March 9, 2pm

I have what I believe to be reliable information that a German Captain and several Germans from the interned vessels in the Gulf of California are planning fitting out as a raider, American vessel ALEXANDER AGASSIZ, now at Mazatlán, between now and March 15th. Germans have machine gun, charts, sextant, et cetera, and expect to take supplies for ninety days. Naval vessel should call at Mazatlán immediately full details.
    CHAPMAN

When Chapman's telegram was delivered to the State Department the following morning, it created a sensation, and resulted in the exchange of a flurry of messages between the State Department and the U.S. Navy. Blue jackets were soon hunched at glowing wireless sets on land and sea, tapping out coded radiograms to the commanders of Naval Operations and the Pacific Fleet:

From: Operations.
March 11, 1918

To : Commander, Division Two.

Following from American Consul, Mazatlán to Secretary of State for information and guidance: "I have what appears to be reliable information that a German captain and several Germans from the interned vessels in the Gulf of California <u>are planning to fit out as a raider the American vessel Alexander Agassiz</u> now at Mazatlán, between now and March 16th. Germans have machine guns, charts, sextants, etc. Navy vessels should call at Mazatlán Consulate for full details."

From: Vicksburg.
March 12, 1918

To : Commander, Division Two.

The American yawl Alexander Agassiz <u>has been refitted is acting suspiciously</u>, and it is reported that she has on board a large amount supplies, including medical stores, sufficient for a three months cruise. Also reported that she has ten Germans on board and is sailing soon. Later news gives Thursday evening. Gardiner, American Vice Consul."

From: Commander, Division Two.
March 12, 1918

To : Vicksburg.

Vicksburg immediately proceed Mazatlán, <u>investigate reports that harbor is mined</u> and that American power boat Agassiz with German crew will leave before March 16th as raider with machine gun. Upon completion duty, coal at Pichilinque or from Brutus at

Acapulco. Submarine Chaser 302 will proceed as directed by you. Acknowledge.

From: Commander, Division Two.
March 13, 1918

To : Operations.

Vicksburg will arrive at Mazatlán at about 10:00 a.m., March 13th in company with Sub Chaser 302. Rainier at Pichilinque. Brutus due there, Yorktown at Ampala, Arctic, Dreadnaught, Undaunted off Magdalena Bay, southbound with tows, Snohomish, Arapaho, Sea Rover, Goliath off Salina Cruz. If Agassiz sails before arrival of Vicksburg <u>all vessels will be employed in search</u>, otherwise Vicksburg will blockade her in Mazatlán.

From: Commander, Division Two.
March 13, 1918

To : Vicksburg.

Operations reports that a small raider will leave Mazatlán on the night of March 14th. Take necessary steps immediately to <u>prevent her escape after departure</u> Mexican waters. Utilize the services of Sub Chaser #302, Brutus, Rainier and tugs at your discretion. Yorktown sailed Ampala 8:00 p.m. Monday for Mazatlán. Acknowledge.

From: Commander, Division Two.
March 13, 1918

To : Vicksburg.

Referring my (last radio) if upon arrival at Mazatlán AGASSIZ is still in harbor <u>board and investigate her in regular manner for American vessel</u>. Vicksburg will prevent her escape from Mazatlán pending action by State Department and at discretion you will direct other vessels proceed on duty assigned. Acknowledge.

From: Vicksburg.
March 14, 1918

To : Commander, Division Two.

Vicksburg will arrive Mazatlán Wednesday midnight and will investigate and attempt report tonight.

At 1:43 a.m. on March 15, the American gunboat USS *Vicksburg* steamed to the northern entry of Mazatlán harbor and dropped anchor. The *Vicksburg* was a formidable coastal patrol vessel, heavily armed with a brace of 4-inch, 6-pounder, and 1-pounder cannons. The 1,010 ton *Annapolis* class gunboat had a maximum speed of 13 knots (15 mph) under steam power, and was equipped with a full barkentine rig of sails for extended cruising.

In the early morning darkness, a launch was lowered from the *Vicksburg*, and Lieutenant Charles Edwin Reordan, the ship's commanding officer, boarded with a contingent of sailors and headed for shore. Although only twenty-nine years old, Reordan was a graduate of the U.S. Naval Academy at Annapolis, and a serious, highly dedicated officer with a command presence that far exceeded his youthful age. His orders from Pacific Fleet headquarters were to prevent the escape of a suspected enemy warship, and he was not going to wait for "normal business hours" to call on the American consul. Leading his men in a march from the wharf through the darkened streets of Mazatlán, Reordan arrived at the consulate at 4:00 a.m. to awaken Chapman and request a full briefing on the situation.

Chapman welcomed the navy men inside and then ushered Reordan to his private office. He gave the young officer an affidavit to read that had been taken from Cornelius Heintz five days earlier, in which the marine engineer had sworn under oath that Fritz Bauman and a group of German accomplices planned to fit out the *Alexander Agassiz* for duty as a German raider.

"Mr. Heintz . . . has gone over with us many of the numerous details as to how the whole matter has been planned for the *Alexander Agassiz* to put to sea as an outlaw," Chapman related, continuing,

He has in very convincing statements shown that the vessel intends to leave port without clearing at this office or at the local port office. He has told us . . . of the ship being too small for the Germans who are to go aboard the *Alexander Agassiz*, which is therefore intended to be used until a larger vessel can be captured. He has shown us such papers as the ship has and explained to us how Miss Maude Lochrane . . . took the papers and wet them with her own hands so that in case they should come into my possession she could make good her excuse that she did not deliver them because they were wet.

Reordan leaned forward in his seat, listening to the consul attentively as he outlined the German scheme.

"He has told us," Chapman continued, "of how they boast of being able to maneuver and run away from any boat the United States has on this coast, of how the Germans laughed at my demand for the ship's papers, and called me and the other American officials impossible names by way of ridicule and contempt for American government organization and of numerous other things which go to prove the claims of Mr. Heintz to the truth of his story that the vessel is about to go on a raiding expedition."

"I must therefore conclude," said Chapman, "that since Miss Lochrane plans as Mr. Heintz says to go on the vessel with these Germans, she is an outlaw, that she is a traitor to and a dangerous enemy of the Government of the United States and that her vessel has been given over by her into the hands of the enemy to be used as an instrument of war against the United States and its allies, and therefore has the status of an outlaw, an enemy of our country."

Reordan questioned Chapman on the particulars of Heintz's story, and then requested that he put his statements in writing and provide him with a copy. He also requested a copy of the affidavit that Heintz had signed on March 9, and asked Chapman to set up a meeting with his informant so that he could learn more about the Germans' intentions. The consul agreed to arrange a meeting at the consulate later that day.

Reordan rose, and after commending Chapman for his vigilance and good judgment, departed with his men for the *Vicksburg*.

Shortly before noon, he returned ashore and called at the consulate to interview Cornelius Heintz. The marine engineer confirmed that Bauman and Madden intended to put to sea on the *Agassiz* armed with small arms and a machine gun to capture a larger ship and initiate a raiding voyage. Reordan questioned him at length about the German plan. Heintz's responses were immediate and consistent with his prior statements. He gave Reordan several dates that the *Agassiz* might attempt to escape, one possible date being Sunday morning, March 17. By the end of the meeting, the naval officer believed Heintz to be a very credible informant.

Reordan next paid a courtesy call on the *Alexander Agassiz* to investigate the suspect schooner, as instructed by a coded dispatch from the Pacific Fleet. He found the *Agassiz* still beached in the saltwater estuary, and approached the craft in a friendly manner, trying not to arouse suspicion. On board were Maude Lochrane, Cornelius Heintz, and "six or seven officer-like looking Germans." Reordan made a routine inspection of the boat, during the course of which he found no incriminating evidence or stores of any kind, but observed that extensive repairs had been made to the sails, hull, and engines, just as Heintz had described.

He struck up a conversation with Maude Lochrane, telling her that he had spoken to Consul Chapman about coming out to look the boat over, and that Chapman had mentioned that the ship's papers were in a drawer that had swollen shut. Maude informed him that earlier that morning she had "broken open the drawer and found the drawer empty—no papers in it." She told Reordan that on a recent voyage the boat had been caught in a very heavy sea and the cabin had become swamped. After returning to port she had found a great many papers that had become "nothing but pulp" and that were strewn about the deck like so many pieces of trash. She had thrown them all overboard, thinking that they were of no importance. Maude now supposed that some of the papers thrown overboard were the ship's papers.

Reordan nodded understandingly, and then excused himself, saying that he had to call on other American boats in the area. He returned to the *Vicksburg* and sent a wireless message to his divisional commander at the Pacific Fleet:

From: Vicksburg.
March 15, 1918

To : Commander, Division Two.

Completed search. Nothing important found. Stores for Agassiz probably assembled onshore. Her papers are not in order. I am confident that she is going to leave either as German raider or else as blind for other operations. Vicksburg will prevent her escape. Reliable information says that other raiders will sail soon.

Reordan dispatched a whale boat and a pair of smaller boats from the *Vicksburg* on "fishing excursions" throughout Mazatlán harbor to maintain watch for any attempt by the *Agassiz* to escape. The boats also used their lines to drag the anchorage areas and entrance ways to the harbor probing for mines, but none were found. It seemed possible that the schooner might attempt to slip out of the harbor that night under cover of darkness; with four exits to watch, it would be impossible to guard them all.

At dusk, he sent Assistant Paymaster Armstrong and Ensign Wrucke ashore to occupy a position at the top of Monte Silla Point, a saddle-shaped hill that stood 250 feet above sea level, where they could easily monitor all four points of exit from the harbor and signal to the *Vicksburg* if the *Alexander Agassiz* should make an attempt to escape. At regular intervals throughout the night, the lookout team sent coded messages to the American gunboat, using a powerful flashlight to keep Reordan updated on the status of their surveillance.

Unknown to the two seamen from the *Vicksburg*, secret activity *was* under way on the *Alexander Agassiz* that night, as items critical to the success of the covert mission were brought on board, including charts, a sextant, the heavy machine gun that Heintz had seen, a container of ammunition, Winchester .30-.30 rifles, and a German naval flag.

Despite these preparations, the purpose behind the *Vicksburg*'s arrival and her boats "fishing" in the harbor had not been lost on Unger and Bauman. Even the signaling atop Monte Silla Point had been noticed by the German plotters. Charles Boston, the draft evader from Missouri who had been recruited for the raider crew, saw "signaling from the shore that night . . . I don't know who they were signaling to or who it was that was signaling . . . It looked like flashes of lightning. I ascertained who it was to and from [through discussion with other crew members] and the answer was that there was a warship in port and that it was a reflection from the signaling of the warship."

Seated at his desk at Melchers Sucs, Unger was not pleased by the "borregos" (slang for rumors) that he had received about the unusual U.S. naval activity in the harbor with the *Alexander Agassiz* on the verge of being dispatched on its mission, and one member of the raider company in particular had become the focus of his displeasure and a cause for concern—Cornelius Adolph Heintz.

Doubts about Heintz's loyalty had been raised by the actions of one of the officials at the American consulate. W. E. Chapman was assisted in his duties by two vice-consuls named Gardiner and Brown. Charles Edwin Gardiner, forty-seven years old, was new to the position, having worked as the foreign representative of a refinery in Argentina before joining the consular service and being posted to Mazatlán. It is unclear what Gardiner did or said to bring Heintz under suspicion by the German plotters. Perhaps it was something as simple as offering a friendly smile or wave to a "slacker" that the Americans were expected to detest, or an indiscreet comment to a German informant, but through some act Gardiner made the conspirators aware that Cornelius Heintz might be more than he appeared to be.

On the evening of March 15, while supplies and equipment were being loaded aboard the *Agassiz* and coded messages being flashed across the harbor between Monte Silla Point and the *Vicksburg*, Heintz was told to report to the German consul. When the engineer arrived at Melchers Sucs, he was given a simple message:

"You had better be shooting square with us—or we will see to it that you are not walking around in the morning."

1. Hilario Malpica, Capitán de Navío. Courtesy of Wikimedia Commons.

2. The Mexican gunboat *Tampico*. Courtesy of the author.

3. The Mexican gunboat *Morelos* at anchor in Mazatlán harbor, with the Islas de las Piedras at left. Photograph taken in 1913. Courtesy of the author.

4. The wharf at Mazatlán harbor. In the foreground, boys with poles stand ready to pull lighters to the dock for unloading cargo. The Mazatlán customs house can be seen in the background; the customs warehouse is at left. Courtesy of the author.

5. The headquarters of the powerful German trading house Melchers Sucesores. The single-story central warehouse stands in the foreground; administrative offices and living quarters are at the rear. From *Guía General Descriptiva de la República Mexicana* (Mexico: Estados y Territorios Federales, 1899).

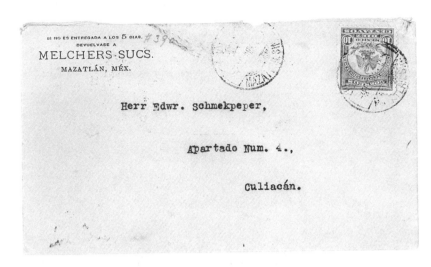

6. Melchers Sucesores business envelope addressed to a customer in Mexico. To circumvent U.S. blacklist restrictions, Melchers Sucs corresponded with American companies using "cloak" intermediaries. Courtesy of the author.

7. The gunboat *Morelos* after being set on fire by Constitutionalist rebel forces in 1914. The foremast has fallen onto the bridge. The discoloration behind the bow shows the point at which the fire ended. Courtesy of the author.

8. German naval attaché Karl Boy-Ed. Courtesy of the author.

9. Shortly before being recalled to Germany for channeling funds to supply German warships from American ports, naval attaché Karl Boy-Ed wrote this check payable to "Cash." Courtesy of the author.

10. A happier time: the Mexican gunboat *Morelos* sails in the Hudson-Fulton Celebration of 1909 in New York Harbor. Her captain is Lieutenant Commander Castellanos, the officer under whom Lieutenant Malpica would later mutiny. Courtesy of the author.

11. Dr. Paul Bernardo Altendorf wears the uniform of a colonel in the Mexican Army. From *Chicago Daily Tribune*, October 31, 1919, 12.

12. General Plutarco Elías Calles. Courtesy of the Library of Congress.

13. German saboteur Lothar Witzke. From *Naugutuck Daily News*, August 26, 1919, 4.

14. German spymaster Kurt Jahnke. Courtesy of the Library of Congress.

15. Badge issued to officers and agents of U.S. Army Military Intelligence during World War I. Courtesy of the author.

16. Altendorf's superior, Byron S. Butcher of the U.S. Army Military Intelligence Division Corps of Intelligence Police. Courtesy of the Library of Congress.

17. An artist's rendering of Maude Lochrane drawn in 1918. From *San Diego Union*, April 3, 1918, 1.

18. The schooner *Alexander Agassiz* is launched by the Marine Biological Association of San Diego, August 1907. Courtesy of Tillie Genter Papers, SMC 30, Special Collections & Archives, UC San Diego Library.

19. U.S. Consul William Edgar Chapman. Courtesy of the Library of Congress.

20. The American gunboat USS *Vicksburg*. Courtesy of the Department of the Navy, Naval Historical Center, Washington DC.

21. The schooner *Alexander Agassiz* after being captured by the USS *Vicksburg* on March 17, 1918. Lieutenant Dorr stands in the foreground. Maude Lochrane is sitting on the coaming at Dorr's left. Submarine Chaser 302 is almost hidden behind the *Agassiz*. Courtesy of the Department of the Navy, Naval Historical Center, Washington DC.

22. *Agassiz* crewmembers Boston, Madden, Volpert, and Brandt stand in irons aboard the *Vicksburg*, guarded by U.S. Navy blue jackets. Courtesy of the Department of the Navy, Naval Historical Center, Washington DC.

23. Officers and seamen of the U.S. Navy inspect the schooner *Alexander Agassiz* in San Diego harbor, March 1918. From *Fort Wayne Journal Gazette*, April 1, 1918. Courtesy of the author.

24. Sand flies through the air as actors in the 1918 Famous Players-Lasky film, *Such a Little Pirate*, dig for pirate treasure on Catalina Island. At right, actress Lila Lee scans the horizon with a spyglass. The schooner *Alexander Agassiz* is at anchor in the foreground. Publicity photo for the film from July 1918. Courtesy of the author.

25. Dr. Paul Bernardo Altendorf in 1919. Photograph from Altendorf's application for entry into the Military Intelligence Corps of Interpreters, dated May 1, 1919, NARA, RG165. Records of the War Department and Special Staffs, Military Intelligence Division, File 51–45.

6 "If You Want to Get the Best of Uncle Sam, Get Up before You Go to Bed"

Long columns of infantry in field-gray uniforms extended as far as the eye could see, as sixty-two German divisions marched toward the front. The final German offensive in France, expected to force a tremendous breakthrough and end the war in victory for the Fatherland, was about to begin. On March 15, the same day that the USS *Vicksburg* arrived in Mazatlán, the ammunition dumps had been completed for the coming assault, code-named Operation Michael. Enormous stockpiles of artillery shells—over 3.2 million rounds would be fired on British troops during the *first day* of the battle—the greatest bombardment in history up to that time, were in position near the German guns. German shock troops were now moving into forward trench positions along the fifty-mile salient that would be the focal point of the attack, to begin a five-day wait for the offensive to begin.

Six thousand miles way, Consul Unger was growing increasingly anxious about the *Alexander Agassiz* expedition. From the general information on the imminent German offensive that had been released to the world press, it was clear to the German officials in Mexico that the war might be over in a very short time. If the raider did not sail now, it might never sail at all. But with Mazatlán harbor under the constant watch of the U.S. Navy, the mission would be in jeopardy from the start.

Fearful that the schooner might be searched by sailors from the *Vicksburg*, Unger ordered that the machine gun, ammunition, and navigational items be removed from the schooner and brought ashore. As long as the Vicksburg remained anchored outside the harbor, it would be impossible to proceed any further. But he had a simple solution for addressing that problem.

On the morning of March 16, W. E. Chapman received a visit from the Mexican captain of the port, Julio Vázquez Schiaffino, who presented him with a written notice demanding that the American warship, USS *Vicksburg*, leave the port of Mazatlán immediately. According to the provisions of the Hague Convention, foreign warships could not remain in the territorial waters of any neutral country longer than twenty-four hours, after which they must otherwise be disarmed. Chapman relayed the message to the *Vicksburg*. To avoid friction with the local authorities, Lieutenant Reordan raised anchor and the *Vicksburg* got under way, steaming out beyond the three-mile limit to patrol offshore.

Reordan sent a wireless message to his divisional commander at the Pacific Fleet:

From: Vicksburg.
March 16, 1918

To : Commander, Division Two.

An American spy who is a member of the crew of the raider here reports that the officers of the raider talked concerning the outfitting of other vessels at Guaymas and Salina Cruz. Other than this nothing further is known. The Raider here is officered by men from the interned German vessels at Santa Rosalía and the navigational instruments are from the same source. They will probably attempt an escape tomorrow, as they appear to be desperate. Ample evidence is at hand justifying their capture at sea. Intense pro-Germanism is shown by local authorities here, who have notified the VICKSBURG to leave port at the expiration of her twenty-four hours. Have procured a fast motorboat to assist and will patrol outside. We have the situation well in hand. Malicious interference with our radio is being carried on by the radio station at Mazatlán.

Despite the confident tone of Reordan's dispatch, his superiors at the Pacific fleet were uneasy about the chance of capturing the *Alexander Agassiz* if it reached the open water. Unlike a freighter or passenger liner bellowing plumes of coal smoke and displaying a prominent outline on the horizon, a small coastal schooner like the *Agassiz*, powered by an internal combustion engine and sails, would be very hard to spot. If the raider managed to slip out of Mazatlán harbor under conditions of poor visibility, and was able to maintain a speed of 12 knots or more, it could prove near impossible for the fleet to track her down across the broad Pacific Ocean.

Reordan's commander at the Pacific Fleet relayed a cautionary wireless message to U.S. Naval Operations:

From: Commander, Division Two.

To : Operations.

Have given orders Brutus, Rainier, Vicksburg, Submarine Chaser 302 near Mazatlán. If the Agassiz escapes at night unobserved and makes a speed of 12 knots, the [gunboat] Yorktown is the only ship in this force that is able to overtake her. 11 knots is reported to be the maximum speed of the Submarine Chaser 302

Shortly after the *Vicksburg* steamed out of view, Heintz received word from Consul Unger that he was to supervise the loading of stores for the raiding mission aboard the *Alexander Agassiz* and ensure that they were brought on board without exciting suspicion. Horse-drawn delivery wagons from Melchers Sucesores arrived at the location where the *Agassiz* was beached in the estuary to deliver the supplies that Bauman and Madden had deemed necessary for the voyage. Under Heintz's diligent supervision, heavy wooden boxes and burlap bags were silently offloaded and manhandled across the sandy terrain onto the dormant craft. Over a ton of provisions were soon taken aboard the schooner, enough to feed the raider crew for ninety days, along with enough fuel for the boat to cruise a radius of five hundred miles—as much as would be needed, since sail power would be employed for most of the journey. The stores included fifty-pound sacks of wheat flour, potatoes, rice, and beans, thirty-eight cases of distillate (two five-gallon cans per case), and over three hundred pounds of wood for the cook stove. After the supplies and fuel had been evenly stowed in the cargo hold below, the navigational instruments and flags were taken on board once again.

The *Agassiz* was now fully loaded, ready to sail at a moment's notice, but the conspirators remained in a quandary. Should they cast the die and head out of port at the risk of being captured if the American gunboat was still lurking offshore, or should they abandon the effort altogether?

On the night of March 16, a compromise was reached. Mate Madden announced that he was game to take a chance and make a dash out of the harbor the following morning at daybreak. A new plan was formulated in which Bauman, who had grown wary of the project, was to canoe out to Venados Island—the farthest island on the northward side of the outer harbor, where he would wait with the machine gun, ammunition, and an additional German crew member. The *Agassiz* would then clear the port with a Mexican pilot at the helm as a camouflage, along with Maude, Madden, Heintz, the remaining members of the raider crew, and several Mexican "passengers" carried as a blind. As soon as the *Agassiz* was safely clear of the harbor, they would proceed to Venados, where Bauman would canoe out to join them with the extra deckhand, the machine gun, and ammunition. The Mexicans would return to the mainland in the canoe, and the *Alexander Agassiz* could then embark on her new career as a raider for the Fatherland. Under this arrangement, if the schooner *was* stopped by an American warship after leaving Mexican waters and boarded, nothing incriminating would be found. If they were not intercepted, they could cruise to Venados and proceed according to plan. No matter what transpired, their bet would be covered.

March 17, 1918, dawned as a beautiful day in Mazatlán, a bright orange sun rising in a clear blue sky. The sea was calm and the currents were light, with a gentle breeze blowing out of the east.

The crew came aboard the *Alexander Agassiz* early, planning to depart the port at 7:00 a.m., but were delayed due to the low tide and a protracted wait to receive final instructions from Unger for contacting Captain Bauman on Venados. The ship's roster included Maude Lochrane, Cornelius Heintz and his wife, Madden, Brandt, Volpert, Koppalla, Boston, the Mexican pilot, and five Mexican passengers. To enable the schooner to exit the harbor without an official clearance, Maude had obtained permission from the captain of the port to take the boat out on a trial run to test her engines. Cornelius Heintz had obtained a similar permission from W. E. Chapman.

By 11:00 a.m., the tide had risen in the esterro, and after Madden received the awaited instructions from the German consul, Heintz turned the engines over and the pilot reversed the *Agassiz* off the tidal flat that had served as her dry dock. The motors throbbed steadily louder as he gradually increased power, and the schooner cruised across the smooth water of the estuary into the harbor. The pilot came from a Mexican gunboat anchored in the harbor and was experienced at running a boat through the hazardous channel, skillfully steering the schooner left and right to avoid obstacles and sunken shoals. In the outer harbor, they passed several small islands with Mexican government buildings on them, watched the Faro lighthouse pass by on the mountainous islet to their right, and at a leisurely 3–4 knots, set course toward the Northwest and Venados Island.

Everything was proceeding according to plan.

Standing on the starboard side of the afterdeck, Richard Brandt pointed out various landmarks on the coast to Mrs. Heintz. As the speed of the schooner increased to 6 knots, Brandt called to Maude Lochrane, "The boat is going pretty fast."

"It can go a whole lot faster," she replied, while heading to the galley to prepare lunch for two of the sailors who would be handling the sails.

As they proceeded into the open ocean, the remaining crew members were situated in various locations around the schooner. Madden stood amidships leaning against the three-foot coaming that lined the inner deck of the *Agassiz*, intently scanning the horizon. Heintz was on deck also, while Koppalla was in the forecastle, busily looking for a line to secure one of the sails. Charles Boston was in the galley cooking some food. Frank Volpert was hiding below in a compartment at the back of the engine room. The instant that Volpert came on board that morning, Madden had taken him aside and instructed him to "Get out of sight and stay out of sight."

At 12:25 p.m., as the *Alexander Agassiz* reached a point about three miles from the bar outside Mazatlán harbor, a large ship appeared in the distance—the USS *Vicksburg*, racing toward them at top speed.

As the *Vicksburg* loomed ever larger, Hendrik Koppalla, the twenty-three-year-old German sailor, spotted a familiar four-quadrant yellow and black checkerboard flag hoisted atop the mainmast—the international maritime signal flag for "stop vessel at once."

"They want us to stop!" Koppalla called out.

The schooner immediately changed course, taking a heading to the west, and built up speed in an attempt to outrun the American warship.

Reordan had anchored the *Vicksburg* two miles north of Mazatlán in Viejo Bay, halfway between the harbor entrance and Venados Island. From that vantage point the American gunboat remained hidden from view, but could still keep watch over the main entryway to the port.

Heintz had given Reordan several dates on which the *Agassiz* might sail, and one of these was Sunday, March 17. The commander of the *Vicksburg* received word from the Pacific Fleet that the supply ship *Brutus* and Submarine Chaser 302 would arrive from the south that afternoon, so he positioned the *Vicksburg* to the north of Mazatlán hoping to lure the unsuspecting schooner out of the harbor. If the *Agassiz* departed toward the north she would be captured by the Vicksburg; if to the south, by the fast Sub Chaser 302.

Shortly after noon, the *Alexander Agassiz* was sighted "standing out" by a lookout on board the *Vicksburg*, and Reordan called the crew to battle stations. As the blue jackets ran to their combat positions, the gunboat's anchor was quickly raised, and the *Vicksburg* got under way, steaming out of Viejo Bay at breakneck speed. When they reached a distance of one and a half miles from the *Agassiz*, the renegade schooner turned sharply away toward the west, and they knew they had been spotted. With its powerful triple expansion steam engine throbbing at maximum revolutions, the *Vicksburg* set off in hot pursuit, and Reordan issued a wireless message to the *Brutus* and Submarine Chaser 302: "RAIDER ESCAPING."

Like an animal trapped in a cage, the *Alexander Agassiz* darted back and forth, her course altered a half dozen times during the chase that ensued.

Finally, in a last-ditch effort to evade capture, the schooner turned south, trying to keep the *Vicksburg* astern while attempting a dash back into port. A distance of fifteen hundred yards now separated the two vessels.

Reordan called out an order to Fire Control on the *Vicksburg*, "Fire a three-inch over her bow!"

Seconds later, a loud bang echoed across the water, as one of *Vicksburg's* one-pounder cannon sent a warning shot over the schooner's bow that produced a white geyser in the sea beyond. The *Agassiz* immediately stopped dead in the water. The *Vicksburg*, still advancing at great speed, came upon the stationary boat quickly, and had to immediately reduce throttle to avoid overshooting the mark. Like the cavalry racing to the rescue, at that very moment, the *Brutus* and submarine chaser appeared in response to the *Vicksburg's* radio message, and also closed on the *Agassiz*.

Reordan would later comment, "The populace ashore could plainly see the three American ships bearing down on the escaping vessel, and this formidable show of force will undoubtedly live long in the memories of the Germans and the Mexicans in that vicinity."

One of the witnesses to the *Agassiz's* capture, standing on the shore that day along the broad Olas Altas near the American embassy, was W. E. Miller, an American who owned a general store in Mazatlán. Miller was acquainted with Cornelius Heintz, and his interest in the events that unfolded that day had begun in the early morning when he became aware that Heintz had mysteriously disappeared.

He described his experiences in a letter to the *Oxnard (California) Daily Courier*:

Heintz was running a boarding house. His China cook came in Sunday morning and said his boss had skipped on the boat. Yes, everything gone. Nothing left in his room; his wife gone too.

Getting interesting. I will investigate. So we ate our dinner and walked down to the bay, only two blocks. No boat. So I started for the American consul—he lives on the waterfront (the ocean is just across the Olas Altas or a wide street). Just as soon as I could see the water I saw a gunboat—our boat—I have not told you the name of it yet, they call it the Alexander Agassiz. And just around the point a submarine chaser going through the water at 20 miles an hour toward them. I looked up: the consul lives in a two-story building and there he was watching the whole business through his field glasses. They were about five miles out from land. He said they signaled to the boat to stop and the boat tried to run away. A shot fired very close made them come to a standstill.

Why was one gunboat south of town and the other north? Why did they have a submarine chaser here? There may be something else going on that I don't know of, but if you want to get the best of Uncle Sam, get up before you go to bed.

On the *Vicksburg*, Reordan ordered the watch officer, Lieutenant J. G. Frederick Dorr, to form a boarding party to search the schooner. Dorr assembled a detail of blue jackets and they clambered aboard a whaleboat that was prepared for launch.

While the gunboat was still some distance from the *Alexander Agassiz*, unusual activity was observed on the dormant vessel, which slowly maneuvered to keep her port side facing the American gunboat. Standing in the foretop, the paymaster of the *Vicksburg*, Edwin Armstrong, trained a pair of binoculars on the schooner and saw several individuals on deck run toward the chart house in the forward part of the ship, then exit on the (blind) starboard side of the structure and toss items over the railing into the water below. Lieutenant Dorr, sitting with the boarding party in the whaleboat swinging high in the davits above the *Vicksburg*'s deck, saw the same thing, and called out to the bridge "They are throwing things overboard on the Agassiz."

Reordan, preoccupied with dodging a rock as he "conned" the *Vicksburg* (issued orders to control the boat's movement through the water), was unable to look up, but when he did a few minutes later, "saw what was apparently two things being thrown overboard." The *Agassiz* crew members engaged in this activity continued to toss items into the sea "for some time," then were seen to disperse and scatter around the deck.

The whaleboat was lowered onto the water and the boarding party made their way to the *Agassiz* and clambered on board. Dorr announced that he wanted to speak to the boat's captain and was surprised when a woman just over five feet tall, Maude Lochrane, stepped forward and told him that *she* was the captain. The naval officer demanded to see the ship's papers. Maude led him to the chart house, where she produced a logbook that contained some entries in Spanish and a letter from W. E. Chapman answering her request to take the *Agassiz* on a trial run to test the engines. With skepticism in his voice, Dorr asked whether the documents represented *all* of the ship's papers. She responded that they did.

Dorr directed Maude to assemble her crew on deck. After assigning two of the rifle-bearing blue jackets to watch them, he headed off with the remaining sailors to initiate a thorough search of the vessel. In the forward crew quarters Dorr discovered a quantity of letters, papers, and miscellaneous correspondence that he handed to one of the sailors accompanying him. In the chart house they found the two Winchester .30-30 rifles, a long-barreled Iver Johnson .32 revolver in a holster, an American double-action .32 revolver in a holster, a Colt .25 automatic, and 150 rounds of ammunition.

Dorr and his men proceeded to the engine room. Looking about the hold, he spotted a compartment that upon inspection proved to be narrow and shallow, and a second compartment that ran to the stern of the ship. Dorr ordered the smallest of the sailors to crawl into the darkened channel and search it. A short time later, the seaman came out and asked for a flashlight, then he reentered the compartment. Crawling on all fours among the tanks in the bilge, he came upon Volpert hiding in a remote opening under the engineer's compartment, and quickly dragged him outside. Dorr asked Volpert his nationality and the tradesman responded "German." They ordered him to empty his pockets, and among the items that he removed was a certificate that stated under the seal of the German consulate that he was a reservist in the German army. Volpert was escorted under guard to join the other members of the schooner's crew on deck.

After completing a preliminary search of the schooner, Dorr and his detail of blue jackets returned to the chart house to conduct a more rigorous inspection. In a closet they discovered a set of international signal flags, and to their great surprise, a large red, white, and black German naval ensign. Examining the flag in the light of the doorway, Dorr saw two rows of odd, hieroglyphic characters written in chalk that extended the length of the ensign. In the center of the first row was a crude drawing of a railroad track. Unable to interpret the markings, he gave the flag to one of his men, and continued rummaging through the chart house. In a coat hanging on the wall they found a leather wallet that had a piece of paper concealed in a hidden pocket. When unfolded, the paper appeared to be part of a cipher:

Hidden Cipher Key Discovered on *Alexander Agassiz*

	9.	8.	7.	6.	5.	4.	3.	2
1.	a	b	c	d	e	f	g	h
2.	i	j	k	l	m	n	o	p
3.	q	r	s	t	u	v	w	x
4.	y	z						

1.	2.	3.	4.	5.	6.	7.	8.	9.	0
m	r	s	k	l	x	a	g	n	i

repeat it

Bauman

1/8	1/9	3/5	2/5	1/7	2/4	t

Source: NARA, RG121, Records of the United States District Courts, U.S. District Court for the Southern District of California, Civil Law Case 622–636, *Alexander Agassiz* Prize Court Trial Records.

Dorr walked out onto the deck and informed Maude Lochrane that she was under arrest. The engines were started on the *Alexander Agassiz*, and the American sailors ran the boat alongside the *Vicksburg*. Dorr called up to Reordan, standing in the bridge of the gunboat, reporting what they had discovered. A "prize crew" from the *Vicksburg* was sent to operate the captured vessel, and the thirteen individuals that had been found on the *Agassiz*, along with the papers, firearms, ammunition, and flags were transported by whaleboat to the American warship.

Once on board, the raider crew members—Madden, Koppalla, Volpert, Brandt, and Boston were placed in irons, and kept under the constant guard of a blue jacket armed with a rifle with fixed bayonet, who paced back and forth near the area where they were confined. With their unshaven faces and rough clothing, wearing dusty fedoras or sailor caps, they were a hard-looking lot. The female prisoners, Maude Lochrane and Mrs. Heintz, were allowed the freedom of the gun deck.

Cornelius Heintz was held apart from the other prisoners. He informed Reordan and Dorr that during the forty-odd minutes that elapsed from the time that the German crewmen spotted the *Vicksburg* and the boarding party came aboard, a large quantity of items had been tossed overboard, including charts, the German code, a commission from the German government authorizing the boat as a raider, and several letters provided to Bauman and Madden for delivery when they reached Germany. The conspirators had been directed to destroy the letters if they did not reach their final destination. Heintz had personally seen Madden throw the sextant and papers overboard; the remaining items had been dropped in the water by other crewmen.

When Heintz was shown the items that had been confiscated aboard the *Alexander Agassiz*, he told the officers that they had overlooked the ship's papers, which remained hidden aboard the schooner. "Miss Lochrane instructed Charlie Boston to hide them in the kitchen underneath a lot of rubbish in the corner of the room," he told them, since Reordan and the American consul had previously been told they had been destroyed. A boat was dispatched to the *Agassiz* with Heintz and a pair of sailors who retrieved the ship's papers from the concealed location and returned to the gunboat.

The *Vicksburg* steamed to Viejo Bay, where a conference was arranged between the American navy and Mexican government representatives to discuss the seizure of the *Agassiz*. Submarine Chaser 302 was used to convey the officials who would attend the meeting to the *Vicksburg*, which included the Mexican captain of the port, Julio Vázquez Schiaffino, Consul Chapman, Vice-Consul Gardiner, and British Vice-Consul Watson.

When the meeting was called to order, Schiaffino demanded that the *Alexander Agassiz* be returned to the port of Mazatlán on the basis that she had not properly cleared the port, and could not clear the port, because of an outstanding balance of several hundred pesos in port charges against her. Reordan, supported by the American and British consular officials, replied that outstanding port charges did not constitute legal grounds for demanding the vessel's return, but in the interest of being conciliatory he offered to pay the port charges against the *Agassiz* if the Mexican officials agreed to remove all complaint against her capture. Schiaffino refused the offer, and demanded to know on what grounds the *Alexander Agassiz* had been captured. With W. E. Chapman acting as his interpreter, the commander of the *Vicksburg* stated his reasons for taking the American schooner as a prize:

1. The *Alexander Agassiz* did not have proper clearance papers and the ship's papers that were on board had been concealed.
2. She had arms and ammunition on board. (These were taken out and displayed for the Captain of the Port to see.)
3. She had several German nationals and a German naval flag on board. (At this, the German prisoners were brought in and Schiaffino looked them over.)
4. The *Agassiz* refused to stop when given the signal to do so, and instead, turned out to sea in an attempt to flee.

Given these circumstances, Reordan explained to Schiaffino, he believed that the *Alexander Agassiz* had become an instrument of war to be used against the United States. The captain of the port remained indignant. In a further attempt to alleviate the situation, Reordan turned over the Mexicans that had been found on the schooner to the port official, convinced that they had taken no part in the German scheme and would have little value as witnesses.

When the three-hour conference ended, Reordan watched the captain of the port depart for Mazatlán "very much afraid that the Germans would mob him when he got ashore for not getting the vessel back." Chapman was also apprehensive about the reaction of the German community, fearing that there would be a German-led demonstration against the American consulate. As Chapman left the *Vicksburg*, Reordan handed the consul a ship's revolver and ammunition "on loan" in case of emergency.

The *Vicksburg* remained in Viejo Bay long enough to coal from the supply ship *Brutus*, and then anchored outside Mazatlán harbor with her "prize" (the *Agassiz*) until the following afternoon, when a coded message was received from the divisional commander:

From: Commander, Division Two.
March 18, 1918

To : Vicksburg.

Vicksburg proceed to San Diego with prize and prisoners.
Acknowledge.

While the *Vicksburg* steamed toward California with the *Agassiz* in tow,
the story of the raider's capture had already become front-page news. The
first reports were published in San Diego, the *Vicksburg*'s next port of call.
Under the headline "American Gunboat Takes Hun Raider off Mexican
Coast," the *San Diego Union* revealed:

> The auxiliary schooner *Alexander Agassiz*, formerly a craft owned and
> operated by the University of California in research work at sea was
> captured off Mazatlan by an American gunboat . . . Germany's first
> attempt to outfit a raider at a west coast Mexican port with which to
> create havoc with Pacific coast shipping has been frustrated . . . An
> astounding mass of intrigue, implicating officials at Mazatlán, is being
> unfolded as a result of the capture of the would-be German corsair . . .
> Attempted revenge on Americans for being blacklisted is said to be one
> of the principal reasons for the outfitting of the *Agassiz* as a raider. Funds
> for the purchase of supplies and munitions were raised by Mazatlán
> German firms whose trade has been seriously curtailed since being
> placed on the American black list.

In a story titled "Women on German Raider Seized at Sea by U.S. Ship,"
the *San Diego Evening Tribune* announced:

> The German raider *Alexander Agassiz*, captured near Mazatlán by a
> United States cruiser will arrive here in a day or two according to
> Washington advices today . . . The raider had 13 persons on board when
> captured, the company including five Germans, two women and six
> Mexicans . . . One woman, at least, is believed to be an American adven-
> turess well-known in San Diego and Los Angeles, who has attempted
> to turn her beauty to great financial account . . . Many merchantmen
> in the Pacific only, do not carry defense guns and it would have been

a comparatively easy task for the men on the *Agassiz* with their rifles and pistols to seize a ship of such type.

National wire services picked up the story. Within days, sensational accounts of the schooner's capture appeared in newspapers across the United States. As word of the foiled German raiding mission spread, published reports grew ever more exaggerated. According to one paper, the schooner was captured "15 miles out of Mazatlán, flying the flag of the Imperial German Navy." Another announced that "typical Teuton methods of sabotage were followed by the Hun raiders uncovered aboard the auxiliary schooner *Alexander Agassiz* to destroy the vessel's engines with dynamite when they were near capture by a United States warship . . . at least two rapid-fire guns were thrown overboard." A further account stated that "a dozen other raiders are today being prepared on the Mexican west coast to prey on Pacific commerce and [will] harass the coast if they can elude the American gunboats."

While the story played out in the press, it also came to the attention of the Justice Department's Bureau of Investigation (renamed the *Federal* Bureau of Investigation in 1935), which quietly opened a criminal investigation titled "Ship Alexander Agassiz—Alleged German Raider" to determine whether any federal laws had been violated by the participants. Bureau agents in San Diego and Los Angeles gathered evidence and interviewed anyone with information about Maude Lochrane, the *Agassiz* crew members, or the Pacific Coast Trading and Shipping Company.

Joseph Mesmer was questioned in his office at the St. Louis Fire Brick Company. A respected industrialist, Mesmer found himself in potentially serious circumstances. Anti-German hysteria was at its peak in the United States, and Mesmer, a second-generation German American, had helped to finance a suspected German commerce raider. He explained to the Justice Department agents that he provided the $5,000 bond for the purchase of the *Alexander Agassiz* as a personal favor to Maude Lochrane, and then turned over all of the private correspondence, letters, telegrams, and legal documents that he had exchanged with the University of California, Maude Lochrane, and government officials relating to the purchase and operation of the vessel. Mesmer's files provided a trove of information for the investigators to use in piecing together the murky history of the *Alexander Agassiz*.

The authorities also interviewed Maude's former partners, William Taylor, her brother Frank Wheeler, and his wife Minnie. Taylor (aka Guillermo Taliferro) had fled from San Francisco in February 1918, shortly before he was to go on trial for "stealing $500 from a negro" and was extradited from a jail cell in Honolulu for questioning and trial. Frank Wheeler, now an auditor with the Gunset Cigar Company of Honolulu, assured investigators that his adopted sister was innocent, as did his wife Minnie. Wheeler contended that either Maude was overcome by force or the Germans had used some form of trickery to gain possession of the boat.

Special Agent V. W. Killick, who interviewed Joseph Mesmer and Minnie Wheeler, summarized in his findings that "Miss Lochrane is reputed to be honest, by both Mesmer and Mrs. Wheeler. Mrs. Wheeler stated that a sister of Miss Lochrane recently died in Michigan leaving two orphan children. Miss Lochrane has undertaken to support and care for these. Neither Mesmer nor Mrs. Wheeler would question the loyalty of Miss Lochrane. They are firm in the conviction that if the *Alexander Agassiz* has actually been used as a German raider, Miss Lochrane was taken advantage of by unscrupulous parties in Mexico, or may have sold it to agents of the Germans unknowingly."

A wealth of information from the public flowed into Bureau field offices after photographs of the schooner's German crew appeared in the press. Edward Gripper, the "Chinese Inspector" in Yuma, Arizona, informed the Bureau's Los Angeles office that Arthur Martens (Madden), pictured aboard the *Alexander Agassiz* in Los Angeles newspapers, had worked in Andrade, California, in early 1917, and was reported to have offered to serve with Mexican General Calles if a war broke out between Mexico and the United States. According to Gripper, Madden "talked bitterly against the United States" while under the influence of alcohol. William Black, the dredge watchman for the Southern Pacific Railroad at Andrade, advised the Bureau's field office in Tucson that Madden had told him "that he [Madden] was on the boat *Maverick* in San Francisco . . . loaded with arms and ammunition to be taken to a German cruiser, but that the

United States government would not permit it. At the time of the Mexican trouble, Madden had been reported as saying that in case of war between the U.S. and Mexico, he would be with the Mexicans over the U.S. in helping the Mexicans to make war on the U.S." Judge Brown, the postmaster at Calipatria, California, advised the San Diego Bureau field office that crewman Richard Brandt had ranched on the outskirts of Calipatria for a year and a half, before leaving the area the previous year. Brown claimed that other parties had told him that at the time the U.S. entered the war, "Brandt had stated that he was a German reservist and that he was going to Mexico to organize a bunch of Mexicans and invade the United States."

The crew of the *Alexander Agassiz* had been confined in shackles on the *Vicksburg* for ten days when the gunboat steamed into San Diego harbor with the schooner in tow. The prisoners were brought ashore by whaleboat and turned over to U.S. Marshal W. C. Carse for delivery to the San Diego county jail. The only exception was Mrs. Cornelius Heintz, who was nearing childbirth and moved to a local hospital. Reporters gathered at the county jail, anxious to interview the "beautiful red-haired adventuress" of the scheme, Maude Lochrane, but were told that she was being held incommunicado—no visitors allowed.

The *Agassiz* was moored alongside the municipal bulkhead, a pier just north of the Broadway dock. Guarded by a detail of armed blue jackets, the German raider quickly became an object of curiosity for hundreds of waterfront visitors. Also paying a visit to view the boat—and be given a guided tour to familiarize themselves with the "evidence"—were the U.S. district attorney and several members of the court who would rule on the legality of her seizure.

The status of the *Alexander Agassiz* as a "prize," whether the schooner and its crew had been lawfully captured, was to be decided by a "prize court." Dating back hundreds of years, a prize court is a legal proceeding conducted by a nation that captures a private ship or merchant vessel in time of war to determine whether it was validly seized and to decide who holds title to the ship and its cargo. In accordance with the provisions of American prize court procedure at the time, two members of the *Agassiz* prize court were appointed by a federal judge, Benjamin Bledsoe of the United States District Court for the Southern District of California: J. E. Fishburn, a Los Angeles banker, and judge W. R. Andrews, the former city attorney for San Diego. The third and final member, and the leader of the prize court, Lieutenant W. R. Cushman, was appointed by the Navy Department based on his extensive experience in international law. United States District Attorney Robert O'Connor would handle the prosecution for the government.

The fate of Maude Lochrane, Cornelius Heintz and his wife, the German crew members, and the schooner *Alexander Agassiz* itself, would unfold in four days at the Federal Building in San Diego when the prize court went into session.

In Mazatlán, the German authorities publicly disclaimed any involvement in the *Alexander Agassiz* affair, and disseminated reports that the raider had not been a raider at all—the schooner's capture by the Americans was entirely due to the failure of her debts being paid in Mazatlán before she sailed off. In private, the mission's failure resulted in anger and recriminations. The blow was softened by the knowledge that five seagoing submarines would soon come through the Straits of Magellan and Smythe's Channel to the Gulf of Fonseca, Honduras, and Salvador, and two of the submarines would continue to cruise stealthily north to the west coast of Mexico. When the salvaged *Morelos* was fit for duty as a submarine tender, the U-boats would commence operations off the western coast of the United States.

And nothing would disrupt *that* plan.

7   "The Germans Are After You"

As the sun descended behind the tree line in the Mazatlán estuary, the birds and reptiles prowling through the darkening mangroves in search of food were startled by a flash of light and strange sounds emanating from the water near the Cervecería del Pacífico brewery. The electric generator on the gunboat *Morelos* suddenly whirred to life, illuminating the vessel in a constellation of incandescent bulbs. On the upper deck, a complement of men carrying rifles could be seen making their rounds of the ship. Señor Arzak had recently added another five guards to the night watch to deter any attempts to seize or sabotage his gunboat.

Louis Arzak was becoming increasingly anxious about the security of the *Morelos*—and with good reason, for he knew that many individuals were now casting covetous eyes on his powerful warship. The Germans had offered him $50,000 in American gold for the gunboat, plus the cost of floating it and repairs to date, most probably to use the *Morelos* as a commerce raider. Arzak had rejected the offer out of hand, certain that the ship would be worth considerably more after the repair work had been completed. His response had left the German representatives far from happy. He suspected that the Mexican government had designs on the vessel as well. The *Morelos* had been the finest warship in the Mexican navy and a symbol of national pride. To reclaim the gunboat and return it to the service of Mexico would bring great honor to the Carranza government. Then there were the Americans to worry about. The American navy was now visiting the port of Mazatlán on a regular basis—never exceeding the twenty-four-hour limit, but still a cause of concern to a man in possession of a ship that was likely viewed as a potential adversary. Perhaps the Americans also wanted to gain control of the *Morelos*?

Arzak's suspicions were well-founded, particularly in regard to the American government's interest in the salvaged gunboat. The U.S. Navy had been maintaining surveillance of the *Morelos* since October 1917, when Consul W. E. Chapman first informed the State Department that a sunken warship had been sold to parties associated with the German trading house, Melchers Sucesores. In the succeeding months, when naval officers visited the American consulate in Mazatlán, the consul kept them updated on the status of the work under way aboard the suspect ship: "A large force is making repairs day and night . . . There is something strange connected with the vessel which is regarded as dangerous. It could put to sea very soon."

After the *Alexander Agassiz* was captured by the *Vicksburg* off Mazatlán, the Navy's concerns over the suspect gunboat only increased. A report by Lieutenant I. M. Graham of the Pacific Fleet forwarded to the secretary of the navy noted: "It is reported that the (*Morelos*) machinery is in good shape, that the bottom is not foul, and that there is some coal aboard. Foundry and repair facilities in Mazatlán belong to the Fundicion De Sinaloa, which is under control of the Germans, and may have been utilized in the repair of the *Morelos* . . . It is considered that there is some danger of her shipping out of port and becoming a raider."

Lieutenant Commander E. J. Minister of the British steamship *Violet*, who managed to get aboard the *Morelos* on March 24, 1918, provided his observations to the commander of the U.S. Navy supply ship *Brutus*:

There were, by actual count, fifty men working on board, five being Germans . . . Her machinery was in very good condition and seemed to be clean. Steam was already up in the donkey boiler. The entire hull outside . . . was in good condition, but many of the deck beams were rusted and also the deck plating . . . Inside the hull, scaling and painting was going on forward . . . the plating seemed to be in fair to good condition. One gun mount was in place and all sponsons and foundations seemed to be good. The vessel was moored stem and stern, head upstream and is expected to be all ready for sea by April 10th.

A few days before Minister visited the gunboat, Dr. Paul Bernardo Altendorf learned of the *Morelos*'s existence and decided to investigate this effort, likely sponsored by the Germans, to restore an old Mexican warship. Losing no time, he called at the place where the most reliable information on German activities in Mazatlán could be found, and where his standing "was still of the highest"—the German consulate. Comfortably seated in Unger's office at Melchers Sucs, through delicate questioning, speaking as one loyal servant of the Fatherland to another, he was able to bring Unger to reveal the complete story of the German plan for the gunboat *Morelos*.

There would soon be submarines off the coast of California and in the Gulf of Mexico, the German consul informed him. Three submarines were intended for operation off Tampico and another two on the Pacific coast. In preparation for this, it had been arranged with President Carranza for the Mexican government to confiscate the *Morelos* as soon as Arzak's team had completed the repairs necessary to make her seaworthy, then the gunboat would be turned over to German representatives for use as a U-boat tender. The fact that the vessel had no armament and was not battle ready was of no consequence; all that mattered was that she be seaworthy and capable of delivering diesel fuel and supplies to the submarines cruising offshore. It was a brilliant plan, Unger confided, a valuable instrument for the destruction of Allied shipping in the Pacific would be acquired at no cost to either government. This would also prevent the *Morelos* from falling into the hands of the Americans. Unger further revealed that a firm based in San Francisco had already opened negotiations with the Arzak brothers for the purchase of the warship.

A proud smile formed on Altendorf's face that masked his inner consternation. The German submarines would arrive within a few weeks. Under these conditions, passing the information on to the U.S. Army Military Intelligence office in Nogales would do little good. He would have to derail the German plan himself.

It was up to me individually to thwart this plot—one lone man among enemies pitted against two unscrupulous governments. Then Unger unwittingly placed the winning card in my hands.

"Arzak brothers are good friends of mine," the consul reflected, "and I do not want to see them get too raw a deal. Suppose you see them and find out what they want for the *Morelos*."

Altendorf agreed to see what he could do.

The doctor-spy returned to his office and arranged for letterhead stationary to be printed in the name of a prominent commercial banking house in Valparaiso, Chile. When it arrived, he wrote himself a letter that authorized "Señor Paul B. Altendorf" to negotiate the purchase of the steamship *Morelos* on the firm's behalf.

With his cover established, he called on Louis Arzak to open "negotiations" for acquiring the gunboat *Morelos*. He showed the beer distributor his letter of introduction and cautioned him that their dealings must be held in strictest secrecy. When Arzak inquired how much Altendorf's firm would be willing to pay for the warship Altendorf replied that he would "cable his principals once he had seen the vessel." He was immediately taken on a detailed inspection tour of the former Mexican gunboat.

After allowing the amount of time to pass that would transpire during an actual exchange of cablegrams, Altendorf wired himself a message stating that the principals of his Chilean firm would be willing to pay 500,000 pesos for the *Morelos*, delivered in good condition and ready for sea duty. Then he notified Louis Arzak that he was ready to talk business, and made a verbal offer to pay him 500,000 *dollars* for the *Morelos*, intentionally inflating the amount that he would pay in Arzak's mind.

When Altendorf returned to Melchers Sucesores, he informed Unger that Arzak was asking $240,000 for the ship and that he had no buyers in sight. It was an amount that Altendorf was certain would ensure little chance of a deal taking place between Unger and his "good customer" Louis Arzak, which would let the beer distributor down easy. Meanwhile, the situation regarding the *Morelos* was communicated through American government channels to Otis McAlister and Company, the San Francisco-based trading company interested in buying the vessel, who were advised "to be on the spot with the money when the proper time came."

On March 24, Altendorf entered the dining room of the Hotel Francia and saw a stranger in deep discussion with some men whom he recognized as local customs officers. Taking a seat at a nearby table, the American spy was able to eavesdrop on their conversation, and learned that the stranger was a Mexican naval officer named Gómez who had been dispatched by Carranza to carry out his order to confiscate the *Morelos*. The customs officials informed him that it would be at least another twenty days before the salvaged warship would be capable of steaming out of port. Gómez announced that he would postpone the confiscation until that time.

"Why waste government funds in fitting out the vessel," Altendorf considered, "when the poor sucker who thought that he owned it was so willing to spend his own money for the purpose?"

The next day Altendorf discovered the name of the Italian engineer who was supervising the restoration of the *Morelos*. Calling on Señor José Leone, Royal Italian naval architect, the American agent introduced himself as being from an unnamed country in South America, there to purchase the *Morelos*, while concealing his true intentions from the Germans under the pretense of practicing medicine. He offered Leone a "commission" of 50,000 pesos if he would support his proposal to purchase the *Morelos*. Altendorf knew that Leone was pro-German, but discovered that a bribe had a wondrous effect in changing his allegiance. The naval architect quickly lost all interest in assisting the Germans.

To further derail the German scheme for the *Morelos*, Altendorf used a close personal friend of Arzak to convey a rumor that Carranza intended to confiscate the gunboat. He wanted Arzak, already anxious about the security of his investment, to grow even more apprehensive so that he might not complete the sale. The doctor was certain that Arzak would find no buyer other than the Americans, and he wanted them to receive a good bargain.

Altendorf's rumor achieved its desired purpose. On April 30, the commanding officer of the supply ship USS *Brutus* sent a wireless dispatch to the commander of the Pacific Fleet:

The following information on the gunboat *Morelos* was obtained from the consulate at Mazatlán: The men who claim to be the owners say that they are very anxious to negotiate a sale to some American, so as to place the ship under the protection of the American government and thereby prevent its being seized by the Mexican authorities, which they understand to be their intention as soon as the vessel has been put into such condition that it could be taken to Vera Cruz for final repairs. Mr. Arzac, [*sic*] who claims to be the real owner, fears that if left in the status of Mexican marine property, seizure will be made and probably without any compensation to him, whereas, if sold to any American with proper documentary evidence of the sale, the Mexican government would be powerless to do anything with the vessel. Mr. Arzac is anxious to negotiate the sale at the earliest possible moment, both parties to acknowledge before the U.S. Consul, thereupon the vessel to be given a provisional registry . . .

V. Manoprio, manager of the brewery at Mazatlan has spoken to Mr. Arzac and said that he ought not to allow the vessel to go into the hands of the Americans, even to be repaired in the United States. The Consul was also informed that the German Consul has said that every effort would be made to prevent this, and the U.S. Consul is of the opinion that the Germans contemplate paying the Mexican government officials to seize the vessel should any development arise that would prevent its coming into their own (German) hands . . . the Consul says that he would not trust Mr. Arzac as being sincere in his proposition to sell the vessel to American interests and have it towed to the States.

During the weeks that followed, Altendorf traveled throughout Mexico on other assignments, then on May 7, he returned to Mazatlán and told Arzak that he was ready to close the deal. The meeting went smoothly until Altendorf informed the beer distributor that he was now ready to transfer 100,000 American dollars to complete the transfer of the warship, which at the current exchange rate was the equivalent of 500,000 Chilean pesos.

Thereupon Arzak protested most violently, saying that I had promised to pay $500,000, but by producing my cablegram, which distinctly said "pesos," he had no alternative but to admit, with many anguished objurgations, that he must have misunderstood me about the "dollars." Then he flatly refused to carry out his part of the bargain.

I assured him that I was very sorry he had misunderstood me; also, I regretted that he was going to lose his steamship altogether, as it was to be confiscated on the 10th; that I had seen a letter to that effect.

This had the desired effect. That very evening Arzak hunted up the two representatives of the San Francisco firm who had been waiting for him to come to his senses and at 7:15 p.m. closed the sale for $129,000 American gold.

I had won the game.

Three days later, on the same date that Altendorf had told Arzak his ship was to be confiscated, the *Morelos* was transferred to Otis McAlister and Company. The gunboat was towed to the outer harbor of Mazatlán by the steam schooner *San Gabriel*, and moored there. Consul Chapman supplied the vessel with a provisional registry as an American ship, transferring the *Morelos* as the "restos" (remains) of a wreck for clearance to be towed to America, and never to serve as a submarine tender of the Kaiserliche Marine.

During the recent mission to the United States with Lothar Witzke in which Altendorf had arranged Witzke's capture by American authorities, the British agent Gleaves had seen Witzke tear a yellow slip of paper into pieces and casually discard the fragments. Gleaves was later able to recover the torn paper and deliver it to the U.S. Army Military Intelligence section at Nogales.

Altendorf and Butcher spent many hours trying to reassemble the scraps of paper to read the message, but it proved a difficult jigsaw puzzle to solve. Some of the pieces were missing and the ink had become smudged after days of rough handling. All they could discern was a date—either January 21 or 22, 1918, and that the message was about the visit of some Germans to Las Tres Marías islands, along with a few recognizable words like "oil" and "gasoline." It did not take a great deal of imagination to infer that the note related to preparations for a possible German submarine base off the coast of Mexico.

On his return to Mazatlán, Altendorf began making cautious inquiries about the islands and learned that five Germans had recently taken a boat to Las Tres Marías. They had stayed on the "big island" several days, before sailing back to port. His curiosity aroused, Altendorf directed an associate to hire a boat for a reconnaissance mission to the island archipelago.

The "Three Marías," today known as the "Islas Marías," consist of a chain of three islands off the coast of the Mexican state of Nyarat that are named after three figures in the New Testament: Mary, the mother of Jesus Christ, Mary Magdalene, and Mary of Clopas, who was present at the crucifixion. In 1918, the largest of the islands, Isla María Madre, was the site of a federal prison colony.

Announcing to everyone within earshot at the harbor that they were leaving on a "fishing trip," Altendorf and his companion departed in a 25-foot sailboat for Las Tres Marias. Seven hours later they sighted the islands, and after sailing around the archipelago, landed at a desolate spot on Isla María Madre. The two men hiked around the area for several hours, but could see nothing through the dense, jungle-like vegetation. They returned to their boat, circumnavigated the island, and moored at a landing where steamers brought provisions ashore for the prison. Once again, they disembarked and reconnoitered the area, but finding nothing of value, returned to the boat and set sail for home.

At a gambling house in Mazatlán, Altendorf uncovered the information that he had been unable to obtain on the fruitless excursion to Isla María Madre. He met a German agent named Graffenberg who introduced him to a fellow spy named Hartmann. While they played the popular German card game of skat, Altendorf engaged the pair in casual conversation on a variety of topics, eventually turning the discussion to Las Tres Marías.

"What do you people think of Las Tres Marías for a submarine base?" he asked.

"Oh, I have been there," Hartmann replied. "It is too small. It is no good unless we could have complete control. There are a lot of prisoners there. The islands would make a good submarine base in one way, but there are so many rocks that approach would be difficult. There are much better places along the coast."

The talkative Hartmann then told Altendorf of his visit to Bahía de Banderas, the "Bay of Flags," a large inlet above Puerto Vallarta that lies two hundred miles south of Mazatlán. It has a most excellent harbor, Hartmann advised, and is approachable by land from both Guadalajara and Tepic. Altendorf learned that the Germans had sent a Spanish engineering team to Bahia de Banderas to scout the area in advance of establishing a submarine base there. A German named Koerner had been in charge of the operation.

Altendorf returned to his office and composed a report on what he had learned for Military Intelligence.

It was typical that Altendorf would find the information that he was seeking in a Mazatlán gaming house, since the port city had become a clearing house for German intelligence and a transit point for many of its agents. Mazatlán provided easy access to the United States by way of Nogales and Calexico, and once over the border, a short trip to San Francisco yielded railroad passage to cities across the United States and Canada, and connection with steamships traveling to Australia, China, Japan, Russia, and South America. Given its geographic location, Altendorf noted that "many things happened in Mazatlán."

One day in the spring of 1918, while waiting to see Unger at the consulate, Altendorf met four German agents who had just returned from Magdalena Bay on the west coast of Lower California where they had been engaged in making maps and collecting information for the German navy. He came upon them in the street the following day, and proposed that they have a beer together. When two of the agents stopped at the Hotel Francia on the way to the beer garden and had a long discussion with a German youth named Karl Jacobson, Altendorf decided to make it his business to learn more about the young man.

He seemed to visit the German consulate oftener than a man on honest business would need to do; and twice I saw him in the American consulate. Not to make a long story of it, Herr Jacobson turned out to be a German secret agent who had been employed through Consul Unger to blow up American factories. Jacobson drew money for travel expenses and advance salary and promptly blew it all at the gambling table. This process was repeated until Unger threatened to have him arrested.

The American consul was induced to stall Jacobson along until he began to confess, little by little, that he was a German secret agent in trouble. In the end, Jacobson went to Rosario and returned with samples of an ingenious chemical apparatus that would explode 35 minutes after it had been primed. Jacobson also had an ingenious plan for carrying explosives concealed in talcum powder tins. Jacobson said he was engaged to take explosives and invisible ink powder in [his] baggage on a tour to California, destroying everything he could.

The youth began to fear for his life in Mazatlán and appealed to W. E. Chapman for help in reaching the United States. The consul gave him the $24 railroad fare for a trip to Nogales, Arizona, deciding that the best place for the German saboteur was in an American prison. After seeing him off, Chapman sent a cable to U.S. border officials alerting them to the danger posed by Jacobson, which concluded: "For God's sake, wake up and keep this man in jail." Through a mix-up at the border, Jacobson passed into the United States without interference and was able to obtain a job at a Nogales saw mill. Altendorf later arranged for him to be apprehended by the Justice Department in Tucson, Arizona, where he once again confessed to being a German spy.

Another dangerous character that Agent A-1 met through the German consulate was a Spaniard named Salvary. The high regard in which the "Austrian" doctor was held by Consul Unger and Vice-Consul Burgmeister inspired great confidence among the enemy agents that he met, and Salvary was no exception. One evening over dinner, Salvary informed Altendorf that he had been recruited by the Germans in Spain for an important assignment in the United States. The mission, which he had recently completed, was so successful that German officials in Mexico City had engaged him to return to the United States again, this time with a fund of $20,000 at his disposal. In a low voice, the Spaniard disclosed his unusual specialty to Altendorf—he was an expert at poisoning cattle.

The movement of Allied soldiers, artillery, and material across the battlegrounds of France was heavily dependent on draft horses and mules from America. Early in the war, German army intelligence had devised a ruthless scheme to disrupt their supply. A German American doctor named Anton Dilger was dispatched to the United States with a hidden cache of deadly anthrax and glanders germ cultures. Dilger established a secret laboratory in Chevy Chase, Maryland, where he used his medical training to propagate the germs into a sizable reserve. Steamer Captain Frederick Hinsch and other German agents in America then hired teams of germ-saboteurs to inject the lethal microbes into draft animals being shipped to Europe, or spread germ-laden liquid into their feed pens and water tanks. The results were devastating. "Within weeks, the first symptoms appeared—staggering, convulsions, skin ulcerations—as the deadly bacteria multiplied inside the unfortunate beasts, and death followed shortly thereafter." The Germans planned to use Salvary to expand the effort, poisoning the cattle herds of the Southwest to deny beef to the Allied armies.

The procedure was quite simple, the Spaniard explained. The poison would be surreptitiously deposited at night into water troughs located throughout cattle country. Salvary informed Altendorf that he was quite anxious to get under way, and planned to leave for America within the next two or three days.

The potential for destruction posed by Salvary appeared so great that Altendorf considered accompanying the saboteur to the border to ensure his arrest. But the agent now faced a common problem—he was short of cash. He had buried a large sum of money ($14,800) in a remote location in Guaymas, but if he traveled there to make a "withdrawal," Salvary would be long gone by the time he returned. Since being sworn in as an operative of U.S. Army Military Intelligence, Altendorf had received a salary of $150 a month and an expense allowance of $3 per day, but this was not enough to finance an expedition to the border with Salvary. To supplement his income he had also been spending his own money freely, but at the moment, was low on available funds.

Agent A-1 sent a wire to his superiors in Nogales requesting an additional stipend to follow the cattle poisoner to America, but received no reply. He sent a second, more urgent telegram, and again there was no response. Altendorf watched Salvary depart on his mission to the United States and never learned what became of him. "But he was not arrested."

One of the assignments that Altendorf had received from Butcher was to learn whether the Germans were operating any radio stations in Mexico. Military Intelligence believed that an enemy wireless station had been established near Tepic, approximately 270 miles south of Mazatlán, where the Germans had established a reservist training camp. Altendorf decided to book passage there to investigate—a trip that he *could* afford—with his Mexican laundry woman Luisita, who had been raised in Tepic and knew the area well.

If he traveled openly as "Paul Bernardo Altendorf, Austrian doctor," the visit was sure to raise questions among his German colleagues in Mazatlán, since he had no legitimate reason for going to Tepic. So he decided to make the journey disguised as a Mexican.

In a second-hand shop he purchased used trousers, sandals, a white cotton shirt without collar, and a battered straw hat. To darken his complexion, he daubed a diluted solution of iodine over his body, from the crown of his head to the soles of his feet. Additional preparations for the trip included concealing his remaining cash, $85 in American gold, in a money belt around his waist, and cutting a thin slit in the side of his cotton shirt that would allow his pistol to remain fully concealed, but readily drawn. Altendorf had recently replaced his worn Colt .45 revolver with a new Colt .45 automatic pistol that he secured under his shirt using two belts hidden beneath his waist band.

The train ride to Tepic was uneventful until they reached Acaponeta where the rebels had destroyed the track, burning a number of bridges in the process. Altendorf hired an automobile that carried them to Santiago, and the following day, the remaining distance to Tepic. He knew that the most important German in the area was Herman Gaedke, an engineer he had met with Schwiertz in Hermosillo. Altendorf left Luisita in Tepic, a small town in the mountains, while he hunted down Gaedke.

The engineer was very surprised to see Altendorf. What was one of Herr Jahnke's secret service men doing in Tepic dressed as a Mexican? Altendorf explained that he had been sent by Mexico City to inspect the German camp, and was traveling in disguise as a precaution against bandits. This seemed to satisfy Gaedke, who informed Altendorf that the training camp had been established on the Hildebrand Farms, five or six miles from Tepic. They were receiving new German recruits daily and had around 240 men for the coming drive into the United States.

At midnight, Gaedke and Altendorf mounted burros and rode five miles into the wilderness to inspect the wireless station, which consisted of a transmitter and receiver, two telescopic steel towers approximately twenty-five feet high, and a forty horsepower gasoline engine to power the generator. According to Gaedke, the station had been built to communicate with submarines in the Gulf of Mexico. The submarines were to hoist their wireless antennae to an effective height for long-distance communication using balloons, and would therefore only operate on moonless nights to avoid discovery. The Germans in Tepic were waiting for the submarines, "which were expected in the Gulf of Mexico any day."

Early the next morning, Gaedke gave Altendorf a ride back to Tepic in his buggy. The doctor located Luisita and they set out on the return journey, stopping in Santiago only long enough to transfer to another hired automobile. They picked up the train at Acaponeta and reached Mazatlán at five o'clock on a Sunday afternoon.

Altendorf went straight to Luisita's house, and after prolonged scrubbing with soap, sand, and water, was able to remove much of the iodine dye from his skin and return it to an approximation of his normal complexion. While Luisita busied herself with the domestic tasks that had come due in her absence, Agent A-1 composed a report for his superiors on the visit to the secret training camp and radio station.

After thanking Luisita for her hospitality, the doctor grabbed his belongings and went to his hotel. The "landlord" of the establishment, a man named Pardo, motioned him to the front desk. There had been an odd occurrence in his absence. A German who would not give any name had been inquiring for him. The proprietor's face held no expression, but his eyes reflected the shrewdness of a life spent in hard circumstances.

"The Germans are after you," he said in a low voice. "You'd better be careful."

It was news that Altendorf had long been expecting. He instructed the hotel keeper to tell anyone who came asking for "Dr. Altendorf" that he had gone to Mexico City, and then immediately headed to his room. The next train north would not arrive for another forty-eight hours, so he had plenty of time to plan his escape. He decided to make a sixty-mile detour to the port of Topolobampo on his way to the U.S. border.

A message that he had received from Washington asked him to go there to see what could be learned about the schooner *Annie Larsen*, which in 1915 had gained notoriety attempting to transport a cargo of arms and munitions for a Hindu uprising in British-controlled India. The ship was believed to have been loaded in Topolobampo under German direction, and the conspirators would soon be coming to trial in the United States. Stopping there would be unexpected, Altendorf reasoned—something his pursuers would be unlikely to plan for.

During the long wait for the train, Altendorf remained out of sight. He could not risk appearing in the hotel dining room, and took his meals in his room. He sent word to another American operative in the city to meet with him and discuss the situation. The man came to his room and agreed to follow up on details related to the Karl Jacobson case, then he departed with Altendorf's final report from Mazatlán.

> The Germans were after me all right. I learned that there was a numerous patrol of them guarding the American consulate day and night, and some even entered and asked clumsy questions regarding my whereabouts, as if I would have no more sense than to hang around so public a place. They also set a watch on the clubs and resorts I had formerly frequented, but I contrived to elude them.

Altendorf could not sleep the night before he left Mazatlán, since he knew that he would face a treacherous passage to America. When morning came, he dressed in old Mexican clothes that would not attract attention, shaved off his moustache, and left the hotel without breakfast, stopping instead at a booth near the train station, where he forced down some dirty tortillas, cheese, and a mug of coffee. He paid a Mexican to buy a third-class ticket for him to San Blas.

Altendorf entered the station and casually made his way to the platform. There were a lot of Germans hanging about, some of whom were no doubt looking for him. He slipped around to the far side of the platform and entered a car near the locomotive just as the train began to move. He had not been recognized, and his departure from Mazatlán was without incident.

At 4:00 p.m. the train arrived at Culiacán. As it drew to a stop, Altendorf spotted a number of Germans he knew in the station. He retreated to a lavatory on the train that was as hot as an oven, where he hid for over an hour until the conductors gave the boarding call and the journey resumed. Overwrought with nervous tension, Altendorf remained awake until the train rumbled into San Blas at four o'clock the next morning. Once there, he hired a livery driver with an ancient Ford automobile "in the last stages of senile decay" to take him the sixty miles to Topolobampo.

When he arrived at the rural seaport, he called on Captain Centemo, the collector of the port, and presented him with a letter of introduction from a mutual friend who lived in La Paz, Lower California. It was late afternoon, and Altendorf remarked in the easy Mexican way that he had a small matter of business to discuss, but would not think of bringing it up until they had something to eat, and invited Centemo and his two-man staff to dinner. Over a fine meal at a local restaurant, Altendorf questioned the captain about the *Annie Larsen*.

"That vessel cleared during the incumbency of the former collector, Captain Cortez," Centemo told him. "I would consider it a pleasure to show you all the records in the customs house, but I am quite sure there are no records of the *Annie Larsen* because Unger, the German consul at Mazatlán, came to Topolobampo, and gave Cortez 3,000 pesos, and each of his staff several hundred pesos each to allow the *Annie Larsen* to sail without clearance. They were ordered to say, if questioned by anyone, that the *Annie Larsen* had never touched there."

After dinner, Centemo led Altendorf to the customs house, where the doctor was given free rein to examine the records, which dated back to 1912. Centemo had been right—there was nothing listed about the *Annie Larsen*. Altendorf returned to the car and headed for the coastal city of Los Mochis, which he reached just before midnight, and continued on to San Blas, arriving at four o'clock the next morning.

When he went to his hotel, he was told that his room was no longer available; it was now reserved for Vice-Consul Burgmeister who was coming up from Mazatlán. Turning away from the desk, Altendorf encountered a Mexican captain named Pérez, who engaged him in a brief conversation. Pérez did not recognize the spy, taking him for the poor Mexican that he was trying to portray. Captain Perez revealed the startling information that Governor Calles had announced a reward of 20,000 pesos for an American agent named Altendorf, dead or alive. Pérez offered to split the reward fifty-fifty with anyone who notified him that they had seen the man. Altendorf assured him that he would be most happy to share the reward if he came across the American spy, and hurried down to San Blas station, arriving just as the train pulled in.

Keeping out of sight myself, I saw Vice Consul Burgmeister, accompanied by three Germans, alight from the train and start toward the hotel . . . Here I was surrounded by enemies hundreds of miles from the nearest place of safety, with only one possible avenue of escape, the railroad, on which only occasional trains were run, and these were carefully watched at all times. Under the stimulus of a large reward offered for my head, vigilance would be redoubled, I had no doubt . . . Catching me seemed so sure and simple an undertaking that nothing but incredible stupidity on the part of my pursuers could have saved my life. Yes there was something more; the intervention of Divine Providence in my behalf.

How otherwise could Burgmeister have been such a bonehead as to stop at San Blas when he was so close on my heels that he moved into my room at the hotel when it was still warm with my breath, figuratively speaking? If he had got wind of my proposed trip to Topolobampo, why did he not send some of his gang down to that port while the rest continued up the main line on the train on which he arrived? And how otherwise, could Captain Pérez . . . have failed to note that I was not of his race and so have seized me on suspicion, instead of babbling about dividing the reward with me for my own head?

One thing was sure: I was determined not to be taken alive. My .45 caliber automatic pistol was concealed under my shirt beneath my left arm with the shirt unbuttoned so that I could draw instantly. If attacked, I proposed to kill as many as possible, but to make sure of an opportunity to blow out my brains at the last. I had seen enough of Mexican and German character to convince me that if I fell into their hands I should be cruelly maltreated. Death by my own hand was preferred to such a fate.

Although he had not slept in three days, Altendorf was abnormally alert, keyed up with adrenaline and nervous tension. He remained out of sight until the train was ready to depart, and then approached the conductor, an elderly American, and speaking in English offered him 10 pesos to allow him to ride in the caboose so that he could "catch some sleep." Altendorf knew that passengers were not allowed in the caboose, and it would enable him to travel unobserved. The conductor agreed, and Altendorf traveled alone in the car all day. On a slip of paper he wrote a farewell message to Byron S. Butcher: "Goodbye, I have done my duty," and put it in a pocket where it would be found if he was killed.

The train reached Esperanza in the late afternoon. Peering through a slit in the blinds, Altendorf saw Governor Calles's son and several other officers he knew on the platform. He retreated to the lavatory, his .45 automatic drawn, waiting for whatever might happen. The soldiers boarded the train and searched the coaches but did not bother to enter the caboose, which they knew was off-limits to passengers. After fifteen minutes, the search ended and they left the station. The period of danger, for the moment, was over.

The train arrived at Empalme four hours later. Altendorf exited on the side opposite the railway platform, and hurried through darkened side streets to the only hotel in town. The contact he had expected to meet was nowhere in sight and, unwilling to risk a telephone call from the hotel, Altendorf returned to the station area. He went to the division headquarters of the American-owned Southern Pacific Railroad and was able to place a call to the man who was supposed to meet him at the station.

Soon a car arrived that drove him a few miles to the outskirts of Guaymas. He jumped out and dodged down darkened streets to the home of his contact, where arrangements were made for him to ride to Nogales on a Southern Pacific freight train. At three o'clock in the morning, he was driven back to the hotel in Empalme. He paid for a room where he sat and smoked until the hour came for the freight train to leave. Altendorf had been without sleep for four days, but could not bring himself to close his eyes; the nervous tension was too great.

He wandered through the railroad yard in the early morning light until he located the train. The conductor was an American who had received orders to place him in the caboose. After departing the station, the slow-moving freight plodded along for three hours until it reached the "passing track" at Escalante, where it pulled onto the siding to make way for the northern-bound passenger train to pass. At this point, Altendorf transferred onto the passenger train. By taking the freight out of Empalme he had avoided the chance of being captured in a search of the passenger train at the station; by switching to the passenger train he avoided the increased risk of traveling on the slow-moving freight. A railroad official on the passenger train who had been briefed on the escape plan guided Altendorf to the caboose and securely locked the door.

Hermosillo would be the supreme test. Like many country towns in Mexico, the populace often suspended their activities to watch the trains come in. Governor Calles himself sometimes joined the throng to see what friends—or enemies—might be passing down the line. The police contingent at Hermosillo station remained ever vigilant in the hope of catching a stray rebel traveling by rail. For the chance to receive a reward of 20,000 pesos they would search every inch of the train, and unbeknownst to Altendorf, Calles had been warned in advance that the American spy would be travelling on that very train.

Shortly after noon, Altendorf felt the train slow as it neared the station. Peering through the blinds of the caboose, he saw Colonel García and several of his men on the station platform. The train was going to be searched. Looking for a place to hide, he spied a closet under the cupola of the caboose where the railway men stored switch ropes, jacks, railing frogs, and dope buckets. He pulled himself into the closet and shut the door behind him. The intelligence agent was forced into a hunched position in the confined space, nearly overcome by the heat and the overpowering stench from the dope buckets.

He remained motionless in the unbearable closet for half an hour, until he heard men at the entrance of the caboose, pounding and shaking the door as they tried to force it open. He drew his .45 automatic and leveled it at the closet door. Seconds passed in agonizing slowness as the clamor continued, then the conductor arrived and assured the men that there was no one in the caboose. The conductor's bluff succeeded, and Altendorf listened to the men stomp away into an adjacent coach.

When the train was miles from Hermosillo, Altendorf dropped out of his hiding place onto the floor of the caboose and breathed in deeply, filling his lungs with fresh air.

Nogales was reached at one thirty in the morning. He was met by Captain Lipscomb, an army intelligence officer, who directed U.S. Consul Ezra Lawton to bring him over to the U.S. side. Under cover of darkness, Lawton guided Altendorf across the border at a stone bridge that was limited to use of consular officers. No immigration officer was consulted. Lawton had been instructed by Lipscomb that "it was not necessary and exceedingly unwise for anyone to know who he [Altendorf] was, or what he was, due to the value of his confidential work to the government."

Lipscomb gave him an Immigration Service form to complete and Altendorf carefully filled in the blanks. Under "Personal Description" he wrote: "Nationality: Austria-Polish, Arrived Via: On Foot, Money: $80, Distinguishing Characteristics: two moles, left cheek, large bullet wound on left shin bone."

Butcher had been wrong—he *had* come back.

8 United States of America vs. *Alexander Agassiz*

The crew of the *Alexander Agassiz* had been in captivity for almost two weeks when they were taken from the San Diego county jail by U.S. marshals and delivered to the federal building for trial. The prisoners were a disheveled and ragged-looking lot, still wearing the clothes that they had on when captured aboard the schooner off Mazatlán. Each was now held in lieu of $10,000 bail.

The preliminary hearings at the courthouse in *United States of America vs. Alexander Agassiz* would establish the facts of the case in order to determine the disposition of the ship's company and the schooner itself. A prize court was a summary matter, in which witnesses were given no opportunity to provide an explanation, and no cross-examination was permitted. The detainees and government witnesses called before the prize court would be sworn in, and after taking the stand, asked forty-three interrogatories, or questions that had been proscribed by the court. The questioning would be conducted by U.S. District Attorney J. Robert O'Connor. Under the rules of the prize court, the accused would not be permitted to see the evidence being held against them, meet with any person with an interest in the case, or consult an attorney. When the questioning was completed, each person who had testified would be given the opportunity to read over their deposition, correct any inaccuracies in the testimony, and then be required to sign the document.

After the discovery proceedings were completed, all of the depositions obtained by the prize court would be turned over to United States

Commissioner Hammack in Los Angeles to determine whether the evidence justified the accused being placed on trial for piracy and whether the schooner *Alexander Agassiz* should be "condemned" and forfeited to the U.S. government.

The first person to be called to the stand for questioning was the government's leading witness, Cornelius Adolph Heintz. During a full day of testimony, the marine engineer described the events that led to the capture of the *Alexander Agassiz* for a rapt audience.

"In the month of February—during the first part of the month—I was called into the office of the German consul, Mr. Unger," said Heintz, in response to interrogatories from District Attorney O'Connor. "He was at the House of Melchers, which is the office of the German consul, with Captain Bauman. At this time it was fully explained to me the purpose for which they were sending this boat out, namely as a raider. I was asked if I would be willing to help out in the expedition. There was a commission from the German government authorizing her to raid, that is, she was authorized by the German government. She was to take over a larger craft if better suited for the purpose and destroy what commerce she could and proceed to Germany. At that time Captain Bauman was sent to Santa Rosalía to obtain all the charts and instruments that were needed for the navigation of the vessel; also to obtain ammunition and arms. He returned with the same about three weeks later. He returned with one machinegun of the very latest make, and with one box of ammunition for the same. I do not know the caliber of that gun, but it shot a shell about the size of a small arm cartridge shell."

"After Captain Bauman's return," Heintz continued, "we immediately started to get the *Alexander Agassiz* ready for sea. We got permission from Miss Lochrane to do it under the pretense of taking the vessel to the South Sea Islands for trading purposes, but the ship was in deplorable condition, so we took her up the esterro [estuary] at Mazatlán where we beached her and overhauled her. We also provisioned the boat for about ninety days. The crew of the ship was picked by Captain Bauman and Madden, Captain Bauman and Madden receiving their instructions in full from Mr. Unger. Most of the provisions came from the House of Melchers, of which Mr. Unger, the German consul, is the head. I might also state that all of the crew knew that she was to be a raider, and all of them excepting one, Charlie Boston, who posed as an American, took an oath before the German consul, Mr. Unger, to give allegiance to the German flag and adhere to the commands of Captain Bauman. The instructions were read before Captain Bauman and to us by Mr. Unger, and he made the boys take an oath that they would stand by Captain Bauman and by the orders which were issued."

"At that time . . . letters were handed to Captain Bauman," Heintz told the court, "several written letters to be delivered when they reached Germany, and if they did not reach Germany they had instructions to destroy them. The substance of them [the letters] was that the boat was to go out as a German raider and destroy all possible comers at sea and then to proceed to Germany. No particular nationality was mentioned at all; in fact, they looked upon all ships on the high seas as enemy ships. Besides these letters, Captain Bauman was given a code whereby he could decipher any messages or letters sent to him. The code was in the German language. As to the pay or consideration, it was this: What the German consul held out to us was that they were to be allowed a percentage of the value of all of ships that were sunk, destroyed, or captured. I was promised five per cent, personally for my share. I do not know what Captain Bauman was to get. I was offered money. That was one of the inducements. I do not think any of the sailors were offered anything. They were simply going for the purpose of showing their allegiance to the flag. This percentage was to be paid to us when we reached Germany, and was to be paid by the German government . . . I had an interest in the cargo and helped put the provisions on board. The total amount of expense that I put in was about $300."

"The crew had in mind to get rid of Miss Lochrane at the earliest opportunity," said Heintz. "I might state that Miss Lochrane had absolutely no information regarding the actions of the Germans as far as the raider was concerned, or as far as the real purpose for which the ship was to go to sea. She was very badly in debt in Mazatlán and was a party to the illicit clearing of the vessel from the port in order to avoid her debts in that place, but that in every other respect her connection with the transaction was a bona fide arrangement with Captain Bauman whereby he was to navigate the vessel, without expense to her, to the South Sea Islands, and upon arrival there, she was at liberty to make what further arrangements she cared to. There was a note in Miss Lochrane's blouse, a note written by Madden to Captain Bauman in the German language and which note I found and which note the captain of the USS *Vicksburg* took away from me. Why the note was written was this: that Bauman had started or began to mistrust something because of our leaving so soon on account of stories that were circulated around the town by Mr. Gardener who was in the government employ. Madden wrote this note to reassure Captain Bauman that everything was O.K., and for Miss Lochrane to go to Melchers in company with Charlie Boston, and tell the same thing to him."

"We did not clear the port, but we simply slid from the port," said Heintz, describing the ship's departure from Mazatlán. "There were thirteen actually on board the vessel and we were to pick up two more, Captain Bauman and one other sailor. I do not remember the name of the island [where they were to pick them up] but it was an island about five or six miles north of Mazatlán. I was acting in the capacity of Chief Engineer. Miss Lochrane was on the ship's papers as the captain of the ship. She was the owner, she was not actually in command. The name of the party actually in command was Madden. We were using the American flag at the time in order to get out of port; we also had the German colors on board, which colors were to signify her nationality after reaching the high seas. No guns were mounted on the vessel. Captain Bauman had a machinegun which he expected to mount. The Germans brought on board several revolvers, also two 30-30 Winchesters that I know of, and plenty of ammunition. The arms came from the German consul and the money to buy the ammunition with was furnished by the German consul."

"We were fired on by the gunboat *Vicksburg*," said Heintz. "We attempted to return to port and we did not heed the gunboat's signal to stop. Those acts were performed by Mr. Madden, who was acting as skipper. I saw them throw one package over. The papers that went overboard, that I know of, were the German code, the charts and two or three letters from the House of Melchers, the German consul. They threw them overboard when they saw that they had no chance of getting away from the USS *Vicksburg*, which was then right on top of us. Mr. Madden threw the papers overboard, and I also witnessed him throw a sextant overboard.

There were charts on board, but when we were captured they were gone, so they must have been thrown overboard, too."

After Heintz answered all of the interrogatories, he stepped down from the witness stand and was taken back to the county jail with the other detainees. The testimony that he gave to the prize court was the same as that which he had previously given in depositions to W. E. Chapman in Mazatlán and Lieutenant Reordan aboard the *Vicksburg*.

The following morning Maude Lochrane was called to the witness stand. She wore the same clothes, her only clothes, that she had worn since the *Vicksburg* steamed into San Diego bay—a plain dress, open at the neck, with fur trimming, that exhibited a good deal of hard wear. Despite weeks of imprisonment, she proved to be an alert and exacting witness, requesting an explanation of any wording in the interrogatories that she did not understand, and displaying an inclination to answer all questions as carefully as possible. Her testimony painted a very different picture of the events surrounding the capture of the *Alexander Agassiz* than was provided by Cornelius Heintz.

"I turned the boat over to a man named Heintz to repair her generally and fix up the engines," Maude said in response to interrogatories from District Attorney O'Connor. "She was not bound for any port; the purpose of her being at sea was for a trial trip in order to test out her sails, her rudder, her wheel, and her engines. The vessel was in very bad condition and made regular letter S's all over [the water]. Permission had been obtained from the American consul, who told me on that trip the ship did not need any papers or any crew or passengers to be signed on."

"There were four in the ship's company that belonged to me at the time she was seized or taken, two sailors, the cook and engineer, also the general contractor, Mr. Heintz, who was remodeling and fixing the boat over," Maude told the court. "There were fourteen people in all on board—I am including myself in that number. Mr. Heintz had been on board about a week superintending the general repair work. Mr. Madden, the Norwegian sailor, came aboard about five or six days before the seizure for the sole purpose of fixing the ropes and the sails. Mr. Madden was on the boat at Mr. Heintz's request, but I intended to pay him for his work. I understand the other men said they were on the boat through the invitation of Mr. Heintz—they were not there by my invitation."

"We were getting ready for a voyage to San Blas on the following day if she was found to be in seaworthy condition, and that is the reason she had fuel and provisions on board," Maude continued. "There were no goods or merchandise on board that I know of except the provisions, a couple of sacks of potatoes, a sack and a quarter of rice, and a sack or perhaps a sack and a quarter of beans and about four sacks or five sacks of white flour. They were 50-pound flour sacks to the best of my knowledge. Also on board at that time were about 36 or 38 cases of distillate, which would be approximately 380 gallons. There may have been 20 gallons or something like that in the tank. The fuel was left from the boat voyage [to Manzanillo for Señor Meistiero]."

"I could not give the exact time of day when the boat was captured," said Maude. "I had just given two of the sailors their meals so that they would be ready to handle the sails. I was in the kitchen baking some biscuits and roasting some coffee at the time the shot was fired. I thought that something was the matter with the engines again, and had stepped out of the door when I caught the smell of powder, and then I knew what had happened. The seizure of the boat was made, to the best of my knowledge, within a mile or a mile and a half of the Mazatlán coast. I do not know anything with regard to the reasons for her seizure except as a matter of hearsay. I heard the lieutenant in charge of the capturing crew say the reason why the boat was captured was because there were no ship's papers on the boat. At the time of her capture I knew of no other colors on board except for the American flag. The lieutenant who searched the boat said that he found a German flag on board the *Alexander Agassiz*—I know of no reason at all why the boat carried such colors."

"I did not have charge of the vessel when captured," she told the court. "In Mexican waters a pilot always takes charge of your boat. At the time of the capture two Mexican government employees had charge of the *Agassiz*. The captain of the port sent the men because he always sends a pilot whenever you notify him that you are ready to move and the tide is up out of the esterro. I understood Mr. Heintz to give an order to the Mexicans that had the boat in charge, through the interpreter, to turn around and we would try the sails. The course of the boat was not altered, to my knowledge. The Mexican had charge of the wheel, and I presume when he saw the American boat heading down on us became frightened. They are very easily frightened, and he might have turned the boat. I don't know what he did."

"I saw nothing at all thrown overboard," she said, "and I do not have any knowledge of anything having been thrown overboard. The lieutenant who came aboard the *Agassiz*, Lieutenant Dorr, I think his name is, said that he found a man down in the engine room, but he was not secreted to my knowledge. I went around and called everyone that I could remember that was on board. Of course, it was all excitement. That man just came on board at Mr. Heintz's invitation, he said, when we were up before the consul."

"There were no guns mounted on the *Agassiz*," Maude said. "There was a shotgun [on board] that is at present with the captain of the port who borrowed it to shoot ducks there in the harbor. Mr. Heintz, from the very first time that he came on board, carried a pistol in his pocket. Those were all the guns I saw. There was no ammunition aboard the boat, to my knowledge."

"The *Alexander Agassiz* was chartered by a man named Sanchez Meistiero for the purpose of trading on the western coast of Mexico. This [the seizure of the boat] makes me lose that contract which would have brought in $7,200 per year by which I expected to pay off all of the boat's debts. It puts me out of employment in the sum of $100 gold per month. I received nothing at all [from Meistiero]. No one has ever assumed to pay any damage and no promise has been made that it will be paid."

When she completed her testimony, Maude stepped down from the witness stand and was taken to the county jail with the other detainees. After being deposed for eight hours, in the course of which she was asked forty-three interrogatories, she had not once mentioned a trip to the South Sea Islands or the name "Fritz Bauman."

Cornelius Heintz and Maude Lochrane had each required a day for questioning by the prize court, but the depositions of the remaining detainees—Madden, Volpert, Brandt, Koppalla, and Boston were taken in sequence within a single day. The first to be called to the stand was German merchant seaman Arthur Martens, aka "Madden."

"I had been on board [the schooner] for four days before it was captured," Madden told the court. "Mr. Heintz told me to come on board to help fix up the ship, but I wasn't getting any wages. The ship was going to make a few trips on the coast and after that it was going to the South Sea Islands. I was going with the ship in the capacity of a sailor. I had talked with Miss Lochrane and she had talked about trading between the islands and we were going to make our money there if she made any money, and if she did make any money she said she would pay us good enough."

"The *Alexander Agassiz* was making a trial trip," Madden continued. "Mr. Bauman was supposed to be the navigator or captain of the boat. I do not know when we were to pick him up. We were to make this trial trip and I think the next day Mr. Bauman was to come on board. He was a captain of one of the German ships in Santa Rosalía. I was on deck [of the *Agassiz*] that morning when the ship was overtaken by the gunboat. We were just coming out of the port and were going to turn around, but Mr. Heintz told us that we should not turn around right away as it would look as if we were afraid of the ship. So we kept right on. Shortly afterwards the man of war fired a shot; it was about a mile out from the port of Mazatlán. Mr. Heintz was giving orders. I don't know what right he had to give orders, but he was in charge of the ship. I was more of a passenger than anything else on board there. One fellow was down in the engine room at the time the boat was captured. His name was Volpert. I do not know why he was hiding down there. I do not know who told him to go down there—I did not tell him to go down there. I did not know before she was captured that she had a German flag. I do not know who brought it on board—I didn't bring it on board. I don't know whether anything was thrown overboard. I didn't see anything. I did not assist in anything being thrown overboard."

"I had one Winchester 30-30 rifle and a Colt .25 automatic pistol on board," said Madden. "I had about fifteen to twenty rounds of ammunition for the rifle. The automatic had two boxes of shells and one clip. I have lost my clothes and some money [as the result of the *Agassiz* being captured].

I didn't have much clothing. I had about six shirts, a [spare] pair of shoes, two pairs of pants and my hat. I was never at the German consul's or any other house in company with Mr. Bauman or Mr. Heintz or any other person talking relative to taking a trip on board the *Alexander Agassiz* as a raider. I never heard of any such thing until I came here to court."

Madden gave no explanation for why he brought a Colt .25 automatic, a Winchester .30-.30 rifle, and two changes of clothes on what was supposed to be a short trial cruise.

"I think Mr. Heintz told me to come on [the *Agassiz*]," German bricklayer Volpert told the court. "He came after me in the park and says, 'come on.' The old lady told me the night before to come on there. I mean the lady who was in here a while ago [deposition: 'indicating Miss Lochrane']. She never told me what I was going to do on board the vessel, she just told me to come and go along with her. I did not get any money. She wanted to go some place else to do some trading. I knew Miss Lochrane through Charley Boston, that American fellow. I knew some others that were on there at the time of the capture. I knew Madden. He asked me if I wanted to go on board. I met Madden in the park. He just came up and said, 'How do you do?' to me. I met him in the park lots of times. I met a lot of fellows in the park. I had known him probably two or three months. He said, 'If you want to go to the South Seas Islands, come and go along.'"

"As soon as I got on board they told me to go down in the engine room," Volpert continued. "I was told to 'get out of sight and keep out of sight.' Mr. Madden told me that. Nobody else told me about that. I am a German and Mr. Madden is a German. I had one revolver on me and some cartridges in my suitcase which I got from a fellow in Mexico. I had had that revolver about three or four months. I was in the habit of carrying it in Mexico. I had a couple of pairs of pants in that suitcase and some other clothes and shirts and some underwear. I did not bring it on board at the time I came on board. Another fellow got it for me before I got on board. His name was Koppalla. He got it where I had been living. I was not in a position to see if anything was thrown overboard. I had been down in the engine room. I never had been on deck [during the cruise]. I did not lift my head above the hatchway to see what was going on."

After providing his curious, conflicting testimony in which he stated that three different individuals had invited him to join the crew of the *Alexander Agassiz*, Volpert left the witness stand.

"I was not a member of the ship's company," said Richard Brandt, the German lumber inspector. "I was invited onto the vessel. Mr. Heintz invited me. I do not know what purpose he had invited me on for. I was working for Mr. Heintz in Mazatlán, and I knew him and he knew me, and he told me he was going to make a trial trip and asked me aboard this boat just about a minute before he went on. There was a little beer garden in front of where the ship was lying and I had been there and Mr. Heintz was there, and he called me over and invited me to have a glass of beer and then asked me if I wanted to go along. I had known Mr. Heintz a long time. I met him first last October. He had not spoken to me about going along before—not a word. I didn't take anything aboard the schooner when I went aboard, no clothing. I only had on a pair of white trousers, this coat and a hat. She was going out on a trial trip, as I was informed, for a two or three hours ride. About five minutes before I left with Mr. Heintz I was offered a position on the gunboat *Morelos* in painting and cleaning the boat. I did not see anything thrown overboard. I am sure of that. From where I was standing I could see right down one side of the whole of the *Alexander Agassiz*. I was pointing out the different points of interest to Mrs. Heintz and I could look down the whole ship. I did not see anything thrown overboard."

"I had known the vessel four or five hours, that is all," the sailor Hendrik Koppalla told the court. "One German fellow took me aboard. He told me to go on board of her. His name was Anderson. He is at Mazatlán now. I was working over there and he came to me and asked me if I wanted to make a trial trip. Anderson is a German. He wanted me to go to look after the engines. Anderson took me on board, and on Sunday morning he told me he wanted a drink of beer and he went away. I don't know whether Anderson is in any way connected with the German consulate at Mazatlán. He never told me that. I was acquainted with Anderson about three weeks while I was working at Mazatlán. There was nothing that I know of thrown overboard. There was nothing thrown overboard. I was not on deck when they captured her. I was in the forecastle. She was only two miles outside Mazatlán when they took her. I have been along there enough at sea to know what two or twenty miles are. There were no guns [mounted on the *Agassiz*], only two rifles. I think those arms and ammunition belonged to the vessel. I don't know why she was so armed. I don't know what those guys wanted to do with the rifles."

"I was one of the crew," said American Charles Boston. "I was in the capacity of cook. I was sent on as a cook, but I did most everything because she, Miss Lochrane, did part of the cooking. I know she made an attempt to get supplies and that Mr. Heintz had made an attempt to get supplies. When the supplies came, I do not know who got them. The goods came down in a delivery wagon. I don't know whose delivery wagon it was, but I know they came from the House of Melchers. I don't know the exact amount, and I couldn't say as to that, but I should say that they would last a crew, with a few more additions, probably two months. The provisions were put on board the night before we started out of the port."

"She [the *Agassiz*] was not bound on any voyage except to make a trip out to the ocean and back in again," Boston told the court. "The purpose of the trip, I was told, was to try out the engines. [The crew] were not all on board. There was to be the captain and three more men on board. The name of the captain was Bauman. He is a German. As to the other two men, one of them was an American and the other was a German. One of the Americans was named Orfila, and the other man's name was Anderson, I believe. The paper from the American consul [authorizing the trial voyage] was considered not true and fair, but at the time it was considered because they changed their mind about the way they were going out of port. They were going to raise anchor and go regardless of anything else. I heard them say that. I heard the ones who were interested in going say that. I don't know any particular one. They were this Mr. Madden, Mr. Bauman, and Mr. Heintz. They never told me what they were going to do. Whenever I overheard something I just remembered it. As to whether I overheard any act that aroused my suspicion or that were in line with what has since happened and would tend to make me suspicious at the time, I would say that there was one remark made. I just forget how it was worded, but one of the boys asked me if Mr. Heintz was on their side or on her side. I didn't pay any attention to it because I thought it was nothing more than a woman not knowing anything about a boat and they wanted to know whether he would take her part in everything or what would happen. I don't remember just who made that remark. It was either the navigator [Bauman] or one of the other Germans. It was a German who made the remark. I am pretty sure of that. That remark was made to me."

On the final day of hearings in San Diego, three naval officers from the USS *Vicksburg* were called to the witness stand to answer the interrogatories: Lieutenant Charles Edwin Reordan, Lieutenant Frederick W. Dorr, and Paymaster Edwin Y. Armstrong.

"The capture was made off Mazatlán, Mexico, about 12:45 p.m.," the youthful Lieutenant Reordan told the court. "The seizure was made on the grounds that the vessel did not have proper ship's papers, also on the ground that the vessel refused to stop when summoned to stop by international flag signal, and on the grounds that there were armed members of the enemy on board. She sailed under American colors. She also had the German colors on board. The master said that she was bound on a trial trip with the intention of returning to Mazatlán. She carried a thousand pounds of foodstuff, three or four hundred pounds of fire wood, and about 150 gallons of distillate. I should say that the arms and ammunition [found] were the only contraband of war aboard. As to whether two revolvers or three revolvers and two rifles among a company of so many was unusual equipment for a merchant vessel, I should say it would be very unusual equipment for a ship so small. I do not know as I have ever heard of merchant ships habitually carrying rifles. It is probably customary for ships' officers on merchantmen to have their own revolvers if they please, but these rifles were supplied with soft nosed bullets, which is another very unusual circumstance."

"There was something thrown overboard but I couldn't say positively what it was," Reordan said. "As to how many times I saw motions made that would indicate that something was being thrown overboard, during the chase Paymaster Armstrong, who was in the foretop, sang down to the bridge, thru the fire control, that the *Alexander Agassiz* was throwing something overboard. At the time I was so busy conning the ship that I could not look up, but I looked up probably two minutes later and then I saw what was apparently two things thrown overboard. I assumed that they had been throwing things overboard ever since the officer in the top had so informed me."

"One party [was] found hiding in a dark hole in the bilge [on the *Agassiz*]," Reordan continued. "His name was Volpert. On him was found a paper under the seal of the Imperial German Consulate at Mexico City stating that he was a reservist of the German Fusilliers. He had a pistol in his possession. The vessel was steering about northwest from Mazatlán. I couldn't say how far offshore she was. Her course was altered probably a half dozen times during the chase. When we took up the chase, the *Alexander Agassiz* changed course so as to head approximately directly away from us, that is, to run away from us. Later she began to haul more to port, apparently with the idea of getting back into Mazatlán. The *Alexander Agassiz* was in the neighborhood of three miles off shore at the time of the capture."

Lieutenant Reordan left the witness stand and Lieutenant Dorr took his place.

"I was detailed to go into a boat that was sent from the ship and board the *Alexander Agassiz*," Dorr told the court, "and I went aboard of her after she had been stopped by the *Vicksburg*. We ran alongside of the *Alexander Agassiz* and I went aboard and asked for the captain, and a woman whom I afterwards found out to be Miss Lochrane, stepped up and said that she was the captain. I then demanded the ship's papers, and I went forward with her to the wheel house where she produced a log book in which some entries were made in Spanish, and also a letter which purported to be from the American Consul at Mazatlán in answer to some request that she had made to take the boat out. I also found a number of papers and letters which I gave to one of my men and they were taken aboard ship. I found in the chart house or in the wheel house some firearms. When I was down in the engine room there was a small compartment aft the engine room. I had one of the men crawl in there and search it . . . he found another member of the crew who was concealed in this compartment. In a coat hanging in the chart house or wheel house I found a leather wallet with a paper concealed there which looked as if it might be a part of a cipher. I took that along with the other papers. While making a search of the vessel, I had one of my men look through the flags in the wheel house, and he found a German flag which I took aboard."

"After we had signaled them to stop, I saw several people on the deck of the *Agassiz* run toward the wheel house, which is in the forward part of the vessel. On the starboard side they seemed to be going out of the wheel house or in that vicinity, and I saw several articles thrown overboard. I actually saw the articles leave their hands and drop into the water, and that was the occasion of my singing out from the bridge that they were throwing things overboard. I was close enough to see that. I had a different view from the people in the forward part of our ship. The whaleboat swings on the after part of the ship, very high, and I could see very plainly that they were throwing something overboard."

Dorr stepped down from the witness stand and was replaced by Paymaster Armstrong.

"My duty at the time was in the control top of the *Vicksburg* where the fire control is maintained," said Armstrong in response to an interrogatory. "We were coming up on the *Alexander Agassiz* at a very increasing rate of speed. I had a pair of binoculars in the top with me, and I had them on the *Agassiz* watching her very closely in her maneuvering. After she came about the first time she continually kept her port side towards the ship that I was on. There was a great deal of activity on the starboard side of the chart house. Two or three men ran up there, and although I could not see the deck on account of the high chart house of the *Alexander Agassiz*, it appeared that they were throwing things over the side. They were at this for some time, and then those sailors dispersed and scattered around the decks. This was previous to the time the boarding officer reached the *Alexander Agassiz*."

"She was steaming on various courses as we pursued her," said Armstrong. "The course was altered many times. They steamed to the south and they tried to keep the *Vicksburg* astern of her most of the time, and after that she kept her port side to us until we came up on her. If she had not been captured and had kept on that course, in my estimation she would have made for the port of Mazatlán."

On April 2, 1918, the prize court proceedings in San Diego were completed. The depositions that had been taken, the exhibits, and other "prize property" seized on the *Agassiz* were turned over to U.S. Commissioner Hammack at Los Angeles to determine whether criminal charges should be brought and to decide the final disposition of the captive schooner.

Since no actual incident of piracy or other belligerent act had taken place, it was already clear that no charge of piracy could be brought against the ship's company. In particular, nothing had been presented that suggested Maude Lochrane had in any way been involved in a scheme to use the *Alexander Agassiz* as a commerce raider, or was even aware that a conspiracy existed. District Attorney O'Connor directed that she be released from jail on her own recognizance until a final determination of the case was made at the U.S. District Court in Los Angeles.

That evening, a Mrs. Gilson called at the county jail and took Maude to dinner in gratitude for the assistance she had once rendered her aging mother when she was ill. They went to Moore's Restaurant in San Diego, a popular eatery that was crowded with diners, and were seated at a table with a U.S. Army lieutenant.

Maude's entire life had been spent in an uphill struggle to achieve financial success and respectability. When she became the sole owner of the Pacific Coast Trading and Shipping Company it seemed that her dream had finally come within reach, only to be dashed, in her mind, by an unwarranted act of the United States Navy. Combined with two weeks of confinement and court deliberations, she was now overwrought and angry—and wanted everyone to know it.

At the restaurant she learned of the wartime rationing under which patrons were only allowed a teaspoonful of sugar to a cup of coffee and families were limited to a purchase of five pounds of the sweetener.

"The United States Navy wastes food in a ridiculous manner," she sneered. "I was not allowed by U.S. officers to buy food for my ship, yet when a naval officer came on board with an inspector on Christmas Day he fined me because I had so little to offer him for Christmas dinner."

"They tried to starve me to death," she said, "and when I finally got a crew and cargo, they forced me out to sea with a heavy load which they hoped would sink my boat."

Maude announced that the navy had taken the *Alexander Agassiz* inside the "two mile limit" and that she had permission from both the American and Mexican consuls to try out the engines.

"I'll make it pretty warm for them before they get through, as they are already much worse scared than I am," she exclaimed. "They are damn fools. If they had only waited until the next morning, they would have gotten something, because I would have cleared that morning and would have had on board the most skilled German pilot that ever went out of a Mexican port. [The *Alexander Agassiz*] could carry enough ammunition to blow up three American warships."

For the remainder of the dinner, the horrified Mrs. Gilson sat in silence while Maude continued her rant against the United States government and the actions of "the Americans"—as if she were no longer to be considered one herself.

The America that Maude Lochrane left in 1917 was not the same country that she returned to a year later. Public sentiment had hardened; to speak out against the U.S. government, the military, or the war was now considered "disloyal" and "pro-German." Two weeks after she departed for Mexico, Congress had enacted the Espionage Act into law, which made it illegal "during time of war, to willfully make or convey false statements with intent to interfere with the operation or success of U.S. forces, promote the success of its enemies, or willfully cause or attempt to cause insubordination, disloyalty, mutiny, or refusal of duty in the U.S. military." Punishment if convicted was a fine of not more than $10,000 or imprisonment for not more than twenty years, or both.

To monitor public expression and silence those making "seditious, disloyal utterances," many Americans volunteered for membership in "vigilance associations" that reported individuals making statements perceived to be "pro-German" to the authorities. The largest private group on the watch for "disloyal" public commentary was the American Protective League (APL). Founded by a Chicago advertising executive, the

APL was a nationwide intelligence-gathering organization consisting of volunteer businessmen that operated under the direction of the Justice Department's Bureau of Investigation. By 1918, the American Protective League had grown to over 250,000 members located in "every occupation, significant company, and industry in the United States," secretly listening for any "seditious utterances" or "pro-German" comments.

On the night of April 3, 1918, an APL operative at Moore's Restaurant overheard Maude's tirade against the U.S. Navy, and filed a report on the incident that was forwarded to the Justice Department. A Bureau of Investigation agent named W. H. Buck was sent to interview Mrs. Gilson and take her statement. Three days later, Maude was arrested on the charge of violating the Espionage Act for making "seditious utterances," and was returned to the San Diego county jail. Ironically, the new charge was potentially more serious than the complaint for which she had been arrested on the *Agassiz*. Judge Charles H. Burch set her bail at $10,000 and announced that she "would not be released on her own recognizance again."

After her brief taste of freedom, Maude felt even more constrained behind bars, and for the first time began giving interviews to the press. In newspaper stories with titles like "Maude Lochrane Is Maid of Mystery" and "Woman Pirate Tells Story of Her Life," she recounted the hardships that she had faced before her arrest:

> I can't begin to tell the trials I passed through down there, a lone woman, handicapped by a load of debt, held by my own government to answer for all my acts and yet denied the protection of my own government; obliged to obey constantly changing rules or pay the penalty; forced to deal with men with whom I could not converse. Oh, it was a merry life, I can assure you . . . Yet I want to go back. I am not an adventuress, as some folks romantically imagine. I went to Mexico and took possession of the Agassiz after my partners Wheeler and Taylor had made a mess of things. My ignorance handicapped me, but I was learning.

Maude described her adventures and answered journalists' questions from a comfortable chair in the matron's office of the San Diego jail, as she placidly knitted socks and "beanies" for servicemen under an assistance program run by the prison.

On April 9, the *Agassiz* prize court hearing was transferred to Los Angeles at the request of District Attorney O'Connor. In the interest of expedience, the Navy transported the prisoners and witnesses from San Diego to LA aboard the now-familiar gunboat, USS *Vicksburg*. The charge of piracy was dismissed, since the *Agassiz* had attacked no ships before it was captured. The only issue to be decided by the court was whether the schooner had been lawfully seized by the *Vicksburg* and subject to "condemnation," confiscation and sale by the government. Maude would be tried for violation of the Espionage Act in a separate hearing.

A public notice regarding the impending legal action was placed in area newspapers advising any individuals with a claim against the *Alexander Agassiz* to appear in court to "interpose their claims." This resulted in a claim being filed by Klauber Wangenheim and Company, a merchant that had sold supplies to Wheeler and Taylor before their departure for Mexico, for several hundred dollars; by trader H. A. Macintosh for $1,175, the balance due on the funds that he had advanced the pair; and by the Regents of the University of California for $5,400 plus interest, the money that was owed the university from the original purchase of the schooner.

In Mexico, port officials in Mazatlán sent W. E. Chapman a note requesting that the U.S. government pay the outstanding claims that remained against the *Agassiz* at the port of Mazatlán. The communiqué was forwarded to Acting Secretary of the Navy Franklin Delano Roosevelt, who responded, "The vessel was so captured as a suspected enemy raider by an American warship and taken to San Diego, California, where it is now in the charge of the United States Marshal, awaiting disposition by a prize court." If the Mexican government had any claims, they were to address them to the prize court.

The change in venue from San Diego to Los Angeles had one unseen, but significant consequence. Los Angeles was a city where industrialist and city father Joseph Mesmer held a great deal of influence and power at all levels of government. Likely with Mesmer's backing, Maude Lochrane would now be represented in court by the law firm of Black, Hammack and Black, whose attorneys would respond on her behalf before the judge hearing arguments in the case, Benjamin F. Bledsoe of the District Court of Southern California.

On May 4, District Attorney Robert O'Connor presented the case for the United States government in the courtroom of the Los Angeles federal building.

"There is evidence in the depositions taken by the Prize Commissioner that the *Alexander Agassiz* was, at the time of capture, acting under the direction and authority of the Imperial German Government through its Vice-Consul at Mazatlán, Mexico," O'Connor began. "Our first contention is that the vessel is subject to condemnation as a neutral vessel upon the grounds which were briefly and pointedly stated by the boarding officer, Lieutenant Dorr: 1. The vessel's papers were not complete, and what papers were aboard were concealed. 2. The vessel attempted to escape after being summoned by international flag signal to stop. 3. The vessel was carrying armed forces of the enemy. 4. There is evidence at hand that the vessel was proceeding to engage in belligerent operations against the United States and its allies."

"Maude Lochrane," O'Connor continued, "had been in Mexico, domiciled there . . . for nearly a year prior to capture. There is absolute absence of evidence of an intent on her part to return to the United States, and the Government contention is that this state of facts clearly establishes a Mexican national character of her for commercial purposes. As such neutral vessel she is undoubtedly subject to condemnation . . . and there can be no question from this evidence that at the time the *Agassiz* was signaled to stop . . . instead of heeding the signal she altered her course and attempted to get away."

"It has also been held," O'Connor argued, "even by our Supreme Court, that where papers are thrown overboard, this, of itself, would justify condemnation. The evidence is practically conclusive that things were thrown overboard."

"While it seems that the foregoing evidence is conclusive and that the Court should condemn the vessel without further proof," O'Connor stated, "there is still the remaining fact that all of the foregoing circumstances tend to strongly corroborate the testimony of C. A. Heintz, a member of the *Agassiz* crew. His testimony is that the ship was outfitted for the purpose of raiding on the commerce of the allies under authority from the Imperial German Government, through the German consul, and that all of the crew except Boston and Miss Lochrane had taken an oath before the German consul to support the German government and aid the German government by the destruction of the allies' commerce with the *Agassiz*, and at the time of the capture she was on her way to pick up Captain Bauman and the necessary machine guns to complete her equipment as a raider."

"Under these facts," said O'Connor, "we believe that if further evidence were needed to justify the condemnation, the testimony of Heintz, supported as it is, by the suspicious actions of the ship at the time of the capture, are sufficient to justify condemnation, on the ground that the boat was acting under the authority of the Imperial German Government, with whom the United States was at that time at war."

"I have no doubt but that the claim will be made that at the time of capture the *Agassiz* was not upon the high seas," he continued. "This is however completely answered by the testimony of the boarding officer, Lieutenant Dorr, in which he states: 'I should say that she was well outside of the three mile limit.'"

"It is respectfully submitted," O'Connor concluded, "that each of the foregoing circumstances, in itself, is a sufficient ground to justify condemnation, and taken together they make out a case for condemnation that is irresistible."

Maude Lochrane's attorney, Mr. Black, rose to present her response to the government's charges, arguing against the confiscation of the *Alexander Agassiz*.

"The vessel '*Alexander Agassiz*' was owned by an American citizen and was flying the U.S. flag, and was of U.S. registry at the time of seizure," Black began. "At such time it was on a trial trip carrying the written permission of the American Consul to make the trip. She had no cargo on board, and but a small amount of gasoline and provisions. She had on board no armament except two rifles and three revolvers, with about

150–200 rounds of ammunition that were found in the possession of the persons on board other than the master. These firearms were suitable for hunting and other like purposes."

"There is no evidence of anything unusual or strange in the vessel and her equipment or in her movements except the evidence of C. A. Heintz," Black continued. "The evidence of Heintz is incredible on its face. It is contradictory, and all the surrounding circumstances demonstrate its falsity. It is flatly contradicted in several material features by the testimony of the other witnesses. It should be disregarded by all rules of evidence in its entirety. The clear preponderance of the evidence shows that the vessel was not on the high seas, but in Mexican waters when the seizure was made. The testimony of the other persons on board, except Heintz, was that the ship was well within the three mile limit. The fact that the Mexicans on board the vessel were released substantiates this position."

"To say that a small forty-ton vessel could escape from a modern gunboat under such circumstances is to state an improbability," said Black. "The fact that the course of the *Agassiz* was changed several times and that it did not stop is not at all unreasonable. The Mexican pilot was undoubtedly confused."

"There is nothing to show, except the testimony of naval officers at a distance, that anything was thrown overboard," Maude's attorney argued. "The persons on board, except Heintz, say that such was not the case. The testimony that Miss Maude Lochrane, while not a party to the plot, was willing to flee from Mexican territory, and was actually fleeing is preposterous. In the first place, the boat would not have gone far on the supply of fuel and provisions on board, and in the second place, the record shows that she had just entered into a profitable contract which made it very desirable for her not to leave."

"If there were questionable characters on board they were either invited by Heintz or were self-invited," Black advised the court. "Mention is made of the fact that the papers of the ship were not regular in regard to her crew, and the non-descript company on board the vessel is referred to as her crew. As a matter of fact, for the purpose of this trip it was not necessary to have a crew nor did she have one. She was not making a voyage and the majority of the people on board were merely 'joy-riding.'"

Black concluded by stating, "As to the contention that the owner of the vessel has lost her rights as an American citizen by reason of her absence from the United States, it is sufficient to us to suggest in reply that during all of the time she was absent she actually resided on the vessel which was as much American soil as the City of Los Angeles."

With Black's concluding statement, the claimants on both sides rested, and it was left to Judge Bledsoe to file his opinion and entry of judgment.

Within the maze of deceptive and contradictory prize court testimony, where did the truth lie? Had the *Alexander Agassiz* been embarking on its maiden voyage as a German commerce raider as Heintz claimed, or was a trip to the South Seas Islands under way, the raiding expedition a fiction concocted by the unscrupulous Heintz? The evidence indicates that at least some of the individuals taken prisoner aboard the *Agassiz* were acting in the service of Germany:

- The leather wallet that Lieutenant Dorr found in the chart house contained two code keys, one written in ink and the other in pencil, for decoding enciphered messages. It is highly unlikely that Heintz created these keys and "planted" them in the hope that they might be discovered during a search of the schooner.
- The German naval ensign unearthed by the boarding party was not an item easily obtained in the Mexican hinterland. In all probability, it was provided by someone other than Cornelius Heintz.
- When the *Agassiz* was stopped by a shot fired over her bow, all of the crew members except Volpert went on deck to see what had happened, yet all except Heintz claimed that they had seen nothing being thrown overboard. The three naval officers from the *Vicksburg* testified that items were thrown overboard by several individuals for "some period of time."
- William Black, the dredge watchman for the Southern Pacific Railroad at Andrade, California, reported to the Bureau of Investigation that Madden (Martens) claimed to have been a crew member on board the oil tanker *Maverick* in San Francisco, a vessel notorious for its involvement in the *Annie Larsen* affair that was later investigated by

Altendorf. It is a remarkable coincidence that Madden was captured aboard a *second* ship involved in a German plot, the *Alexander Agassiz*, after having come on board with a Winchester .30-30 rifle and an automatic pistol.

- Frank Volpert was hiding in the engine room of the American-registered ship, carrying a document from the German embassy in Mexico City that identified him as a reservist in the German Fusiliers.
- The *Alexander Agassiz* was heading northwest when it was challenged by the *Vicksburg*, in the direction of Venados Island, where Heintz claimed that Fritz Bauman was waiting with an additional sailor and a machine gun.

But at the same time, the schooner *Alexander Agassiz* was an unlikely choice for a commerce raider. With a single deck-mounted machine gun and a top speed of only 9 knots, it could be outrun by even the slowest oceangoing steamship, and would have posed little threat to Allied merchantmen.

It is more probable that the schooner was to be used as a means for repatriating German reservists stranded by the Allied naval blockade to their homeland, in a mission sanctioned by Consul Unger. In the course of achieving this end, the German crew was authorized to take a larger "prize" if possible, by playing the part of a ship in distress or other trickery. The news that a small German "raider" was loose in the Pacific would distract the Allied navies from the Mexican coast, where Unger knew German submarines would soon be operating. Given this scenario, it is only natural that Unger would have called the departing reservists to the consulate to swear an oath to obey the commands of Captain Bauman during the voyage. In a statement H. A. Macintosh provided to the Bureau of Investigation after the *Agassiz* was captured, the trader cautioned, "As relates to Mr. Unger, the German consul at Mazatlán, I know him well and would not put anything of this nature beyond him. The house of which he is the head, Melchers Sucs, during my presence in Mazatlán, were repeatedly making inquiries of me as to the speed of the *Alexander Agassiz*, her seaworthiness, etc."

What part did Cornelius Heintz play in the affair? It is hard to imagine a witness with less personal integrity and credibility than government informant Cornelius Adolph Heintz. He had fled to Mexico from the United States to avoid the draft in the employ of Bernard Hilbing, a man later interned as a dangerous enemy alien under a presidential warrant. One of his first acts in Mazatlán was to purchase the gunboat *Morelos* with the backing of Melchers Sucs, a blacklisted German firm. Heintz was renowned as a shady operator in Mexico, where he had left a long trail of worthless checks. (W. E. Miller, the American store owner who witnessed the capture of the *Agassiz* from shore, held a bad check of Heintz for $20. G. Davidson, the American businessman who provided information to Chapman on blacklisted companies, had also received a bad check from Heintz in the amount of $50.) By his own admission, Heintz had invested $300 in the raider scheme, and was to have earned 5 percent of the value of Allied ships captured or destroyed. Was Heintz a trusted government informant, a reluctant participant, an active member of the conspiracy, or an agent provocateur—the driving force behind the scheme? Perhaps Heintz was "playing both ends against the middle"; if the Americans seized the *Agassiz*, the young engineer could return to the United States as a valued government informant and avoid prison time for draft evasion; if the schooner escaped to sea, he could claim honors for the raiding expedition in Germany. Although some of Heintz's testimony concerning the German plans for the *Agassiz* was undoubtedly true, it is likely that some of his claims were fictitious, created to serve his own purposes. Heintz's lack of credibility as an eyewitness would have a significant impact on the outcome of the *Alexander Agassiz* prize court hearing.

On July 15, 1918, Judge Bledsoe issued his opinion in the case of *United States of America vs. Alexander Agassiz*.

"Unusual pressure of other duties makes it impossible for the Court to do other than merely indicate in skeletonized form, it's conclusions in this case," Bledsoe began. "I am persuaded first, that the capture of the vessel was affected on the high seas, that is, outside of the three mile limit. The testimony on this point is conflicting, but in the first place, the Court may rely on the presumption of official duty properly performed. It is to be assumed that an officer of the United States Navy would not knowingly, endeavor to intercept a vessel under circumstances herein indicated, unless she were at the time outside the three mile limit."

"I am firmly of the belief that the vessel, together with her owner, Miss Lochrane, were endeavoring to effect what might be termed a 'get-a-way' to the South Seas Islands or some other distant locality, in order, probably, that she might escape the payment, or at least the immediate pressure for payment, of debts owing by her in and about Mazatlán and perhaps elsewhere . . . If it was the fact that witness Heintz was intending to inaugurate a privateering or other belligerent venture of some sort, I am persuaded that this intention on his part had in no way been communicated to Miss Lochrane, the owner and Flag Captain of the vessel, and that she was in consequence no party to it."

"The detention of the vessel, was justified, nay under the circumstances was required, because of the suspicious movements of the vessel previous to her capture, because of the almost complete absence of ship's papers, and the secreting of those on board," said Bledsoe, "because of the presence of an incriminating cipher of apparent German origin and letters indicating a connection of some sort between Miss Lochrane and German agents, and because of the secreting of an armed member of the forces of the enemy in the hold on board the vessel, because of the unnecessary and unexplained possession of a German flag, apparently the only national flag besides an American flag on board, and lastly because of the statements and assertions of the witness Heintz, seemingly in actual command of the vessel at the time, with respect to their present determination to engage in belligerent operations against the United States and its Allies."

"Owing, however to the fact that no overt act was committed," the judge stated, "that no privateering or other belligerent operations had been indulged in, that the owner and Flag Captain of the vessel was in ignorance of any intent so to do, that no arms were on the vessel in sufficient numbers or quality to justify the inference that belligerent operations were intended and owing to the further facts that the vessel was actually unsuited, either in the way of provisions or fuel or munitions, to enter upon any scheme of belligerent operations, even on a small scale, the Court is led to the conclusion that condemnation of the vessel would not be proper or just, although the conditions detailed herein before amply justified her search and consequent seizure and detention."

"In this case, I feel that justice would be done by ordering a restitution of the vessel," Bledsoe concluded, "each party to pay its own costs thus far incurred, with this proviso, however, the cost of the Prize Commission being, as I understand it, the reasonable fee to be allowed to Commissioner Andrews of San Diego, and which the Court feels to be reasonably worth the sum of $150.00 should be paid, half by Claimant [Maude Lochrane] and half by the United States Government. A sale of the vessel to be ordered in satisfaction of the expenses incurred and herein above referred to if payment thereof be not made or security given within ten days."

Shortly after Judge Bledsoe issued his opinion, charges were dropped against Maude Lochrane for making seditious statements in violation of the Espionage Act. She was released from jail, along with the two other American detainees, Cornelius Heintz and Charles Boston. The German crew members captured on the *Agassiz*, Frank Volpert, Richard Brandt, and Arthur Martens, were interned as alien enemies and transferred to Fort Douglas, Utah, where they became respectively, War Prisoners No. 1028, 1029, and 1030.

Maude borrowed the $75 needed to pay her share of the Prize Court costs and the *Alexander Agassiz* was released to her by the United States marshal in San Diego. The court ordered that all goods, papers, and possessions that had been seized by the navy on the schooner also be returned to her—except for the German flag and cipher code, which were retained by the government. She was even given the two rifles and three pistols that had been confiscated by the boarding party.

After five months of imprisonment, having lost everything but the clothes on her back, and facing charges that could have kept her in a federal prison for the rest of her life, Maude had emerged from the trial victorious. She was free once more, and the master of the schooner *Alexander Agassiz*, of which she remained the sole and undisputed owner.

9   Going For Broke

At the same time that Maude was reclaiming the *Alexander Agassiz* in San Diego, on the other side of the world, the final attack of the great German spring offensive was being driven back by the Allied forces. The German campaign captured substantial French territory and inflicted heavy casualties, but in the end, was stopped forty miles from Paris. German manpower was exhausted in the futile effort, while the Allies were bolstered by the arrival of 300,000 fresh American troops each month. The German army began a broad retreat, and by August 1918, even the Kaiser recognized that the war was lost.

In Mazatlán, reports of the initial success of the spring offensive had brought great rejoicing in the German community, and a banquet had been held to celebrate the Fatherland's impending victory. Now the atmosphere had grown sullen, as it became clear that the initiative had passed to the enemy. With the change in fortune, there could be no German Mexican invasion of the United States, and the submarines that were expected on the Pacific coast failed to materialize. In the final months of the war, German secret service operations in Mexico quickly drew to a close.

To the managing directors of Melchers Sucesores and their countrymen, the news of the German surrender was almost overwhelming. But along with despair came the hope that the end of hostilities would bring the return of normal business conditions, and allow the firm to regain its former prominence.

The first signs were positive. On April 29, 1919, the U.S. War Trade Board announced that the Enemy Trading List (the "blacklist") was formally rescinded. Two years later, Melchers Sucs celebrated its seventy-fifth year in operation, giving renewed confidence in the future. The partners expressed their belief, "strong and optimistic, that the future is bright and promising . . . We are hopeful that the future will be prosperous and fruitful for future generations. A healthy optimism makes us expect that we will reach the century mark driven by the same trends of advancement and continuous improvement as in the past."

But the decade of the 1920s proved difficult for Melchers Sucesores. In 1922, a general economic depression spread across Mexico and the trading company's business declined significantly. At the same time, the Weimar Republic, struggling to pay war reparations to the Allied governments, was forced to use unsupported paper marks to buy foreign currency on the open exchanges, creating a severe hyperinflation that lasted three years and destabilized the nation's economy. The mark became virtually worthless, which disrupted Casa Melchers' ability to conduct financial transactions in Germany, its leading source of supply. Mexican customers saw the price of German goods increase, while deliveries could not always be depended upon.

The wartime isolation of the German trading houses by the Allied blockade and enemy trading lists resulted in American companies making strong inroads into the Mexican market. The expansion of the Southern Pacific Railroad down the west coast of Mexico further increased competition from merchants in California, and trade reverted to the United States in ever-growing proportions.

The final straw came with the Wall Street crash in 1929, which triggered a worldwide depression. Melchers Sucesores was forced to declare bankruptcy. With Casa Melchers gone, Consul Friedrich Unger took a position with the Cervecería del Pacífico brewery. He died of a heart attack in Mazatlán in 1940 at the age of sixty-five.

Maude's immediate concern after the war was how to keep the *Alexander Agassiz* from being seized again—by the U.S. Marshal for nonpayment of outstanding claims against the vessel. The mortgage owed on the schooner to the University of California alone had ballooned to almost $8,000, and the problem remained that the *Agassiz* could not pass inspection to carry cargo for hire in the United States.

The financial outlook brightened somewhat when an offer to charter the schooner arrived from an unlikely source. The Famous Players-Lasky Corporation (later renamed Paramount Pictures) was planning to film a comedy-romance titled *Such a Little Pirate* about an innocent young girl who sails off in search of her great-grandfather's pirate treasure, and along the way, nearly falls prey to the machinations of her cutthroat crew. The picture would feature one of the studio's rising stars, a talented young actress named Lila Lee, who went on to star in blockbuster hits like *Blood and Sand* with Rudolph Valentino, and became one of the few stars of the silent era to successfully transition to "talkies" a decade later. Executives at the studio had read about Maude Lochrane and the *Alexander Agassiz* in Los Angeles newspapers, and recognizing the publicity potential, chartered the former German raider for use in the film. Four months after Maude and the raider crew were captured off Mazatlán, the *Agassiz* returned to the sea again, sailing between San Pedro and Catalina Island with Lila Lee and a company of "pirate" actors to film scenes for the movie. But when the production ended, so did the charter income, and the Pacific Coast Trading and Shipping Company once more teetered toward bankruptcy.

In desperation, Maude hatched a "go-for-broke" scheme to take the *Agassiz* on a sealing expedition to the Santa Cruz Islands. She hired a captain, W. J. Saunders, to pilot the boat, an engineer named Harry Tripp to handle the engines, and two seamen, Charley Grass and Hans Nelson to catch the seals. She borrowed money for supplies from Miss Vive Lorie, an acquaintance in Los Angeles, and set sail for Santa Cruz.

The voyage was a financial disaster; few seals were caught and Maude returned to port owing $854 that she didn't have to Saunders, Miss Lorie, and the crew. Her newest creditors filed a legal action, which resulted in the *Alexander Agassiz* being seized by the U.S. Marshal in San Diego. For the next six months the schooner was moored under the watch of a keeper, until June 24, 1919, when Maude was able to reach an agreement to settle their claims and obtain the schooner's release.

Undeterred by the sealing fiasco, "the 'skippertress' of the good ship *Alexander Agassiz*," as Maude was now known in the press, continued a vain search for freight contracts that would help pay off the mounting debt, but it was a losing battle. Within a year the *Agassiz* was seized once again, this time by the U.S. marshal in Los Angeles, and put up for auction to pay off Maude's creditors.

Joseph Mesmer had supported Maude in her efforts to run a shipping company from the beginning, both out of friendship and his personal desire to assist the disadvantaged. But the industrialist recognized that the Pacific Coast Trading and Shipping Company was destined for failure; a freight carrier with a vessel that could not legally carry cargo for hire was not a viable business proposition. When the *Alexander Agassiz* came up for sale at the U.S. Marshal's auction, Mesmer purchased the schooner for $4,200 to help settle some of the outstanding claims against the vessel. He then recovered part of his outlay by selling the *Agassiz* to the Halfhill Tuna Packing Company of San Francisco, the largest tuna processor on the Pacific Coast. The *Alexander Agassiz* was gone, but until her death in the mid-1940s, it would be remembered by Maude Lochrane as the greatest adventure of her life.

Cornelius Adolph Heintz finished the war safe at home in Los Angeles. After giving his deposition at the Prize Court hearing, he was released on his own recognizance. On April 5, 1918, Heintz registered for the draft, claiming an exemption for having a dependent wife. Following Judge Bledsoe's ruling that no overt act of privateering or other belligerent operations had been indulged in by the *Agassiz*'s crew, Heintz was released from custody, a free man.

Unlike the others captured on board the schooner, for Cornelius Heintz, the *Alexander Agassiz* saga had a happy ending. He was no longer a slacker, no longer subject to the penalty of one year in jail for draft evasion, and with a dependent wife, would not be called to serve in the U.S. armed forces.

In the years after the fateful voyage, Heintz would continue to find employment as an engineer. He developed a smokeless incinerator, and in the 1930s capitalized on the growing demand for air conditioning by forming his own air conditioner manufacturing company. Heintz later remarried and had four sons. His first son, Cornelius A. Heintz Jr., was a hero during World War II. An Army Air Corps navigator, young Heintz's bomber was shot down over France in 1943, and he spent the following two years in a German prisoner-of-war camp.

Cornelius Adolph Heintz Sr. died in Los Angeles in 1958 at the age of sixty-eight.

Lieutenant Charles Edwin Reordan's actions during the capture of the *Alexander Agassiz* would add to his reputation as a capable naval commander. In the decades that followed, his career in the navy would steadily progress, as he rose from lieutenant, to lieutenant-commander, commander, and finally to captain. He was the commanding officer of a number of U.S. Navy vessels, from the USS *Henderson*, a 12,000-ton troop transport, to the USS *Farragut*, one of the newest destroyers in the fleet. In 1935, Reordan was selected to attend the U.S. Naval War College and graduated in the senior class. Six years later, he was the captain of the USS *Tennessee*, a powerful 33,000-ton battleship with a ship's company of over 1,000 men.

One peaceful Sunday morning in December 1941, Captain Reordan was enjoying shore leave on the island of Oahu, Hawaii, when the sound of distant explosions and gunfire signaled the opening of the surprise attack on Pearl Harbor. Wave after wave of Japanese dive bombers, torpedo planes, and fighters descended upon the unsuspecting American warships, and within minutes, the *Tennessee*, moored on Battleship Row along Ford Island with seven other battleships, was struck by two armor-piercing bombs that disabled a gun and killed several sailors. As the *Tennessee* responded with a barrage of defensive fire, a terrific explosion occurred aft of the warship, as the battleship *Arizona* was torn apart by a bomb that dropped down her funnel, showering the *Tennessee* with burning debris and leaving the surface of the water "a mass of flaming oil from millions of gallons of (released) fuel oil." As the battle continued to rage, the *Tennessee* was singled out for attack, and became the target of additional bombs, while her deck was raked with machine-gun bullets from low-flying Japanese planes.

Without stopping to change out of his civilian clothes or remove the straw hat that he was wearing, Reordan rushed back to his ship to take command. The burning oil from the *Arizona* threatened to engulf the *Tennessee*, and he gave orders to advance at slow speed into a better defensive position. But no movement could occur—the *Tennessee* was now pinned against a dock by the stricken battleship *West Virginia* and frozen in place. At that moment, Reordan noticed that the wash from the *Tennessee*'s propellers was holding back the burning oil released by the *Arizona*. He directed that the engines be run at full speed, which kept the flaming mass away from the *Tennessee* and saved the ship. The whirring propellers continued to protect the *Tennessee* for the next twenty-four hours until the flames subsided. The battleship was finally freed when the dock was dynamited, and the *Tennessee* returned to sea within a few days of the Japanese attack.

For his performance at Pearl Harbor, Captain Reordan received a commendation from Admiral Chester W. Nimitz, the commander of the Pacific Fleet, and he would later receive the Legion of Merit from President Truman for his work as commandant of the Key West Naval Operating Base. Charles E. Reordan died in Miami, Florida, at the age of fifty-eight, on March 23, 1947.

After his harrowing escape from Mexico, Dr. Paul Altendorf reported to the Military Intelligence office in Nogales, Arizona, where he spent the next several weeks monitoring the movement of suspected enemy agents across the border. In August 1918, he was called to Fort Sam Houston in San Antonio, Texas, to testify at the trial of Lothar Witzke, the German saboteur-assassin he had delivered into American hands. Altendorf provided damning firsthand testimony, telling the court of Witzke's confessing to multiple acts of sabotage on American soil. At the conclusion of the trial, the German agent was sentenced to death, and only escaped the hangman's noose when President Wilson commuted his sentence to "confinement at hard labor for the rest of his natural life." Witzke was sent to Leavenworth penitentiary. Three years later, under intense pressure from the Weimar Republic, the U.S. government released Witzke and he was deported to Germany.

Witzke would remain one of a score of men who wanted to see Dr. Paul Bernardo Altendorf *dead*. In 1928, lawyers representing the Lehigh Valley Railroad, owners of Black Tom Island, the munitions storage terminal destroyed in 1916 by a group of saboteurs that included Jahnke and Witzke, located the former saboteur in Venezuela. Although Witzke refused to divulge any information about the missions that he had undertaken for Germany during the war, the lawyers found him to be amiable and courteous—until Dr. Altendorf was introduced into the conversation. At the mention of Altendorf's name, Witzke's demeanor changed in an instant. "With eyes flashing fire, he referred to Altendorf, stating that he had once had him at the point of a pistol and regretted that he had not put him out of the way then."

While Altendorf was at San Antonio, Major Barnes, the head of military intelligence for the Southern Department, told him to "look around and see what you can do." Forty-eight hours later, Altendorf had become a member of the Tannhauser Halle, the leading German club in San Antonio. He subsequently investigated several cases for the department, including that of Dr. Ludwig Reuter, a suspect German chemist, and Count Pierre Fremonte E. Rodyke, a Russian-born German agent, obtaining evidence that sent both men to prison.

As the war drew to a close, the army's military intelligence branch was drastically reduced in size. The unit in which Altendorf served, the Corps of Intelligence Police, which had fielded over a thousand investigators during the war, was soon left with just a handful of men. Altendorf's superiors attempted to retain their star agent as an interpreter, or obtain permission to hire him for another secret mission, but without success. The doctor-spy was demobilized from the service in April 1919.

Altendorf left the military intelligence branch on the best of terms. A letter of recommendation from Brigadier General J. A. Ryan stated:

> Dr. Altendorf is a fine linguist and a man of exceptional talent for secret service work. His splendid work in Mexico resulted in important developments and important captures by the Government. He is devoted to the American Forces and I deem him competent to perform the duties of a Captain of the Intelligence Department, to which Department he would be a valuable acquisition. Dr. Altendorf is possessed of experience way beyond his years and should not be placed under men who have less experience and less ability. He should by all means be secured for the U.S. Secret Service.

Major Barnes confirmed:

> Dr. Altendorf displayed much energy in the discharge of his duties. He is an excellent linguist and is otherwise well qualified for this class of work. The results which he secured while connected with the service were very gratifying.

The division superintendent of the Bureau of Investigation in San Antonio, Charles E. Breniman, provided a further endorsement:

> Dr. P. B. Altendorf has been known to me personally for the past several months through his connection with the Intelligence Office of the Southern Department. He is a man who possesses exceptional ability as an investigator, speaks a number of foreign languages, is painstaking and careful in his work, and his reports are always received with the most implicit confidence. His wide experience, splendid education and natural qualifications would make him a most valuable man to any investigating branch of the Government.

Breniman recommended Altendorf for a job with the Bureau of Investigation, which he accepted and held for a period of six months. Altendorf then moved to New York in pursuit of something more lucrative—an offer that he had received from the McClure Newspaper Syndicate for publication rights to the story of his wartime adventures as a secret agent. In the months that followed, the former spy penned a complete account of his exploits, from being chased out of Yucatán by Salvador Alvarado to his escape from Mexico and eventual departure from military intelligence. Altendorf pulled no punches in identifying his enemies in the narrative—Schwiertz, Calles, Jahnke, Witzke, and Unger—but concealed the names of American agents and their operating methods. Altendorf's memoir *On Secret Service in Mexico* was syndicated as a thirty-installment series in newspapers from coast to coast. It detailed the extraordinary degree to which he had infiltrated the German secret service, while also revealing the duplicity that existed during the war between German representatives in Mexico and members of the Carranza government.

In his syndicated series, Altendorf claimed that he had received official approval from Brigadier-General Marlborough Churchill, the director of

Military Intelligence, to publish the articles. But when pressed for approval, Churchill had merely stated that Military Intelligence had no legal means to prevent their publication because Altendorf was no longer in their employ, but that he regretted the articles being published and would not vouch for their accuracy. When Altendorf's syndicated memoirs appeared in the press less than a year after the Armistice, the man who had been seen as "an invaluable asset to the American government . . . [who] provided more information of real value than any other dozen informants" fell rapidly from grace. The legendary agent had dishonored the service by revealing secret operations for money and burned many of his bridges to U.S. military intelligence in the process.

Among the public at large, Altendorf became recognized as an authority on current conditions in Mexico. The former spy was invited to make an address on the Mexican situation before the Society of American Wars in New York City, whose members included President Wilson, ex-President Taft, and General Pershing. He gave a series of interviews to the National Association for the Protection of American Rights in Mexico, a powerful business group consisting of banks, oil companies, and miners with interests in Mexico that were printed and widely distributed to news organizations. Altendorf stated:

Since 1914 I have been in 22 of the 27 states constituting the former Mexican Republic, and in most of them in the last two years, traveling almost continuously on foot, on mule back, in boats and on the few trains that are still running. I traveled as a German; for no one but a German is safe in Mexico. Speaking from the fullness of first hand knowledge thus acquired, it seems to me a joke to call Carranza's administration a "government." No real government exists south of the Rio Grande, except such authority as a thug with a gun exercises over an unarmed victim. Mexico is nothing more than an agglomeration of anarchist gangs who kill and plunder with no restraint but their own caprices . . . The men at the top get the largest share of the swag; make no mistake about that. Carranza is reputed to have $15 million on deposit in Chilean banks . . . General Calles, former governor of Sonora, now in command of the troops there and consequently the real ruler, saved more than a million dollars in two years out of a government salary . . . In Mexico, as in Russia, the sinister hand of Germany is to be found pulling the strings.

In January 1920, Dr. Altendorf was called to give testimony before Senator Fall, the chairman of a U.S. Senate Foreign Relations Committee investigating affairs in Mexico. After being sworn in, he made a strong impression on the committee, describing the interwoven relationship that existed between the Mexican and German governments during the war, and provided as an example, Mario Méndez, the minister of telegraph, who Alterndorf alleged was in the pay of Germany and provided von Eckhardt with copies of cables sent by the U.S. government to the American ambassador.

Altendorf had made a great many enemies in Mexico after being exposed as an American spy, and continued to stoke the flames of their enmity through his writings and public statements. Two years after he escaped across the border, he took a step that was wholly unexpected and would prove extremely unwise: Dr. Altendorf returned to Mexico.

By the summer of 1920, the former secret agent was once again short of cash. The money that he had been paid for *On Secret Service in Mexico* by the McClure Syndicate was running low, and he now had a wife to support. Altendorf had married Mrs. Wallace M. Woody, the widow of an army lieutenant killed in France. To add to his frustration, his life savings of $14,800 remained buried on the Pacific coast of Mexico—the last place on earth that he could go to recover it. If Altendorf returned to Mexico, he would be walking to almost certain death.

The only alternative would be to send someone to retrieve the money for him; someone that he could trust implicitly. Altendorf contacted his former superior, Captain Dickey at Fort Sam Houston in San Antonio, and explained the situation, offering to pay him $4,000 to travel to Guaymas and bring back the buried cash. The adventurous captain readily agreed. Altendorf gave Dickey $125 to cover expenses and provided him with a detailed map showing exactly where the money was hidden. The intelligence officer departed for Mexico, and a week later returned to inform Altendorf that he had encountered a major problem when he arrived at the destination—a landslide had covered the burial spot with a small mountain of earth. He would not be able to do anything without another four or five men to help excavate.

Altendorf came to the conclusion that he would have to go to Guaymas himself to retrieve his savings, but then encountered another obstacle, when he learned that he could not obtain a U.S. passport for travel to Mexico. In desperation, he formulated a risky plan for obtaining safe passage through Mexico. Altendorf visited Teodulo Beltrán, the Mexican Consul in San Antonio and advised him that he had obtained information about a counterrevolution brewing in Mexico. He told Beltrán that he wanted to personally convey details of the plot that he had uncovered to the Mexican authorities, and requested a letter of recommendation and a guarantee of safety for him to travel to Mexico City. The consul agreed to the request, and gave Altendorf a letter addressed to President de la Huerta, and a second addressed to the president's chief of staff, Colonel Gaxiola.

Altendorf crossed into Mexico through the port of Nuevo Laredo, arriving in the Mexican capital on August 6, and proceeded directly to the Hotel Regis, where he registered under the name Pablo Heitke. The next day he went to the National Palace and requested an audience with the president. An aide brought the documents that he had received from Beltrán to de la Huerta, and word was relayed back to the captain of the guard for Altendorf to call again later in the afternoon. He waited at the palace for his appointment with the president and met a number of old acquaintances, telling them that he had come to see de la Huerta on personal business. At the appointed hour, he excused himself and went to see Colonel Gaxiola about his meeting with the president. He was announced to President de la Huerta, but word was returned that the Mexican leader was not feeling well and would be unable to see him. Could the doctor come back tomorrow?

He returned the next day and received the same message.

On Monday, August 9, Altendorf once again called at the National Palace and asked to see the president. At half past one, instead of being taken to de la Huerta, he was ushered into the office of General Plutarco Elías Calles, now the powerful minister of war and marine—the same man whom Altendorf had tricked into dismissing Major Schwiertz, a loyal officer on his staff; the same man who had been Altendorf's superior in the Mexican Army before he deserted to America as a wanted spy; and the same man that he had subsequently denounced as a corrupt scoundrel in his syndicated memoirs and public statements.

Altendorf reached out to shake Calles's hand, but the general turned away sharply, and barked an order to a major and two soldiers armed with rifles to take the doctor to the military prison of Santiago Tlatelolco. If the prisoner made a move to escape, they were to use their rifles. Stunned, Altendorf tried to provide an explanation, but Calles cut him off, telling him to "keep quiet and not say one more word." Then he was briskly escorted from the room.

At Santiago prison, Altendorf's personal effects were confiscated and he was clapped into a small cell with an iron bed called a "gridiron." He had no visitors until eight o'clock in the evening, when two captains came to check on him in his cell. Altendorf asked if he could have a mattress for the bed. One of the officers responded, "No. Prisoners are allowed to buy their own mattress and blankets, but I have orders from General Calles not to allow you to buy anything; you are to remain as you are in the cell."

The other officer flashed Altendorf a sign that he did not understand. Fifteen minutes later he returned and said that he could give him a pencil and paper if he wanted to send out any messages. Altendorf scribbled a quick note to the Hotel Regis and a second to the American consul informing him of his arrest and handed them to the officer.

The next day, Calles sent some reporters from the *Universal* newspaper to interview the "American spy." They asked Altendorf if it was true that he had deserted from the Mexican Army in 1917.

"I was in the Mexican Army only 2–1/2 months and resigned in Hermosillo, Sonora in October 1917," Altendorf told them. "The general knows this perfectly well."

They informed him that Calles intended to have him court-martialed and shot. One of the reporters said, "Doctor, I have orders to take some pictures of you." Altendorf refused, and the captain of the guard, a man named Rodolfo Vela, was called and the pictures were taken by force.

A second group of reporters, this time from the *Excelsior* newspaper, arrived to interview Altendorf, but he refused to speak with them. They directed his attention to a wall outside his cell. "You see that wall, Doctor? If you refuse to talk they are going to put you there at half past four in the morning, and shoot you like they do the rest." Altendorf maintained his silence and they left without a story.

Calles next sent an undercover informant to visit his cell in an attempt to trap him into revealing something incriminating. "He presented himself in a very suspicious way and I had very little confidence in him," Altendorf recalled later. "He began to talk to me in English, very broken English. He said, 'Doctor, I come here to help you. You need not be afraid of me.'"

But the former spy would not be fooled.

Every time the man spoke to him in English he answered in Spanish. After several minutes spent going back and forth this way, Altendorf grew tired of the game and told the stranger, "You are young and have little experience. You will have to know a lot more than you know now, before you can get into any conversation with me."

He left him at the door and walked back into his cell.

On his second Sunday in prison, Altendorf was allowed into the yard, at Santiago prison called "the patio":

It was ten o'clock in the morning and the captain opened my cell and told me to walk out and have some exercise. When I walked out into the yard, I noticed that I was being watched by some of the guards to see if I would attempt to speak to somebody . . . After making two rounds in the patio, Colonel Feta with several of the soldiers who were prisoners walked up to me and grabbed me and threw me into a water tank that used to be a fountain in the yard, and shouted "throw him into the water, that gringo." Every time that I tried to come up and get some air, they hit me in the head with sticks and dived me down into the water for about ten minutes. I got up again at last without any assistance and went back to my cell.

At six o'clock that evening, Colonel Farel, who was in charge of the prison, walked by on inspection. Altendorf called him to his cell and complained about his near-drowning in the fountain.

"You're all right," Farel replied, sarcastically. "You can stand this. Think that you have been out in the rain." For registering a complaint, Altendorf was denied the black coffee that they called "supper" that night and had to go without food until morning.

The days at Santiago Tlaltelolco prison were filled with tension as Altendorf waited to be taken away for a quick trial and an even quicker execution. After being held incommunicado for over a week, his face was now covered with a heavy growth of black beard.

Early one morning, without any advance notice, two army officers came to his cell—Colonel Santos Mendoza and Major Jiménez. The captain of the guard unlocked the door, and Altendorf was informed that President de la Huerta had ordered him deported under Article 33 of the Mexican Constitution as a "pernicious foreigner" for maligning Mexico in his writings and Senate testimony. He was told that they would depart in one hour on a train for Juárez.

Altendorf breathed a sigh of relief. The message that he had sent to the U.S. consul had apparently done the trick. Not wanting trouble with the Americans for executing their spy, Calles had decided to have him deported instead.

Following a train ride that lasted two days with little food and water, they reached Juárez, and Altendorf was taken to see Mr. Harper, the American consul. The Mexican officers informed Harper that Altendorf was being deported back to the United States.

> The American Consul asked me if I was an American citizen and if I had a passport. I told him I had taken out my first naturalization papers in 1918 and that I have my papers in San Antonio. He consulted with the Immigration Officer and after a while he told me that he was very sorry but he could not allow me to cross the border without having this paper. I wired to my wife in San Antonio; she brought up the paper and there I found more trouble. I am a Pole, born in Austrian Poland before the war, and because I was born in Austrian Poland, I was again an alien enemy.

The U.S. officials refused to allow Altendorf to pass onto American soil. Colonel Mendoza sent a wire to his superiors that Altendorf had been denied entry into the United States, requesting further instructions. On August 31 the colonel received an ominous reply—"Bring Altendorf back to Mexico City at once." It was now clear to the Mexican officials that the Americans were not concerned about the fate of their spy after all.

The meaning of the message was not lost on Altendorf, who began to plan his escape.

That afternoon, the three men returned to the hotel suite that they were sharing, and Mendoza and Jiménez started drinking heavily. At eight o'clock Altendorf went into his room, undressed, and went to bed. After an appropriate amount of time had passed, he peered into the outer room and saw the officers sitting in their chairs, drunk and nodding off to sleep. He dressed quickly, then slipped past his slumbering escort and walked outside into the darkened street. There was no one in sight. During the previous two days, Altendorf had been allowed to go about the streets of Juárez while accompanied by Major Jiménez and was now familiar with the area. He found a horse that he was able to bridle, mounted it bareback, and cantered off into the night. He knew the direction of the border from a map that he had studied in the American consul's office, and rode through brush and mud until he reached the Rio Grande. He abandoned the horse on the Mexican side of the river and swam across the cool water into the United States.

For the second time in as many years, Altendorf had escaped from his enemies in Mexico.

He walked along a country road for two and a half miles, and then caught a ride into El Paso. It was raining, and he used his handkerchief to shine his shoes, trying to make himself appear somewhat more presentable. He was able to check into a room at the Hotel Fisher, where he was joined by his wife the following day.

Altendorf went to the office of the Bureau of Investigation and confessed to having "entered the United States at a place other than a regular point of entry and without the knowledge or consent of duly authorized officers of the United States." The U.S. Attorney was consulted, and a complaint was filed against him for violation of the Passport Control Act. He was released on a $300 bond to ensure his appearance at a Grand Jury hearing.

Months later, after learning the details of Altendorf's work as a Military Intelligence agent during the war and of his life being in danger at the time of his escape from Mexico, the San Antonio Grand Jury decided not to indict Altendorf for illegally entering the United States.

For a year, Dr. Altendorf disappeared from public view and his whereabouts remained a mystery. Then he returned to the spotlight once again during the investigation of one of the most infamous crimes of the 1920s.

Shortly before noon on September 16, 1920, a red horse-drawn wagon slowly made its way through the financial district of New York and came to a stop in front of the headquarters of the J. P. Morgan Bank at 23 Wall Street, the busiest location in the district. As lunchtime crowds surged along the sidewalks, the wagon driver exited his vehicle and hurried away, apparently to arrange a delivery. Minutes later, a fifty-pound charge of blasting gelatin exploded, blowing the horse and wagon to bits and sending hundreds of cast-iron window sash weights tearing through the area. The concussion of the blast was terrific, and was quickly followed by a searing wall of flame. After the smoke cleared, the financial district had been transformed into a battleground: a demolished car lay on its side burning fiercely, the pavement was coated with glass shards from hundreds of shattered office windows, and mangled bodies were scattered in every direction. Thirty-eight people died as a result of the blast and over a hundred were injured, while property damage ran into the millions of dollars.

Responsibility for the deadly "bomb outrage" was quickly directed at foreign-inspired anarchists and radicals. In a mailbox located a few blocks from the scene, a postal letter carrier discovered five circulars printed on cheap 7 x 11 paper that read:

Remember
We will not tolerate any longer
Free the political prisoners or it will be death to all of you
American Anarchist Fighters

A year earlier, on June 2, 1919, smaller package bombs had been detonated in eight U.S. cities—one was planted outside the Washington townhouse of Attorney General A. Mitchell Palmer—that were wrapped in circulars signed "Anarchist Fighters." The June explosions had been the catalyst that led to the Palmer "red raids" in which thousands of foreign-born communists and anarchists with no connection to the incidents had been arrested.

Investigations into the Wall Street bombing were launched by the Justice Department's Bureau of Investigation, the New York City Police, the Fire Department, and several insurance companies, but they quickly stalled due to lack of evidence. The night after the explosion, cleaning crews swept through the area to allow business to resume the next day, removing physical evidence that could have helped investigators locate those responsible for the crime. The remains of the dead horse were carted off to a rendering plant. Many eyewitnesses dispersed after the explosion, and the recollections of those who could be located were vague and uncertain. Promising leads went nowhere. Yet public officials still announced that those responsible would be brought to justice and that "arrests were imminent," which only served to heighten public pressure for a speedy resolution to the crime.

One of the investigators at work trying to apprehend the culprits was William J. Burns, the president of the Burns International Detective Agency and the most famous detective in America. Burns had spent a lifetime solving "unsolvable" crimes of every sort: arson, counterfeiting, murder, robbery, land theft—even the 1910 bombing of the *Los Angeles Times* building. He had been hired by the American Bankers Association to investigate the Wall Street blast. On the afternoon of the explosion, the detective went to the scene to personally pick through the debris in search of clues. While the authorities debated whether the destruction was the result of an accident or an "infernal machine," Burns knew at once that it was a premeditated crime.

"We have evidence to prove that it was the work of time-lock bombs," Burns told the Associated Press, "placed by anarchists or 'reds' as a gesture to startle the world."

Two months later, the Burns International Detective Agency announced that it would pay a $50,000 reward for information leading to the conviction of the individuals responsible for the deadly attack. By this time, Burns was convinced that the Wall Street bombing had been inspired by the leaders of the Communist International in Moscow.

One of his chief sources of information on radical activities was a Polish immigrant named Wolfe Lindenfeld, also known by the alias William Linde.

Lindenfeld had a long history of involvement in fringe political and labor groups, and was variously described as a half-brother of German socialist Rosa Luxemburg, the managing editor of the radical Slavic Press Bureau, and a representative in America of Lenin and the Third International. He had been recommended to the Burns Detective Agency as "the man who knew most about the Wall Street explosion," and Burns later declared, "careful checking had borne this out." Lindenfeld had been an informant on "red" activities for the New York police department, and later applied for a position with the Burns Detective Agency, where he was hired "to keep the agency in touch with the activity of anarchistic circles."

Three weeks before the Wall Street explosion, confidential sources had informed the Burns Agency that a bombing would occur shortly. When asked to verify the information, Lindenfeld told Burns that the rumor was true, but denied that he knew where the bombing would take place. After the bomb wagon exploded in the financial district, Burns was convinced that Lindenfeld knew the full story behind the deadly act.

In March 1921, Burns entrusted Lindenfeld with the mission of searching out the Wall Street bombers. He provided the informant with $3,000 in expense money and sent him to Europe, where the ex-radical claimed the perpetrators had fled after the explosion. For months Lindenfeld traveled across the continent attending communist party gatherings in Moscow, Zurich, Berlin, and Warsaw. As time passed without Burns receiving any word from Lindenfeld, newly discovered evidence in the United States suggested that rather than being a turncoat, Lindenfeld was in fact an active communist and perhaps a conspirator in the Wall Street bombing himself.

Burns needed to locate Lindenfeld *fast*. Fortunately, he had just the man to track him down: Dr. Paul Bernardo Altendorf.

A month after Altendorf swam across the Rio Grande to escape from Mexico, he moved to New York and obtained employment as an operative with the Burns Detective Agency at a salary of $8 per day. Burns now gave the former intelligence agent an important assignment—travel to Europe and find Wolfe Lindenfeld.

Altendorf had already been dispatched to Europe in search of information earlier that year. Just as the doctor-spy had worked his way into the confidence of the German secret service in Mexico City, he had traveled to Russia and Poland posing as a dedicated Marxist to gain the confidence of the Communist International. On his return to New York City, Altendorf made the acquaintance of Dr. Isaac Hourwich, a legal adviser to L. C. Martens, the representative of the Soviet government in the United States. Hourwich arranged for him to join the American Benevolent Committee for Child Relief in Poland, a communist front organization, at a salary of $20 per week. He was given credentials that would enable him to visit Poland as a member of the committee and (the communists believed), to obtain information for the Soviet bureau directed by Hourwich.

With his cover as a Bolshevik secret agent firmly established, Altendorf booked passage on a steamship for Poland, arriving in his homeland in late August 1921. He traveled extensively and met with communist interme- diaries throughout the country, attempting to learn more about the Wall Street bomb plot and the whereabouts of Wolfe Lindenfeld. His suspicious activities quickly brought him to the attention of the Polish authorities. When he was detained by the Poles for questioning, Altendorf resorted to a strategy that had yielded great success in his secret operations in Mexico. He exaggerated his level of authority, informing the officials that he was a representative of the U.S. Department of Justice on an official mission for the government. To support his claim, Altendorf showed them documents that described his service in American military intelligence.

But postwar Warsaw was a European metropolis, not the hinterlands of Mexico, and the Poles immediately contacted the U.S. Legation to learn whether Altendorf was, in fact, on an official mission. The Polish inquiry resulted in a flurry of awkward exchanges between the U.S. State Department, the Justice Department, and William Burns, which resulted in Altendorf's becoming persona non grata at the legation. To the U.S. diplomats in Warsaw, Altendorf was an unprincipled troublemaker whose false claims and misrepresentations threatened to create a diplomatic inci- dent. Henceforth, the "Burns agency man" would receive no assistance in his investigation from the American Mission in Warsaw.

Despite the lack of cooperation from the State Department officials, Altendorf sent word to Burns that he was making considerable progress on the case. Then Altendorf, like Lindenfeld, mysteriously disappeared . . .

Growing increasingly frustrated with the status of the investigation, William Burns, who had recently been appointed the director of the Bureau of Investigation, dispatched a special agent named Silvester Cosgrove to Poland to "get in touch with Altendorf, find out what Altendorf has and knows, and transmit it to the Justice Department."

Cosgrove was able to track down Altendorf, and then Lindenfeld, who was arrested by the Polish police. Lindenfeld turned state's evidence and provided a ten-thousand-word written statement in which he claimed that although he was not a participant in the crime, he knew the complete story. According to Lindenfeld, the Soviets in Moscow had promised a $30,000 payment for the job, which was carried out by five principals. Their intended target in the attack had been banker J. P. Morgan, but the plotters were foiled when the bomb had exploded prematurely due to "a mechanical mistake." Lindenfeld's sworn statement provided a mass of details, including the New York addresses of various individuals involved in the plot, and even the location where the cash was to be paid.

When news of Lindenfeld's arrest reached the United States, it appeared that the mystery surrounding who was behind the Wall Street bombing had at last been solved. All of the pertinent facts in the case were disclosed in Lindenfeld's written confession, and the authorities announced that further arrests were expected.

In recognition of the part that he had played in the capture of Wolfe Lindenfeld, Altendorf was hailed as a hero. His picture appeared in the nation's newspapers once again, beneath headlines like "Dr. Paul B. Altendorf, Former Soldier of Fortune, Balked Berlin's War Lords at Every Step, Adds to Laurels." Journalists wrote glowingly that Lindenfeld stood little chance against Altendorf, the "Nemesis of German Plotters" whose "services as a super-spy in the war days were immeasurable."

The news seemed too good to be true—and it was. Within days of the stories' release, accolades turned to indignation, when Wolfe Lindenfeld was exposed as a fraud. Far from being a valued informant for the New York City Police Department, it turned out that the police considered Lindenfeld to be a "hot air artist," and had given him the nickname "Windy Linde." Although he had worked with radicals "of every shade and degree" while acting as a stool pigeon for the New York police, neither side really trusted him. A cursory investigation of Lindenfeld's claims revealed them to be pure fiction, and "Windy Linde" later recanted his testimony to the Polish police.

The Lindenfeld episode was a personal disaster for William J. Burns. Renowned as "America's Sherlock Holmes," overnight the new director of the Bureau of Investigation became a subject of scorn and ridicule.

It also brought an end to the amazing career of Dr. Paul Bernardo Altendorf. In 1918, he had been a legend in military intelligence, but in the years since, his star had taken a precipitous decline. He had drawn the ire of his wartime superiors by publishing his memoirs in the newspapers. He caused further embarrassment by foolishly returning to Mexico and getting himself tossed into prison, then was charged with illegally entering the United States on his return. Now the man who had outfoxed the German secret service while serving as an American spy in Mexico had been taken in by the shameless deception of a con man. Altendorf, the "man of mystery," quietly disappeared from the public stage, this time, never to return.

By the late 1920s, Altendorf's descent seemed nearly complete as rumors surfaced that the former spy was in Havana, mixed up with a gang of prohibition rum-runners "something worse than a lot of rum-runners." When he heard the news, Vaughn Cooper, a lieutenant-colonel in the Military Intelligence Division said of Altendorf, "His service with G2 during the war was very valuable; but after the war he seems to have followed the usual course of adventurers and gotten into trouble." Marlborough Churchill gave a more succinct appraisal: "Altendorf is an adventurer out of luck."

In the fall of 1920, Captain Roy Stevens hoped his luck would hold as he cautiously edged his fishing schooner, the *Alexander Agassiz*, closer to the coast. He was heading for San Francisco from San Pedro in late November, and it was a tough time to be out on the water. In the early morning darkness, there was a heavy fog blowing in over Drake's Bay that made taking bearings impossible. He was now almost feeling his way toward the San Francisco channel.

Stevens had bought the *Agassiz* from the Halfhill Tuna Packing Company, which in turn had acquired it from Joseph Mesmer. Halfhill Tuna, named after Albert Halfhill, the pioneer of the California tuna industry, was the largest tuna cannery in the state. The company bought boats like the *Agassiz* and then sold them on time payments to fishermen, taking a share of the albacore that they caught in payment.

The 1920 albacore season had been a disappointment, forcing boats to go out in weather that would otherwise have kept them in port. The rocky waters of the lower coast, combined with unpredictable weather, made tuna fishing a precarious way to make a living. Three Halfhill boats had been lost around the California channel islands in the past five years. The *Agassiz* herself had been driven onto the rocks of the Long Beach harbor jetties by heavy groundswells the previous August, and three boats owned by other packers had either been damaged or gone onto the jetties themselves trying to help free the stranded schooner. Fortunately, the *Agassiz* had been pulled to safety without much damage.

As the *Alexander Agassiz* cruised closer to the coast in the heavy fog, Captain Stevens suddenly felt the boat lurch and heard a sickening crash, as the schooner ran aground on the rocks near Point Reyes at the tip of the bay. He ordered the engines reversed in an attempt to pull away, but soon realized that it was a hopeless task—the schooner was stuck fast on the rocks.

At daybreak, Mate Herman Derham and another member of the crew swam ashore in search of help, but there was none to be found. Later that morning, Steven's wife, the engineer's wife, and five of the crew went ashore in a small boat, while Captain Stevens and three other men remained on board trying to free the stricken vessel. No matter what was attempted the boat would not budge and they were forced to abandon the effort.

The schooner *Alexander Agassiz*, which had collected marine specimens for University of California biologists, hauled cargo between Mexican ports while captained by Maude Lochrane, had been commissioned as a commerce raider by Germans in Mazatlán, starred in a pirate movie filmed off Catalina Island, and finally, used to fish for tuna in southern California waters, had been lost. Within days, the schooner was pounded to pieces by the action of the surf and disappeared beneath the waves.

Like the other participants of the secret war in Mexico, the *Alexander Agassiz* quickly faded from memory and was forgotten, as if it had never existed at all.

NOTES

PROLOGUE

1 **The mutiny on board**: Information on the *Tampico* mutiny is from "Rebel Warship Sunk," *Washington Post*, June 18, 1914, 1; J. H. Klein Jr., *United States Naval Institute Proceedings, The Career of the Mexican Gunboat Tampico* (Annapolis: United States Naval Institute, 1921), 527–55.

1 **As the *Tampico* steamed away**: Klein, *United States Naval Institute Proceedings*, 527.

2 **The mutiny on the gunboat**: Background information on the Mexican Revolution is from Ronald Atkin, *Revolution! Mexico 1910–1920* (New York: John Day, 1970), 103–16, 117–26.

2 **When a courageous senator**: Atkin, *Revolution!* 150.

3 **Hilario Malpica Rodríguez Saliva**: Biographical information on Malpica is from C. G. Marciano Valdez Martinez and Raymundo Bautista Contreras, *Héroes y Próceres del Ejercito, Fuerza Aerea y Armada de Mexico* (Mexico City: Secretariat of National Defense and Secretary of the Mexican Navy, 2011), 291–95.

4 **The *Tampico* steamed into**: Additional information on the aftermath of the *Tampico* mutiny is from Klein, *United States Naval Institute Proceedings*, 528–31.

4 **The U.S. Navy alone**: "Sixteen Warships Sent to Mexican Ports," *New York Times*, June 19, 1916, 1.

6 **The port city of Mazatlán**: *The United States Naval Medical Bulletin, 1915 v.9* (Washington DC: U.S. Government Printing Office, 1915), 167.

6 **The harbor was a hazardous**: *Mexican and Central American Pilotage, Pacific Coast*, 5th ed. (Washington DC: U.S. Hydrographic Office, 1918), 150.

6 **As the *Morelos* steamed**: "Only a Third of Mexican Navy Is Left on Pacific," *San Francisco Chronicle*, May 31, 1914, 4.

6 **"The *Morelos* will be ours"**: "Only a Third of Mexican Navy Is Left on Pacific," 4.

6 **Shortly after five o'clock**: "Former Marion Boy in Mexico," *Marion Daily Star*, June 27, 1914, 9.

7 **Frank Smith, a young Marine**: "Former Marion Boy in Mexico," 9.

7 **Artillery from the Federal fort**: "Only a Third of Mexican Navy Is Left on Pacific," 4.

7 **On the morning of May 7**: "Former Marion Boy in Mexico," 9.

7 **Recognizing the hopelessness**: "Only a Third of Mexican Navy Is Left on Pacific," 4.

8 **"the bridge and foremast became"**: "Only a Third of Mexican Navy Is Left on Pacific," 4.

8 **To speed the *Tampico*'s return**: Klein, *United States Naval Institute Proceedings*, 532–35.

9 **"Can you tow us"**: Klein, *United States Naval Institute Proceedings*, 532.

10 **At about 5:30 p.m.**: Klein, *United States Naval Institute Proceedings*, 532.

11 **True to his vow, Malpica**: Klein, *United States Naval Institute Proceedings*, 538.

11 **"Those boobs on the *Tampico*"**: Klein, *United States Naval Institute Proceedings*, 537.

12 **Captain Malpica stood at the bow**: Information on the capture and death of Malpica is from Klein, *United States Naval Institute Proceedings*, 541–42; Martinez and Contreras, *Héroes y Próceres del Ejercito, Fuerza Aerea y Armada de Mexico*, 294–95; "Rebel Warship Sunk," 4.

12 **We met the captain**: Klein, *United States Naval Institute Proceedings*, 543.

13 **Malpica's body was taken**: Martinez and Contreras, *Héroes y Próceres del Ejercito, Fuerza Aerea y Armada de Mexico*, 295

1. A SIMPLE BUSINESS TRANSACTION

15 **The average depth in the harbor**: "The West Coast of Mexico," *Journal of Electricity*, January 15, 1917, 393.

15 **When the tide was out**: "The West Coast of Mexico," 394.

15 **Over $5 million worth**: "Mazatlán," *Annual Report of the Board of Harbor Commissioners of the City of Los Angeles* (Los Angeles: The Board of Harbor Commissioners of the City of Los Angeles California, 1917), 19.

16 **A seemingly endless line**: Welford Beaton, *Frank Waterhouse & Company's Pacific Ports: A Commercial Geography* (Seattle: Terminal, 1917), 93.

16 **Before it was sunk**: "Mexican Gunboats Bravo and Morelos," *Marine Engineering*, December 1905, 520–21.

17 **The Finance Ministry dutifully placed**: "Minutes of the Meeting Held August 14, 1917," *Diario Oficial de la Federación*.

17 **All parties interested in bidding**: Information on the auction of the gunboat *Morelos* is from Memorandum from W. E. Chapman to State Department, "Supplement No. 1 to Despatch No. 54 of October 17, Subject: Sale of the Mexican Gunboat *Morelos*," October 26, 1917, U.S. National Archives and Records Administration (NARA), State Department Record Group 59 (RG59), Neutrality, M367, Roll 0184, Document No. 763.72111m57/53.

18 **"outcasts from home and country"**: "Slackers Are Now Outcast," *San Bernardino News*, January 8, 1918, 3.

18 **Heintz's stated purpose**: Statement of Cornelius A. Heintz sworn before C. E. Reordan on the USS *Vicksburg* at Sea, March 20, 1918 ("Vicksburg Statement"), NARA, RG59, Neutrality, M367, Roll 0184, Document No. 763.72111m57/60, 1.

18 **At one time Hilbing**: Report by George T. Holman, "Re: Bernard Hilbing," September 28, 1917, NARA, M1085, BI Files, Old German Files, Case No. 8000–6968, 13.

19 **Heintz worked at overhauling**: Heintz, "Vicksburg Statement," 1.

19 **Hilbing had sailed**: Report by F. F. Webster, "Re: Bernard Hilbing," August 27, 1917, NARA, M1085, BI Files, Old German Files, Case No. 8000–6968, 18.

19 **In October 1917 Hilbing's detention**: Memorandum from Attorney General T. W. Gregory to Robert J. O'Connor, United States Attorney, October 16, 1917, NARA, M1085, BI Files, Old German Files, Case No. 8000–6968, 11.

19 **In Mazatlán, Heintz called on**: Heintz, "Vicksburg Statement," 2.

20 **The largest and most powerful**: *Melchers Sucs Mazatlán 1946–1921* [corporate history published to commemorate the company's seventy-fifth anniversary] (Mazatlán: Casa Melchers Sucs, 1921), 1–82; J. Figueroa Doménech, "Melchers Sucesores," *Guía General Descriptiva de la República Mexicana* (Mexico: Estados y Territorios Federales, 1899), 567–70; Brigada Von Menz, Verena Radkau, Beatriz Scharrer, and Guillermo Turner, *Los Pioneros del Imperialismo Aleman en Mexico* (Tlalpan, Mexico: Ediciones de la casa chata, 1982), 132–34. (Originally called "Melchers Hermanos y Cia," the firm was renamed "Merchers Sucesores" in 1869.)

22 **The new law made it illegal**: *Trading with the Enemy* (New York: Guaranty Trust Company of New York, 1917), 41.

22 **Prominent among the enemy firms**: *Trading with the Enemy, Enemy Trading List* (Washington DC: War Trade Board, 1917), 25.

22 **The two managing partners**: *Melchers Sucs Mazatlán 1946–1921*, 7, 20, 21.

23 **Now alone and abandoned**: *Melchers Sucs Mazatlán 1946–1921*, 36–39.

23 **In San José del Cabo**: Report of Commanding Officer of USS *Brutus* to Commander Pacific Fleet Division 2, Subject: Additional Report on Conditions—Mazatlán, March 26, 1918, NARA, RG59, Neutrality, M367, Roll 0184, Document No. 763.72111m57/45, 3.

23 **Vessels flying the American flag**: Report of Commanding Officer of USS *Brutus* to Commander Pacific Fleet Division 2, 3.

23 **U.S. postal authorities would**: Memorandum from W. E. Chapman to State Department, August 5, 1917, NARA, RG59, Neutral Commerce, M367, Roll 0214, Document No. 763.72112/4429; Report by C. L. Keep, "Re: Melchers Sucs Alien Enemy Black List," April 3, 1918, Investigative Reports of the Bureau of Investigation 1908–1922, NARA, M1085, Roll: boi_german_257-850_0041, Old German File 1909–1921, Case No. 8000–111649, 1–7.

23 **In some cases, local companies**: American Consul B. F. Yost to State Department, "Possible Enemy Activity and Trading at San Jose del Cabo, Lower California," August 5, 1917, NARA, RG59, Neutrality, M367, Roll 0230, Document No. 763.72112/9794.

24 **"the business of the most important"**: *Report of the War Trade Board* (Washington DC: Government Printing Office 1920), 57.

24 **Their first product was**: Even today, Cerveza Pacífico Clara remains one of Mexico's most popular beers.

24 **The senior partner**: Heintz, "Vicksburg Statement," 2.

25 **It was a thrilling spectacle**: "Only a Third of Mexican Navy Is Left on Pacific," *San Francisco Chronicle*, May 31, 1914, 4.

25 **After examining the wreck**: Paul Bernardo Altendorf, "U.S. Agent Foils Carranza Plot to Supply Germans with Tender for U-Boat off California Coast," *El Paso Herald*, November 29, 1919, 1, 20.

25 **There had been no dynamiting**: Description of the condition of the gunboat Morelos from Report of Commanding Officer of USS *Brutus* to Commander Pacific Fleet Division 2, 2.

26 **Based on the positive appraisal**: Altendorf, "U.S. Agent Foils Carranza Plot," 1.

27 **Hinsch's plan to obtain**: Henry Landau, *The Enemy Within* (New York: Putnam's, 1937), 182–83, 245, 247.

27 **"Tell 2584 [Hinsch]"**: Landau, *The Enemy Within*, 245.

27 **Pochet would later tell**: Landau, *The Enemy Within*, 182–83.

27 **When the war began**: Dan van der Vat, *Gentlemen of War: The Amazing Story of Karl von Müller and the SMS* Emden (New York: William Morrow, 1983), 42.

28 **"You are hereby . . . detached"**: van der Vat, *Gentlemen of War*, 41.

28 **During the next three months**: van der Vat, *Gentlemen of War*, 119.

28 **The landing party from the *Emden***: van der Vat, *Gentlemen of War*, 125–40.

29 **As the war progressed**: E. Keble Chatterton, *The Sea Raiders* (London: Hurst and Blackett, 1931), 193–95.

29 **The first of these disguised**: Richard Guilliatt and Peter Hohnen, *The Wolf* (New York: Simon and Schuster, 2010), 27.

29 **"Her masts had been rebuilt"**: Guillatt and Hohnen, *The Wolf*, 27.

29 **The *Wolf* was armed**: Guillatt and Hohnen, *The Wolf*, 32–36.

30 **the ever-present need for coal**: Chatterton, *The Sea Raiders*, 18–20.

30 **The German navy had anticipated**: Chatterton, *The Sea Raiders*, 25–28; van der Vat, *Gentlemen of War*, 34–35.

30 **The man in charge**: John Price Jones, *The German Spy in America* (London: Hutchinson, 1917), 113–31.

31 **In August 1914 a cable**: "$2,000,000 Spent by Boy-Ed Here on German Plot," *New York Times*, November 24, 1915, 1, 4; John Price Jones, *The German Spy in America*, 113–31.

32　**Boy-Ed arranged for the Deutsche Bank**: "$2,000,000 Spent by Boy-Ed Here on German Plot," 4.

32　**Shortly before dawn**: "German Warship Coaled by Trick," *Trenton Evening News* (Trenton NJ), October 6, 1914, 2; "Mazatlán Is Held with Her Cargo of Coal," *San Francisco Chronicle*, August 21, 1914, 14.

33　**In loading a cargo of coal**: "Neutrality Not Violated," *San Francisco Chronicle*, November 28, 1914, 1.

33　**In the estuary**: Report of Commanding Officer of USS *Brutus* to Commander Pacific Fleet Division 2, 2.

2. "I WILL SHOOT YOU DOWN LIKE A DOG!"

35　**The streets of old Mazatlán**: "Miller Finds Mexico Safe," *Oxnard Courier* (Oxnard CA), January 19, 1917, 3.

35　**He spoke Spanish**: "Miller Finds Mexico Safe," 3.

36　**Unger walked to his desk**: Report by H. B. Mock, "In re: One Connors: Pro-German Subject and Espionage Act Investigation," September 28, 1917, NARA, M1085, BI Files, Old German Files, Case No. 162413, 9.

37　**Their conversation was interrupted**: Paul Bernardo Altendorf, "Calles Discovers German Agents Robbing Him," *El Paso Herald*, November 18, 1919, 10.

37　**That evening, the pair met**: Altendorf, "Calles Discovers German Agents Robbing Him," 10.

38　**Dr. Altendorf made a strong**: Report by William Neunhoffer to A. Bruce Bielaski, Number 30 for week ending October 2, 1917, NARA, M1085, BI Files, Old German Files, Case No. 54263, 65–66.

38　**Altendorf had been born**: Background information on Paul Bernardo Altendorf is from Paul Bernardo Altendorf, Questionaire for Applicant for the Corps of Interpreters, May 1, 1919, NARA, RG165, Records of the War Department and Special Staffs, Military Intelligence Division, File 51–45; Captain Henry G. Pratt, Memorandum for Colonel Martin, April 10, 1919, NARA, RG165, Records of the War Department and Special Staffs, Military Intelligence Division, File 51–45.

39　**When the world war began**: Paul Bernardo Altendorf, "On Secret Service in Mexico," *El Paso Herald*, November 3, 1919, 4.

39　**"if only because of the fact"**: Atkin, *Revolution!* 296.

39　**The governor of Yucatán**: *Investigation of Mexican Affairs: Preliminary Report and Hearings of the Committee on Foreign Relations United States Senate Pursuant to S. Res. 106* (Washington DC: Government Printing Office, 1920), 1229–30.

39　**Altendorf moved to Frontera**: *Investigation of Mexican Affairs*, 1229–30.

39　**From Veracruz, Altendorf set out**: Altendorf, "On Secret Service in Mexico," 4.

40　**I handed one of my**: Altendorf, "On Secret Service in Mexico," 1.

40 **The train had traveled**: Altendorf, "On Secret Service in Mexico," November 4, 1919, 1, 7.

41 **I sprang to the ground**: Altendorf, "On Secret Service in Mexico," November 4, 1919, 7.

41 **As the train drew slowly**: Altendorf, "On Secret Service in Mexico," 1.

41 **In the days that followed**: Altendorf, "On Secret Service in Mexico," November 5, 1919, 1.

42 **Four days after Altendorf**: Altendorf, "On Secret Service in Mexico," November 5, 1919, 1.

42 **Following a genial conversation**: Altendorf, "On Secret Service in Mexico," 1.

43 **He evidently wanted to size me up**: Altendorf, "On Secret Service in Mexico," 10.

44 **After his dinner meeting**: Altendorf, "On Secret Service in Mexico," 10.

44 **At the Hotel Cosmos**: Altendorf, "On Secret Service in Mexico," 1.

45 **The year before, a raid**: Charles H. Harris III and Louis R. Sadler, "The Witzke Affair: German Intrigue on the Mexican Border 1917–1918," *Military Review*, February 1979, 36.

45 **When they had obtained**: Altendorf, "On Secret Service in Mexico," 10.

45 **"It may come in handy"**: Paul Bernardo Altendorf, "German Spy Agents Get Warm Reception from Mexicans as They Travel across Country Plotting against the U.S.," *El Paso Herald*, November 7, 1919, 1.

46 **"We will drive the American"**: Altendorf, "German Spy Agents Get Warm Reception," 1.

46 **It was the bandit attack**: Altendorf, "German Spy Agents Get Warm Reception," 1.

46 **Schwiertz haggled with a Turk**: Altendorf, "German Spy Agents Get Warm Reception," 10.

47 **When they reached Hermosillo**: Paul Bernardo Altendorf, "German Secret Spies Plot in Mexico to Murder for Money As Well As to Make War on U.S. from Sonora," *El Paso Herald*, November 8, 1919, 3.

47 **"General, let me introduce"**: Paul Bernardo Altendorf, "Calles Admits to American Agent That Invasion of the United States from Mexico Is Secretly Planned," *El Paso Herald*, November 10, 1919, 5.

47 **"Oh yes, we have enough men"**: Altendorf, "Calles Admits to American Agent," 5.

48 **When they reached**: Paul Bernardo Altendorf, "American Deserter Put a Crimp for Time Being into Efforts of Germans to Invade United States," *El Paso Herald*, November 11, 1919, 1.

49 **"You must help me"**: Paul Bernardo Altendorf, "Renegade Americans Start Mutiny among German-Mexican Plotters Planning an Invasion of the U.S.," *El Paso Herald*, November 12, 1919, 1.

49 **It was late afternoon**: Altendorf, "Renegade Americans Start Mutiny," 1.

50 **Altendorf immediately called on**: Altendorf, "Renegade Americans Start Mutiny," 10.

50 **The next day, a telegram**: Paul Bernardo Altendorf, "American Spy Has German Banished into United States against Which He Has Been Plotting from Mexico," *El Paso Herald*, November 13, 1919, 1.

50 **He arranged for**: Altendorf, "American Spy Has German Banished," 1, 5.

51 **Schwiertz was evidently surprised**: Altendorf, "American Spy Has German Banished," 5.

51 **Altendorf would later learn**: Paul Bernardo Altendorf, "American Agent Is Forced to Fight for Life against Kaiser's Spies But Builds a Backfire under Them," *El Paso Herald*, November 14, 1919, 1, 3; Schwiertz's escape to Lower California noted in letter from R. H. Van Deman to A. Bruce Bielaski, May 4, 1918 NARA, M1085, Investigative Reports of the Bureau of investigation 1908–1922, Roll: boi_german_257-850_0065, Old German File 1909–1921, Case No. 8000-480, 305.

52 **In late 1917 a courier**: Paul Bernardo Altendorf, "American Agent Cures General Calles and Falls In with Female German Spies Smuggling Goods to Mexico," *El Paso Herald*, November 15, 1919, 1.

52 **Altendorf went "shopping"**: Paul Bernardo Altendorf, "German Submarines as Effective in Commerce as in Murder at Sea; Carried Food Cargoes from Mexico," *El Paso Herald*, November 28, 1919, 1.

52 **Altendorf informed Governor Calles**: Paul Bernardo Altendorf, "American Secret Agent Discovers a German Plot in Mexico to Bomb El Paso and Other Cities on Border," *El Paso Herald*, November 17, 1919, 3.

53 **This man has been continuously**: Memorandum from Major S. W. Anding, 35th Infantry Intelligence Officer to Department Intelligence Officer, Fort Sam Houston, Texas, "Subject: Informant A-1," December 16, 1917, NARA, RG165, Records of the War Department and Special Staffs, Military Intelligence Division, File 51–45.

53 **Jahnke suggested that Altendorf**: Paul Bernardo Altendorf, "U.S. Agent in Mexico Invades German Spy Files; El Paso Letter Reveals Plot to Blow Up Canal," *El Paso Herald*, November 21, 1919, 1, 7.

54 **Alone in the house for thirteen days**: Altendorf, "U.S. Agent in Mexico Invades German Spy Files," 7.

54 **He also had the opportunity**: Altendorf, "U.S. Agent in Mexico Invades German Spy Files," 7.

54 **The train carrying Jahnke**: Paul Bernardo Altendorf, "U.S. Agent Is Ordered to Join Mission to Border to Arrange Mexican-German Invasion of U.S.," *El Paso Herald*, November 22, 1919, 1.

55 **"Well, Witzke," the spymaster began**: Altendorf, "U.S. Agent Is Ordered to Join Mission," 1.

55 **Witzke's assignment was**: Altendorf, "U.S. Agent Is Ordered to Join Mission," 1, 12.

55 **"and subvert the Black 9th and 10th Cavalry"**: Harris and Sadler, "The Witzke Affair," 37.

56 **"Doctor, listen very carefully"**: Altendorf, "U.S. Agent Is Ordered to Join Mission," 12.

56 **"You must do away with"**: Altendorf, "U.S. Agent Is Ordered to Join Mission," 12.

56 **The agents gathered later**: Altendorf, "U.S. Agent Is Ordered to Join Mission," 12.

57 **Turning to face Altendorf**: Altendorf, "U.S. Agent Is Ordered to Join Mission," 12.

57 **On January 16, 1918**: Paul Bernardo Altendorf, "U.S. Agent Gets German Agent Drunk Making Copies of Secret Papers; Finds British Agent Trailing Spy," *El Paso Herald*, November 25, 1919, 1.

57 **They reached Irapuato**: Altendorf, "U.S. Agent Gets German Agent Drunk," 1.

58 **The steamship docked at Mazatlán**: Altendorf, "U.S. Agent Gets German Agent Drunk," 10.

58 **January 26th, 10 a.m. to Butcher**: Landau, *The Enemy Within*, 118.

58 **Would you not have Joe Bru**: Joe Bru was a Rumanian also employed by the Military Intelligence office in Nogales to report on German activities in Sonora. Bru's code name was "Agent B-1."

58 **Calles received them cordially**: Altendorf, "U.S. Agent Gets German Agent Drunk," 10.

58 **A few days later, Witzke**: Altendorf, "U.S. Agent Gets German Agent Drunk," 10.

59 **When he reached Nogales**: Letter from A. J. Milliken, Inspector in Charge, to the Supervising Inspector, Immigration Service, July 12, 1918, NARA, RG165, Records of the War Department and Special Staffs, Military Intelligence Division Correspondence 1917–1941, File 41–161 to 51–57, Box 39, 1.

59 **Learning that Witzke**: Landau, *The Enemy Within*, 119.

59 **As soon as Witzke passed**: Landau, *The Enemy Within*, 120; Altendorf, "U.S. Agent Gets German Agent Drunk," 10.

59 **Now safe in America**: Paul Bernardo Altendorf, "U.S. Agent's Work Traps at Border German Spy on Mission of Murder; Captured Papers Bare German Code," *El Paso Herald*, November 26, 1919, 10.

60 **"The mission is exceedingly"**: Paul Bernardo Altendorf, "U.S. Agent Disguised as Doctor, Returns to Mexico to Trail Spies, Knowing Mission May Mean Death," *El Paso Herald*, November 27, 1919, 1.

60 **Butcher outlined the objectives**: Altendorf, "U.S. Agent Disguised as Doctor," 1.

60 **"Doctor, I might as well"**: Altendorf, "U.S. Agent Disguised as Doctor," 5.

60 **"Where is Witzke?"**: Altendorf, "German Submarines as Effective in Commerce," 10.

61 **I am in Los Angeles**: Altendorf, "German Submarines as Effective in Commerce," 10.

61 **The laborer stopped by**: Paul Bernardo Altendorf, "U.S. Agent Foils Carranza Plot to Supply Germans with Tender for U-Boat off California Coast," *El Paso Herald*, November 29, 1919, 1.

62 **The Carranza government would**: Altendorf, "U.S. Agent Foils Carranza Plot," 1.

3. THE *ALEXANDER AGASSIZ*

63 **The contract signed with**: Information on the charter voyage for Señor Meistierro from Deposition of Miss Maude M. Lochrane, March 30, 1918, Alexander Agassiz Prize Court Trial Records, NARA Riverside, RG21, Records of the United States District Courts, U.S. District Court for the Southern District of California, Civil Law Case–622–636, Folder Title 624, Box 59, 9–14; Report by V. W. Killick, "Re: Ship Alexander Agassiz, Letter from Maude Lochrane to Joseph Mesmer," March 26, 1918, NARA, M1085, BI Files, Old German Files, Case No. 170046, 24; Report by Robert Burrous, "In Re: Fred F. Osborn," March 13, 1918, NARA, M1085, BI Files, Old German Files, Roll 568, Case No. 170046, 5; Report by David Gershon, "In Re: Power Boat Alexander Agassiz, Interview with Maude Lochrane," April 5, 1918, NARA, M1085, BI Files, Old German Files, Case No. 170046, 7–16.

64 **Maude Lochrane was ahead**: Background of Maude Lochrane from Report by V. W. Killick, "Re: Ship Alexander Agassiz," March 23, 1918, NARA, M1085, BI Files, Old German Files, Case No. 170046, 39–43; Detroit City Directory 1903; San Bernardino City Directory 1906 and 1908.

65 **One man who knew her**: "Former Oxnard Man Sees Capture of Raider Agassiz," *Oxnard Daily Courier*, March 29, 1918, 3.

65 **Maude was "quite an entertaining talker"**: Report by Robert Burrous, "In Re: Fred F. Osborn," March 13, 1918, NARA, M1085, BI Files, Old German Files, Roll 568, Case No. 170046, 5.

65 **Her rising stature became**: "Syndicate Is Formed," *San Bernardino Daily Sun*, November 14, 1907, 1–2.

66 **One reader took particular interest**: "Is Anxious to Find a Girl," *San Bernardino Daily Sun*, September 18, 1908, 3.

67 **Whether Maude Lochrane**: El Paso City Directory 1910, 1911, and 1912; Los Angeles City Directory 1915.

67 **At this point she met**: Report by V. W. Killick, "In Re: Ship Alexander Agassiz, letter from William Taylor to Joseph Mesmer, dated June 8, 1917," April 23, 1918, NARA, M1085, BI Files, Old German Files, Roll 568, Case No. 170046, 2.

68 **In 1903 a Harvard-educated**: Elizabeth N. Shor, "How Scripps Institution Came to San Diego," *San Diego Historical Quarterly* 27, no. 3 (Summer 1981): 1–6; Helen Raitt, "Alexander Agassiz," SIO Subject Files, 81–26. Special Collections & Archives UC San Diego Library, Alexander Agassiz 1908–1910, Box 58, Folder 11, 1–4.

68 **Named after an eminent**: Raitt, "Alexander Agassiz," 2; "Biographic File–Fred Baker," SIO Subject Files, 81–26. Special Collections & Archives UC San Diego Library, Folder 30, January–March 1907, and Folder 32, November–December 1907.

69 **"the boat is above criticism"**: Letter from Fred Baker to Dr. Ritter, November 9, 1907, SIO Bibliographical Files, 81–17. Special Collections & Archives UC San Diego Library, 81–26, Folder 32, November–December 1907, 5.

69 **On February 13, 1912**: Shor, "How Scripps Institution Came to San Diego," 6.

69 **One of the assets transferred**: *Biennial Report of the President of the University on Behalf of the Regents to His Excellency the Governor of the State 1910–1912* (Berkeley: University of California Press, 1912), 254.

69 **Now part of the state**: Raitt, "Alexander Agassiz," 3.

69 **Then in late 1916**: Letter from William Taylor to W. C. Crandall, December 7, 1916, SIO Subject Files, 81–26. Special Collections & Archives UC San Diego Library. "Alexander Agassiz 1916–1920," Box 58, Folder 10.

70 **After conferring with university**: Letter from the Business Manager, Scripps Institution, to Pacific Coast Trading and Shipping, December 8, 1916, SIO Subject Files, 81–26. Special Collections & Archives UC San Diego Library. "Alexander Agassiz 1916–1920," Box 58, Folder 10.

70 **Maude contacted her brother**: Report by V. W. Killick, "Re: The Ship Alexander Agassiz," March 23, 1918, NARA, M1085, BI Files, Old German Files, Case No. 170046, 41–43.

70 **Joseph Mesmer was the president**: Background of Joseph Mesmer is from James Miller Guinn, *A History of California and An Extended History of Los Angeles and Environs, Biographical Volume III* (Los Angeles: Historic Record Company, 1915), 925–26.

71 **Maude became acquainted**: Report by V. W. Killick, "Re: The Ship Alexander Agassiz," March 23, 1918, 44.

71 **Maude, Frank Wheeler, and**: Report by V. W. Killick, "Re: The Ship Alexander Agassiz," March 23, 1918, 41–42.

71 **With a $5,000 surety bond**: *Annual Report of the President of the University on Behalf of the Regents to His Excellency the Governor of the State 1916–1917*, 287.

72 **The *Alexander Agassiz* was immediately**: Letter from W. C. Crandall to Joseph Mesmer describing alterations that Pacific Coast Trading made to Alexander Agassiz, undated, SIO Subject Files, 81–26. Special Collections & Archives UC San Diego Library. "Alexander Agassiz 1916–1920," Box 58, Folder 10.

72 **events were unfolding in Washington**: "Transfer of American Vessels to Foreign Registry," *Second Annual Report of the United States Shipping Board, December 1, 1918* (Washington DC: Government Printing Office, 1918), 36–37.

73 **To improve their ability**: Report by David Gershon on Maude Lochrane interview, "In Re: Power Boat Alexander Agassiz, Interview with Maude Lochrane," April 5, 1918, NARA, M1085, BI Files, Old German Files, Case No. 170046, 17.

73 **"Change that flag back"**: Letter from Maude Lochrane to Joseph Mesmer, dated January 10, 1918, enclosed with report by V. W. Killick, "Re: Ship Alexander Agassiz," March 25, 1918, NARA, M1085, BI Files, Old German Files, Case No. 170046, 4.

73 **The most exciting part**: "Former Oxnard Man Sees Capture of Raider Agassiz," 3.

73 **After hours spent wandering**: Letter from Maude Lochrane to Joseph Mesmer, dated June 5, 1917, from report by V. W. Killick, "Re: Ship Alexander Agassiz," March 25, 1918, 21.

74 **They contacted the French consul**: Statement written by H. A. Macintosh to David Gershon, March 28, 1918, NARA, M1085, BI Files, Old German Files, Case No. 170046, 36.

74 **Wheeler and Taylor bond the boat**: Letter from Maude Lochrane to Joseph Mesmer, dated November 25, 1917, included in report by V. W. Killick, "Re: Ship Alexander Agassiz," March 26, 1918, NARA, M1085, BI Files, Old German Files, Case No. 170046, 6.

74 **H. A. Macintosh, an American trader**: Information on Wheeler and Taylor's dealings with trader H. A. Macintosh from Statement written by H. A. Macintosh to David Gershon, March 28, 1918, NARA, M1085, BI Files, Old German Files, Case No. 170046, 33–37.

75 **"Wheeler and Taylor had made a mess"**: "Woman Pirate Tells Story of Her Life," *Daily Twin Falls Times*, April 23, 1918, 6.

76 **Taylor informed her**: Report by David Gershon on Maude Lochrane interview, "In Re: Power Boat Alexander Agassiz, Interview with Maude Lochrane," April 5, 1918, NARA, M1085, BI Files, Old German Files, Case No. 170046, 16.

76 **When Maude returned to Mazatlán**: Letter from Maude Lochrane to Joseph Mesmer, dated January 31, 1918, included in report by V. W. Killick, "Re: Ship Alexander Agassiz," March 25, 1918, 30.

77 **Gaining full ownership**: Information on the transfer of Frank Wheeler's and William Taylor's interest in Pacific Coast Trading to Maude Lochrane from Deposition of Miss Maude M. Lochrane, March 30, 1918, Prize Court Trial, Civil Law Case-622-636, Folder Title 624, Box 59, 11–13; Bill of sale, dated August 6, 1917, from William Taylor to Miss Maude M. Lochrane, Prize Court Trial, Civil Law Case-622-636, Folder Title 624, Box 59.

77 **"The *Alexander Agassiz* is an American boat"**: Letter from Maude Lochrane to Joseph Mesmer, dated January 10, 1918, included in report by V. W. Killick, "Re: Ship Alexander Agassiz," March 25, 1918, 27–28.

77 **She appealed by wire**: Letter from Maude Lochrane to Joseph Mesmer, dated January 10, 1918, included in report by V. W. Killick, "Re: Ship Alexander Agassiz," March 25, 1918, 28.

78 **In the American store**: Report by Robert Burrous, "In Re: Fred F. Osborn," March 13, 1918, NARA, M1085, BI Files, Old German Files, Roll 568, Case No. 170046, 4–5.

78 **At this dark moment**: Report by David Gershon, "In Re: Power Boat Alexander Agassiz, Interview with Maude Lochrane," April 5, 1918, NARA, M1085, BI Files, Old German Files, Case No. 170046, 12, 15.

79 **Maude placed great confidence**: Report by V. W. Killick, "Re: Ship Alexander Agassiz," March 23, 1918, 40.

4. FOR HONOR AND FATHERLAND

This chapter detailing German Consul Fritz Unger's involvement in planning the *Alexander Agassiz* raider expedition, is based on the three sworn statements of Cornelius Heintz:

1. Affidavit of Cornelius Adolph Heintz sworn before W. E. Chapman at the U.S. Consulate at Mazatlán, March 9, 1918 ("Consulate Affidavit"), NARA, RG59, Neutrality, M367, Roll 0184, Document No. 763.72111m57/60, 8.
2. Statement of Cornelius A. Heintz sworn before C. E. Reordan on the USS Vicksburg at Sea, March 20 ("Vicksburg Statement"), NARA, RG59, Neutrality, M367, Roll 0184, Document No. 763.72111m57/60, 9–14.
3. Deposition of C. A. Heintz sworn before the U.S. District Court for the southern district of California, San Diego, March 29, 1918 ("Prize Court Deposition"), Alexander Agassiz Prize Court Trial Records, NARA Riverside, RG21, Records of the United States District Courts, U.S. District Court for the Southern District of California, Civil Law Case–622–636, Folder Title 624, Box no. 59.

81 **In September 1917**: Report by David Gershon, "In Re: Power Boat Alexander Agassiz, Interview with Maude Lochrane," 8.

81 **"Melchers Sucs, during my"**: Statement written by H. A. Macintosh to David Gershon, March 28, 1918, NARA, M1085, BI Files, Old German Files, Case No. 170046, 33.

81 **He would later recall**: Information on Unger's meeting with Cornelius Heintz and Fritz Bauman from Heintz, "Vicksburg Statement," 1–6; Heintz, "Prize Court Deposition," 1–20.

84 **The proposal from the two Norwegians**: Heintz, "Prize Court Deposition," 17–18.

84 **Madden was, in fact**: Background of Madden (Arthur Martens) from Report by David Ross, "In Re: Arthur Martens, on Board Alexander Agassiz, German Raider," April 9, 1918, NARA, M1085, BI Files, Old German Files, Case No. 174275,

1; Report by C. L. Keep, "In Re: Ship Alexander Agassiz," April 6, 1918, NARA, M1085, BI Files, Old German Files, Case No. 170046, 20; Memorandum from Executive Officer USS *Vicksburg* to Commanding Officer, "Subject: Statements of Prisoners Taken from Alexander Agassiz March 18, 1918," NARA, RG59, Neutrality, M367, Roll 0184, Document No. 763.72111m57/60, 16.

85 **At the insistence of**: Letter from Maude Lochrane to Joseph Mesmer, dated January 31, 1918, included in report by V. W. Killick, "Re: Ship Alexander Agassiz," March 25, 1918, 29–30.

85 **The port city of Santa Rosalía**: G. A. Martin, "Some Still Remain in Port on Gulf of California at Santa Rosalía," *El Paso Herald*, April 12, 1921, 1.

86 **Bauman knew the officers**: Information on Captain Bauman's visit to Santa Rosalía and the briefing of the *Agassiz* crew by Unger from Heintz, "Vicksburg Statement," 1–6; Heintz "Prize Court Deposition," 1–20.

87 **Frank Volpert was**: Background of Frank Volpert from Deposition of Frank Volpert, Prize Court Trial, Civil Law Case–622–636, Folder Title 624, Box 59; Memorandum from Executive Officer USS *Vicksburg* to Commanding Officer, "Subject: Statements of Prisoners Taken from Alexander Agassiz March 18, 1918," NARA, RG59, Neutrality, M367, Roll 0184, Document No. 763.72111m57/60, 16.

87 **Hendrik Koppalla was**: Background of Hendrik Koppalla from Deposition of Hendrik Koppalla, Prize Court Trial, Civil Law Case–622–636, Folder Title 624, Box 59; Memorandum from Executive Officer USS *Vicksburg* to Commanding Officer, "Subject: Statements of Prisoners Taken from Alexander Agassiz March 18, 1918," NARA, RG59, Neutrality, M367, Roll 0184, Document No. 763.72111m57/60, 16.

87 **Richard Brandt was**: Background of Richard Brandt from Report by W. A. Weymouth, "In Re: Richard Charles Brandt, German Activities," NARA, M1085, BI Files, Old German Files, Roll 602, Case No. 197038, 1; Report by V. W. Killick, "Re: Ship Alexander Agassiz," March 25, 1918, 3; Deposition of Richard Brandt, Prize Court Trial, Civil Law Case–622–636, Folder Title 624, Box 59; Memorandum from Executive Officer USS *Vicksburg* to Commanding Officer, "Subject: Statements of Prisoners Taken from Alexander Agassiz March 18, 1918," 15.

87 **Charles Boston was**: Background of Charles Boston from Deposition of Charles Franklin Boston (Prize Court Deposition), Prize Court Trial, Civil Law Case–622–636, Folder Title 624, Box 59, 1; Memorandum from Executive Officer USS *Vicksburg* to Commanding Officer, "Subject: Statements of Prisoners Taken from Alexander Agassiz March 18, 1918," 15.

89 **A few miles from the German**: Letter from Maude Lochrane to Joseph Mesmer, dated February 24, 1918, included in report by V. W. Killick, "Re: Ship Alexander Agassiz," March 25, 1918, 22; Report by V. W. Killick, "Re: Ship Alexander

Agassiz," May 6, 1918, NARA, M1085, BI Files, Old German Files, Roll 568, Case No. 170046, 13.

5. "SHE IS AN OUTLAW AND A DANGEROUS ENEMY"

91 **William Edgar Chapman was born**: Background of William Edgar Chapman from "Biographical Statement Respecting Persons Serving under Appointment of the Department of State," *Register of the Department of State 23 December 1918* (Washington DC: Government Printing Office, 1919), 94. (The population of Mount Pisgah in 2014 was 101.)

93 **He was to consult with**: Memorandum from Wilbur J. Carr to William E. Chapman, April 17, 1918, NARA, RG59, Neutrality, M367, Documents No. 763.72112A/9735 and 763.72112A/1463x.

93 **On July 31, 1917, Chapman**: Memorandum from Henri Claisse to W. E. Chapman, July 31, 1917, NARA, RG59, Neutrality, M367, Roll 0214, Document No. 763.72112/4429 (file date: August 5, 1917).

93 **A communiqué with similar information**: Letter from Theodore Watson to W. E. Chapman, August 4, 1917, NARA, RG59, Neutrality, M367, Roll 0214, Document No. 763.72112/4429 (file date: August 5, 1917).

94 **After receiving information from**: Telegram from Chapman to the Secretary of State, September 7, 1917, NARA, RG59, Neutrality, M367, Roll 0215, Document No. 763.72112/4679 (file date: September 7, 1917).

94 **I am told by an American**: Memorandum from Chapman to the Secretary of State, "Supplement to Despatch No. 29 of August 5, 1917, Subject: Prohibition or Regulation of Exportation to Anti-American Firms in Mexico," October 24, 1917, NARA, RG59, Neutrality, M367, Roll 0218, Document No. 763.72112/5418.

95 **In response, Chapman's superiors**: Letter from Herman Oliphant to Marion Letcher, November 15, 1917, NARA, RG59, Neutrality, M367, Roll 0218, Document No. 763.72112/5575.

95 **During the summer of 1917**: Letter from Wilbur J. Carr acting for Secretary of State to W. E. Chapman, August 17, 1917, NARA, RG59, Neutrality, M367, Document No. 763.72/5606.

96 **Mr. Chapman, the American Consul**: Report for the Commanding Officer of the USS *Brutus* to Commander Division Two, Pacific Fleet, February 25, 1918, NARA, RG59, Neutrality, M367.

96 **On December 15, Chapman wired**: Telegram from W. E. Chapman to Dr. Oliphant, War Trade Board Fleet, December 15, 1917, NARA, RG59, Neutrality, M367.

97 **"the consul [Unger] is furious"**: Report of Commanding Officer of USS *Brutus* to Commander Pacific Fleet Division 2, Subject: Additional Report on Conditions–Mazatlán, March 26, 1918, NARA, RG59, Neutrality, M367, Roll 0184, Document No. 763.72111m57/45, 2.

97 **Chapman also gained**: Affidavit of Gustaf Danielson sworn before W. E. Chapman, March 5, 1918, NARA, RG59, Neutral Commerce, M367, Roll 0225, Document No. 763.72112/7770.

98 **Chapman contacted the State Department**: Telegram from Chapman to the Secretary of State, October 11, 1917, NARA, RG59, Neutrality, M367, Roll 0170, Document No. 763.72111/5655.

99 **"I kept the American consul"**: Heintz, "Vicksburg Statement," 2.

99 **Heintz paid a surprise visit**: Heintz, "Vicksburg Statement," 3.

100 **Chapman instructed Heintz**: W. E. Chapman statement to Captain C. E. Reordan, March 14, 1918, NARA, RG59, Neutrality, M367, Roll 0184, Document No. 763.72111m57/45 (file date: March 20, 1918); Heintz, "Prize Court Deposition," 7.

101 **Chapman responded by sending**: Telegram from W. E. Chapman to the Secretary of State, March 9, 1918, NARA, RG59, Neutrality, M367, Roll 0184, Document No. 763.72111m57/56.

101 **Blue jackets were soon hunched**: U.S. Navy radiogram messages are from: W. F. Fullam to the Secretary of the Navy (Operations), State Department, "Re: Complaint of Mexican Ambassador of Action of United States Naval Vessels Lying off Port of Mazatlán, Enclosure: File of Radiograms," August 23, 1918 NARA, RG59, Neutrality, M367, Roll 0184, Document No. 763.72111m57/45, 11–14.

104 **At 1:43 a.m. on March 15**: Report from C. E. Reordan to Secretary of the Navy (Operations)—"Subject: Capture of Auxiliary Yawl 'Alexander Agassiz,'" March 20, 1918, NARA, RG59, Neutrality, M367, Roll 0184, Document No. 763.72111m57/45.

104 **Reordan arrived at the consulate**: Information on meeting between C. E. Reordan and W. E. Chapman from Report from C. E. Reordan to Secretary of the Navy (Operations)—"Subject: Capture of Auxiliary Yawl 'Alexander Agassiz.'"

106 **Reordan next paid a courtesy**: Information on inspection of *Alexander Agassiz* by C. E. Reordan from Report from C. E. Reordan to Secretary of the Navy (Operations)—"Subject: Capture of Auxiliary Yawl 'Alexander Agassiz,'" 1.

106 **He returned to the *Vicksburg***: W. F. Fullam to the Secretary of the Navy, State Department, "Re: Complaint of Mexican Ambassador, File of Radiograms," 15.

107 **At dusk, he sent**: Report from C. E. Reordan to Secretary of the Navy (Operations)—"Subject: Capture of Auxiliary Yawl 'Alexander Agassiz,'" 1.

107 **"signaling from the shore"**: Boston, "Prize Court Deposition," 1.

108 **Doubts about Heintz's loyalty**: Heintz, "Vicksburg Statement," 6; Heintz "Prize Court Deposition," 13.

108 **"You had better be"**: Heintz, "Vicksburg Statement," 6.

6. "IF YOU WANT TO GET THE BEST OF UNCLE SAM"

109 **Operation Michael**: Information on Germany's Michael Offensive from John Toland, *No Man's Land* (New York: Ballantine Books, 1980), 14–18.

110 **On the morning of March 16**: Report from C. E. Reordan to Secretary of the Navy (Operations)—Subject: Capture of Auxiliary Yawl 'Alexander Agassiz,' " 2.

110 **Reordan sent a wireless message**: W. F. Fullam to the Secretary of the Navy, State Department "Re: Complaint of Mexican Ambassador, File of Radiograms," 15.

111 **Reordan's commander at the Pacific Fleet**: W. F. Fullam to the Secretary of the Navy, State Department, "Re: Complaint of Mexican Ambassador, File of Radiograms," 17.

111 **Heintz received word from Consul**: Information on the provisioning and departure of the *Alexander Agassiz* from Heintz, "Vicksburg Statement," 4–5; Heintz, "Prize Court Deposition," 6, 10, 17; Deposition of Lt. Charles Edwin Reordan ("Prize Court Deposition"), Prize Court Trial, Civil Law Case–622–636, Folder Title 624, Box 59, 6.

113 **Standing on the starboard**: Deposition of Richard Brandt ("Prize Court Deposition"), Prize Court Trial, Civil Law Case–622–636, Folder Title 624, Box 59, 14.

113 **"It can go a whole lot faster"**: Brandt, "Prize Court Deposition," 14.

113 **As they proceeded**: Information on the location of crewmembers before the capture of the *Agassiz* from individual prize court depositions of Martens, Heintz, Koppalla, Boston, and Volpert, Prize Court Trial, Civil Law Case–622–636, Folder Title 624, Box 59.

114 **"They want us to stop!"**: Deposition of Hendrik Koppalla ("Prize Court Deposition"), Prize Court Trial, Civil Law Case–622–636, Folder Title 624, Box 59, 10.

114 **Shortly after noon**: Information on the capture of the *Alexander Agassiz* from Report from C. E. Reordan to Secretary of the Navy (Operations)—"Subject: Capture of Auxiliary Yawl 'Alexander Agassiz,' " 2; Reordan, "Prize Court Deposition," 2, 3, 10–12.

115 **He described his experiences**: "Former Oxnard Man Sees Capture of Raider Agassiz," *Oxnard Daily Courier*, March 29, 1918, 3.

116 **While the gunboat was**: Deposition of Paymaster Edwin Y. Armstrong ("Prize Court Deposition"), Prize Court Trial, Civil Law Case–622–636, Folder Title 624, Box 59, 5–6; Deposition of Lt. Frederick W. Dorr ("Prize Court Deposition"), Prize Court Trial, Civil Law Case–622–636, Folder Title 624, Box 59, 6–7; Reordan, "Prize Court Deposition," 10.

116 **The whaleboat was lowered**: Information on the search of the *Alexander Agassiz* from Dorr, "Prize Court Deposition," 2–9; Heintz, "Prize Court Deposition," 13.

119 **The *Vicksburg* steamed to**: Report from C. E. Reordan to Secretary of the Navy (Operations)—"Subject: Capture of Auxiliary Yawl 'Alexander Agassiz,' " 2–3; Reordan, "Prize Court Deposition," 2.

120 **The *Vicksburg* remained in**: W. F. Fullam to the Secretary of the Navy, State Department, "Re: Complaint of Mexican Ambassador, File of Radiograms," 18.

121 **The first reports were published**: "American Gunboat Takes Hun Raider Off Mexican Coast," *San Diego Union*, March 23, 1918, 1; "Women on German Raider Seized at Sea by U.S. Ship," *San Diego Evening Tribune*, March 23, 1918, 1.

122 **Another announced that**: *Hawaiian Gazette*, April 2, 1918, 6.

122 **Joseph Mesmer was questioned**: Report by V. W. Killick, "Re: Ship Alexander Agassiz," March 23, 1918, 43.

123 **Wheeler contended that**: *Hawaiian Gazette*, April 2, 1918, 6.

123 **Edward Gripper, the "Chinese Inspector"**: Report by C. L. Keep, "In Re: Ship Alexander Agassiz," April 6, 1918, NARA, M1085, BI Files, Old German Files, Case No. 170046, 20.

123 **William Black, the dredge watchman**: Report by David Ross, "In Re: Arthur Martens, on Board Alexander Agassiz, German Raider," April 9, 1918, NARA, M1085, BI Files, Old German Files, Case No. 174275, 1.

124 **Judge Brown, the postmaster**: Report by W. A. Weymouth, "In Re: Richard Charles Brandt, German Activities," NARA, M1085, BI Files, Old German Files, Roll 602, Case No. 197038, 1.

124 **The crew of the *Alexander Agassiz***: "Prize Court to Begin Trial Tomorrow," *San Diego Evening Tribune*, March 29, 1918, 7; "Woman Is First Witness to Be Called," *San Diego Evening Tribune*, March 30, 1918, 14.

124 **The *Agassiz* was moored**: "Lieutenant Cushman Will Head Prize Court on Agassiz," *San Diego Union*, March 30, 1918, 5.

124 **The status of the *Alexander Agassiz***: "Hun Raider with Prisoners Aboard Convoyed to Port by U.S. Warship," *San Diego Union*, March 28, 1918, 5.

125 **In Mazatlán, the German authorities**: "Extract from report of Commanding Officer of USS Yorktown, Subject: Military Operations," April 9, 1918, NARA, RG59, Neutrality, M367, Roll 0184, Document No. 763.72111m57/45 (file date: March 26, 1918).

125 **The blow was softened**: Report of Commanding Officer of USS *Brutus* to Commander Pacific Fleet Division 2, Subject: Additional Report on Conditions–Mazatlán, March 26, 1918, NARA, RG59, Neutrality, M367, Roll 0184, Document No. 763.72111m57/45 (file date: March 26, 1918).

7. "THE GERMANS ARE AFTER YOU"

127 **Señor Arzak had recently added**: Report from W. E. Chapman to the Secretary of State, "Re: Naval Report on Conditions at Mazatlán," April 1, 1918, NARA, RG59, Neutrality, M367, Roll 0184, Document No. 763.72111m57/58 (file date: April 1, 1918).

127 **The Germans had offered**: W. F. Fullam to the Secretary of the Navy, State Department, "Re: Complaint of Mexican Ambassador, File of Radiograms," 27.

128 **A report by Lieutenant I. M. Graham**: Report by Lieutenant I. M. Graham U.S. Navy to Commander Division 2 Pacific Fleet, "Subject: Comments on Mexican

Gunboat Morelos," March 22, 1918, NARA, RG59, Neutrality, M367, Roll 0184, Document No. 763.72111m57/10 (file date: April 4, 1918).

128 **Lieutenant Commander E. J. Minister**: Report of Commanding Officer of USS *Brutus* to Commander Pacific Fleet Division 2, Subject: Additional Report on Conditions—Mazatlán.

129 **There would soon be submarines**: Altendorf, "U.S. Agent Foils Carranza Plot," 1.

129 **It was up to me individually**: Altendorf, "U.S. Agent Foils Carranza Plot," 1.

130 **When Altendorf returned**: Altendorf, "U.S. Agent Foils Carranza Plot," 20.

130 **On March 24, Altendorf entered**: Altendorf, "U.S. Agent Foils Carranza Plot," 20.

131 **The next day Altendorf discovered**: Altendorf, "U.S. Agent Foils Carranza Plot," 20.

131 **The following information**: "Extract from the Report of the Commanding Officer of the USS Brutus on Conditions of Mexican Coast between Salinas Cruz and Mazatlán Inclusive," April 30, 1918, NARA, RG59, Neutrality, M367, Roll 0184, Document No. 763.72111m57/45 (file date: March 28, 1918).

132 **Thereupon Arzak protested**: Altendorf, "U.S. Agent Foils Carranza Plot," 20.

133 **Consul Chapman supplied the vessel**: Report from C. P. Snyder to the Secretary of the Navy (Operations), "Report of Commander Snyder on the Cruise of the Oregon from May 5th to May 8th 1918," May 22, 1918, NARA, RG59, Neutrality, M367, Roll 0184, Document No. 763.72111m57/63 (file date: March 22, 1918). (In 1920, the *Morelos* returned to service in the Mexican Navy as the gunboat *Blanquet*. It was decommissioned five years later.)

133 **It did not take a great deal**: Information on Altendorf's investigation of German submarine base from Paul Bernardo Altendorf, "U.S. Agent Finds 14 Shiploads Munitions Interned by Mexico Ready for German Thrust at U.S.," *El Paso Herald*, December 1, 1919, 1, 9.

135 **When two of the agents**: Information on Altendorf's investigation of Karl Jacobson from Paul Bernardo Altendorf, "U.S. Agent on Mexico Discovers Spaniard Engaged by the Germans to Come to U.S. and Poison Cattle," *El Paso Herald*, December 2, 1919, 10.

136 **Another dangerous character**: Information on Altendorf's investigation of Salvary from Altendorf, "U.S. Agent on Mexico Discovers Spaniard," 10.

137 **"Within weeks, the first symptoms"**: Bill Mills, *The League: The True Story of Average Americans on the Hunt for WW1 Spies* (New York: Skyhorse, 2013), 49.

137 **Military Intelligence believed**: Information on Altendorf's mission to Tepic in search of a German radio station from Paul Bernardo Altendorf, "Germans Hold American in Mexico for Ransom as Bandits Get Blame," *El Paso Herald*, December 3, 1919, 1, 5; Paul Bernardo Altendorf, "U.S. Agent Learns Germans Incited Mexicans to Kill Americans, Saying Mexico Was at War with the U.S.," *El Paso Herald*, December 4, 1919, 1.

139 **"The Germans are after you"**: Information on Altendorf's escape from Mexico from Altendorf, "U.S. Agent Learns Germans Incited Mexicans," 1, 8; Paul Bernardo Altendorf, "U.S. Agent in Mexico, with Reward on His Head, Eludes His Pursuers; Finds Himself Betrayed at Border," *El Paso Herald*, December 5, 1919, 1, 13.

145 **He was met by Captain Lipscomb**: Letter from A. J. Milliken, Inspector in Charge, to the Supervising Inspector, Immigration Service, July 12, 1918, NARA, RG165, Records of the War Department and Special Staffs, Military Intelligence Division Correspondence 1917–1941, File 41–161 to 51–57, Box 39, 1.

145 **"it was not necessary"**: Letter from A. J. Milliken, Inspector in Charge, to the Supervising Inspector, Immigration Service, July 12, 1918, 2.

145 **Lipscomb gave him**: U.S. Department of Labor Immigration Service Alien Arrival Form for Paul Altendorf, Mexican Border District, Nogales, Arizona, June 20, 1918, NARA Records of the Immigration and Naturalization Service, RG85, M1769, Index and Manifests of Alien Arrivals at Nogales, Arizona, July 1905–1952.

8. UNITED STATES VS. *ALEXANDER AGASSIZ*

147 **The preliminary hearings**: Background information on the *Alexander Agassiz* prize court trial procedures from Certification of the prize court trial proceedings sent by William Andrews and W. R. Cushman to Judge Bledsoe, April 19, 1918, Prize Court Trial, Civil Law Case–622–636, Folder Title 624, Box 59.

148 **The first person to be called**: Testimony of Cornelius Heintz from Heintz, "Prize Court Deposition," 1–20.

151 **The following morning Maude Lochrane**: Testimony of Maude Lochrane from Lochrane, "Prize Court Deposition," 1–23.

154 **The first to be called to the stand**: Testimony of Madden (Arthur Martens) from Martens, "Prize Court Deposition," 1–18.

155 **"I think Mr. Heintz told me"**: Testimony of Frank Volpert from Volpert, "Prize Court Deposition," 1–13.

156 **"I was not a member"**: Testimony of Richard Brandt from Brandt, "Prize Court Deposition," 1–19.

156 **"I had known the vessel"**: Testimony of Hendrik Koppalla from Koppalla, "Prize Court Deposition," 1–12.

157 **"I was one of the crew"**: Testimony of Charles Boston from Boston, "Prize Court Deposition," 1–22.

158 **"The capture was made"**: Testimony of Lt. Charles Edwin Reordan from Reordan, "Prize Court Deposition," 1–13.

159 **Lieutenant Reordan left**: Testimony of Lt. Frederick W. Dorr from Dorr, "Prize Court Deposition," 1–9.

160 **Dorr stepped down**: Testimony of paymaster Ewin Y. Armstrong from Armstrong, "Prize Court Deposition," 1–9.

161 **They went to Moore's:** Information on alleged "disloyal" statements made by Maude Lochrane at Moore's Restaurant from Report by W. H. Buck, "In Re: Power Boat Alexander Agassiz German Raider," April 16, 1918, NARA, M1085, BI Files, Old German Files, Roll 568, Case No. 170046, 11, 12.

162 **Public sentiment had hardened:** Information on "disloyalty" in America during World War 1 from Mills, *The League*, 157–65.

162 **"during time of war":** Mills, *The League*, 157–65.

163 **Judge Charles H. Burch set her bail:** "Maude Lochrane Faces Grave Charge," *San Diego Evening Tribune*, April 8, 1918, 3.

163 **I can't begin to tell:** "Woman Pirate Tells Story of Her Life," *Daily Twin Falls Times*, April 23, 1918, 6.

164 **A public notice regarding:** Publisher's affidavit, April 9, 1918, Prize Court Trial, Civil Law Case–622–636, Folder Title 624, Box 59; Claims by Klauber Wangenheim & Co., H. A. Macintosh, and the Regents of the University of California, Prize Court Trial, Civil Law Case–622–636, Folder Title 624, Box 59.

164 **"the vessel was so captured":** Letter from Franklin D. Roosevelt to the Secretary of State, April 17, 1918, NARA, RG59, Neutrality, M367, Roll 0184, Document No. 763.72111m57/19.

165 **On May 4, District Attorney:** District Attorney Robert O'Connor's summary presentation from "Points and Authorities of Government for Condemnation," undated, Prize Court Trial, Civil Law Case–622–636, Folder Title 624, Box 59, 1–19.

166 **Maude Lochrane's attorney:** Mr. Black's response on behalf of Maude Lochrane to the government's claims from "Memorandum of Facts and Authorities in Behalf of Maude M. Lochrane," undated, Prize Court Trial, Civil Law Case–622–636, Folder Title 624, Box 59, 1–4.

168 **With Black's concluding statement:** Judge Bledsoe's opinion from "Opinion of the Court," July 15, 1918, Prize Court Trial, Civil Law Case–622–636, Folder Title 624, Box 59, 1–4.

9. GOING FOR BROKE

173 **In Mazatlán, reports of:** "Extract from Report of Commanding Officer of USS Yorktown, Subject: Military Operations," April 9, 1918, NARA, RG59, Neutrality, M367, Roll 0184, Document No. 763.72111m57/45 (file date: March 26, 1918).

173 **the Enemy Trading List (the "blacklist"):** *War Trade Board Journal, No. 21–May 1919* (Washington DC: Government Printing Office 1919), 36.

174 **The partners expressed their belief:** *Melchers Sucs Mazatlán 1846–1921*, 81.

174 **But the decade of the 1920s:** U.S. Department of Commerce, *Mexican West Coast and Lower California, A Commercial and Industrial Survey* (Washington DC: Government Printing Office, 1923), 267–69.

175 **The financial outlook brightened**: "Agassiz Again Plows the Briny," *San Diego Evening Tribune*, July 22, 1918, 5.

175 **In desperation, Maude hatched**: Information on the *Alexander Agassiz* sealing expedition from "Woman Skipper Meets More Trouble," *San Diego Evening Tribune*, February 6, 1919, 1; "Woman Skipper Once More Has Command," *San Diego Evening Tribune*, June 24, 1919, 1; "Miss Lochrane Gets Possession of Vessel Again," *San Bernardino Daily Sun*, June 25, 1919, 6.

176 **When the *Alexander Agassiz* came up**: Information on the purchase of the *Alexander Agassiz* by Joseph Mesmer at auction from "Historic Launch Sold by U.S. Marshal," *San Diego Evening Tribune*, May 25, 1920, 22.

176 **On April 5, 1918, Heintz registered**: Draft Registration Card for Cornelius Heintz, dated April 5, 1918, Precinct 403, Los Angeles, California, NARA, World War I Selective Service Sysem Draft Cards, M1509, Roll 1530899, Draft Board 17, Los Angeles.

176 **In the years after the fateful voyage**: Postscript information on Cornelius Heintz from "Obituary for 'Cornelius Heintz Sr.,'" *Los Angeles Times*, June 21, 1958, 28.

177 **In the decades that followed**: Postscript information on Charles Edwin Reordan from "Capt. Reordan Dies; 'Tennessee' Skipper during Pearl Harbor," *Sunday Star* (Washington DC), March 22, 1947, A-5; "Naval Officer in Civilian Garb, Straw Hat Directed Warship at Pearl Harbor," *Morning World-Herald* (Omaha NE), April 12, 1944, 18; *United States Navy Cruise Book 1941–1945*, Ship BB-43 USS Tennessee (publisher unknown), 11–17; "Wore 'Civvies' on Battleship," *The Milwaukee Journal* (WI), April 14, 1944, 18.

177 **"a mass of flaming oil"**: *United States Navy Cruise Book 1941–1945*, 12.

178 **After his harrowing escape**: Information on Altendorf's appearance at the trial of Lothar Witzke from Landau, *The Enemy Within*, 126–28.

179 **"With eyes flashing fire"**: Landau, *The Enemy Within*, 185.

179 **"look around and see what you can do"**: Paul Bernardo Altendorf, "U.S. Agent in San Antonio Traps Austrian with Scheme to Destroy Whole Armies with Disease Germs," *El Paso Herald*, December 6, 1919, 1.

179 **Altendorf's superiors attempted to retain**: Memorandum from Captain H. S. Dickey to Director of Military Intelligence Division, "Subject: Paul Bernardo Altendorf–Informant A-1," November 6, 1918, NARA, RG165, Records of the War Department and Special Staffs, Military Intelligence Division, File 51-45; Memorandum from Colonel J. M. Dunn to Mr. R. W. Flournoy, Chief, Division of Passport Control, December 13, 1918, NARA, RG165, Records of the War Department and Special Staffs, Military Intelligence Division, File 51-45.

179 **Brigadier General J. A. Ryan stated**: Letter from General J. A. Ryan, addressed "To Whom It May Concern," October 23, 1918, NARA, RG165, Records of the War Department and Special Staffs, Military Intelligence Division, File 51-45.

180 **Major Barnes confirmed**: Letter from Major R. L. Barnes, addressed "To Whom It May Concern," April 7, 1919, NARA, RG165, Records of the War Department and Special Staffs, Military Intelligence Division, File 51–45.

180 **The division superintendent**: Letter from C. E. Breniman, addressed "To Whom It May Concern," October 26, 1918, NARA, RG165, Records of the War Department and Special Staffs, Military Intelligence Division, File 51–45.

180 **Breniman recommended Altendorf**: Report by P. W. Lamb, Bureau of Investigation, "In Re: Paul Bernardo Altendorf–Information for the San Antonio Office," July 16, 1921, NARA, RG59, Records of the State Department 1910–1929, 811.108/1152 to 811.108 F11/1, 7370.

181 **But when pressed for approval**: Letter from Marlborough Churchill to Alexander B. Coxe, September 9, 1920, NARA, RG165, Records of the War Department and Special Staffs, Military Intelligence Division, File 51–45.

181 **The former spy was invited**: "Here with Big Price on Head," *Los Angeles Times*, February 7, 1920, 1.

181 **Since 1914 I have been**: *Investigation of Mexican Affairs: Preliminary Report and Hearings of the Committee on Foreign Relations United States Senate Pursuant to S. Res. 106*, 463–64.

182 **After being sworn in**: *Investigation of Mexican Affairs*, 1229–31.

182 **Dr. Altendorf returned to Mexico**: Information on Altendorf's return to Mexico and escape to the U.S. from "Statement Dictated by P. B. Altendorf at San Antonio, Tex., on September 8, 1920, Relative to His Journey to the City of Mexico, His Imprisonment while There, and His Re-entry into the United States," NARA, RG59, General Records of the Department of State, Office of the Counselor/Under Secretary and Chief Special Agent, General Records 1916–1928, 812.0–651 / 812.0–739, Entry 535 Box 81; Memorandum from W. A. Wiseman titled "Dr. Paul B. Altendorf—Mexican Matter," August 20, 1920, NARA, M1085, Investigative Reports of the Bureau of Investigation 1908–1922, Roll: boi_german_257-850_0103, Old German File 1909–1921, Case No. 8000–233186, Roll 645, 77.

188 **the San Antonio Grand Jury decided**: Telegram from Special Agent in Charge Louis DeNette to Chief, Bureau of Investigation, January 18, 1921, NARA, RG59, Records of the State Department 1910–1929, 811.108/1152 to 811.108 F11/1, 7370.

188 **Shortly before noon on September 16, 1920**: Information on the 1920 Wall Street bomb explosion from "Wall Street Disaster Caused by Time Bomb According to Experts," *Dallas Morning News*, September 17, 1920, 1, 3; "Bomb Caused It," *Kansas City Star*, September 17, 1920, 2, 1; "31 Killed, 225 Injured in Wall Street Explosion," *Anaconda Standard* (MT), September 17, 1920, 8, 1; "See Bomb Plot in New York Explosion," *Miami Herald*, September 17, 1920, 1, 2.

188 **In a mailbox located**: "'Reds' Responsible for Blast, First Tangible Clue Is Obtained in Metropolis Explosion which Caused 35 Deaths and Hurt 300," *Albuquerque Journal*, September 18, 1920, 1, 3.

189 **Investigations into the Wall Street bombing**: Beverly Gage, *The Day Wall Street Exploded* (New York: Oxford University Press, 2009), 141–44.

189 **"We have evidence to prove"**: "Wall Street Disaster Caused by Time Bomb," 1

189 **would pay a $50,000 reward**: "Big Reward for Solving Bomb Blast," *San Diego Evening Tribune*, November 23, 1920, 9.

189 **One of his chief sources**: "Wall Street Bomb Plot Cleared with Arrest in Poland," *Evening Star* (Washington DC), December 17, 1921, 1; "Capture of Wall Street Bomber Result of 15 Months Still Hunt by Burns' Men," *Duluth News-Tribune* (MN), December 18, 1921, 1.

190 **Three weeks before the Wall Street**: "Capture of Wall Street Bomber Result of 15 Months Still Hunt," 1.

190 **In March 1921, Burns entrusted**: "Warsaw Arrest of Lindenfeld Puts Clever 'Red' Agitator and 'Double-Crosser' in Toils," *Fort Worth Star-Telegram*, December 22, 1921, 9.

190 **A month after Altendorf swam**: Report by P. W. Lamb, Bureau of Investigation, "In Re: Paul Bernardo Altendorf–Information for the San Antonio Office," July 16, 1921, NARA, RG59, Records of the State Department 1910–1929, 811.108/1152 to 811.108 F11/1, 7370.

191 **On his return to New York**: Memorandum for file from J. Edgar Hoover, July 19, 1921, NARA, RG59, Records of the State Department, central decimal file 1910–1929, decimal 811.108 A1 72/2.

191 **When he was detained**: Memorandum from Benjamin Thaw Jr., Secretary of Legation to W. L. Hurley, August 13, 1921, NARA, RG59, Records of the State Department 1910–1929, 811.108/1152 to 811.108 F11/1, 7370.

191 **The Polish inquiry resulted**: Memorandum from Benjamin Thaw Jr., Secretary of Legation to W. L. Hurley, August 13, 1921.

192 **Growing increasingly frustrated**: Letter from William L. Hurley to Richard E. Pennoyer, American Commission Berlin, October 6, 1921 NARA, RG59, Records of the State Department 1910–1929, 811.108/115 to 811.108 F11/1, 7370.

192 **Lindenfeld turned state's evidence**: "Held for Hand on Wall Street Bomb Horror," *Boston Herald*, December 17, 1921, 1.

192 **Altendorf was hailed as a hero**: "U.S. Agent, Nemesis of German Plotters, Caught Wall Street Bombers," *New York Evening Telegram*, December 18, 1921, 7.

192 **The news seemed too good**: "To Sift Linde's Story of Bomb," *Springfield Daily News* (MA), May 9, 1922, 10. No one was ever tried for the Wall Street bombing, but it is widely believed to have been carried out by confederates of an Italian anarchist named Luigi Galleani, possibly in reprisal for the indictment of anarchists Nicola Sacco and Bartolomeo Vanzetti five days earlier.

193 **By the late 1920s**: Letter from Lieutenant-Colonel Vaughn M. Cooper to Major James C. Schwenck, American Embassy Havana Cuba, November 25, 1928, NARA, RG165, Records of the War Department and Special Staffs, Military Intelligence Division, File 51–45.

193 **"Altendorf is an adventurer"**: Letter from Marlborough Churchill to Alexander B. Coxe, September 9, 1920, NARA, RG165, Records of the War Department and Special Staffs, Military Intelligence Division, File 51–45.

194 **As the *Alexander Agassiz* cruised closer**: Information on the loss of the *Alexander Agassiz* in Drake's Bay from "Power Schooner Beached in Fog Alexander Agassiz Goes Ashore in Drake's Bay," *San Francisco Chronicle*, November 21, 1920, 58; "Schooner Ashore," *San Diego Union*, November 21, 1920, 17; "Boat Is Wrecked," *Los Angeles Times*, August 13, 1920, 28.

REFERENCES

Annual Report of the Board of Harbor Commissioners of the City of Los Angeles. Los Angeles: The Board of Harbor Commissioners of the City of Los Angeles California 1917.

Annual Report of the President of the University on Behalf of the Regents to His Excellency the Governor of the State 1916–1917. Berkeley: University of California Press, 1917.

Atkin, Ronald. *Revolution! Mexico 1910–1920*. New York: John Day, 1970.

Beaton, Welford. *Frank Waterhouse & Company's Pacific Ports: A Commercial Geography*. Seattle: Terminal, 1917.

Biennial Report of the President of the University on Behalf of the Regents to His Excellency the Governor of the State 1910–1912. Berkeley: University of California Press, 1912.

Chatterton, E. Keble. *The Sea Raiders*. London: Hurst and Blackett, 1931.

Detroit City Directory 1903. Detroit: R. L. Polk, 1903.

Doménech, J. Figueroa. *Guía General Descriptiva de la República Mexicana*. Mexico: Estados y Territorios Federales, 1899.

El Paso City Directory (Worley's Directory of El Paso) 1910, 1911, and 1912. El Paso: John F. Worley Directory Company.

Gage, Beverly. *The Day Wall Street Exploded*. New York: Oxford University Press, 2009.

Guilliatt, Richard, and Peter Hohnen. *The Wolf*. New York: Simon and Schuster, 2010.

Guinn, James Miller. *A History of California and an Extended History of Los Angeles and Environs, Biographical Volume III*. Los Angeles: Historic Record Company, 1915.

Investigation of Mexican Affairs: Preliminary Report and Hearings of the Committee on Foreign Relations United States Senate Persuant to S. Res. 106. Washington DC: Government Printing Office, 1920.

Jones, John Price. *The German Spy in America*. London: Hutchinson, 1917.

Klein, J. H., Jr. *United States Naval Institute Proceedings, the Career of the Mexican Gunboat Tampico*. Annapolis MD: The United States Naval Institute, 1921.

Landau, Henry. *The Enemy Within*. New York: G. P. Putnam's Sons, 1937.

Los Angeles City Directory 1915. Los Angeles: Los Angeles Directory Company, 1915

Martinez, C. G. Marciano Valdez, and Raymundo Bautista Contreras. *Héroes y Próceres del Ejercito, Fuerza Aerea y Armada de Mexico*. Mexico City: Secretariat of National Defense and Secretary of the Mexican Navy, 2011.

Melchers Sucs Mazatlán 1946–1921 [corporate history published to commemorate the company's 75th anniversary]. Mazatlán: Casa Melchers Sucs, 1921.

Mexican and Central American Pilotage, Pacific Coast, 5th Edition. Washington DC: U.S. Hydrographic Office, 1918.

Mexican West Coast and Lower California, A Commercial and Industrial Survey. Washington DC: Government Printing Office, 1923.

Mills, Bill. *The League: The True Story of Average Americans on the Hunt for WW1 Spies*. New York: Skyhorse, 2013.

Register of the Department of State 23 December 1918. Washington DC: Government Printing Office, 1919.

San Bernardino City Directory 1906 and 1908. Los Angeles: San Bernardino Directory Company.

Second Annual Report of the United States Shipping Board, December 1, 1918. Washington DC: Government Printing Office, 1918.

Shor, Elizabeth N. "How Scripps Institution Came to San Diego." *San Diego Historical Quarterly* 27, no. 3 (Summer 1981): 1–6.

Toland, John. *No Man's Land*. New York: Ballantine Books, 1980.

Trading with the Enemy. New York: Guaranty Trust Company of New York, 1917.

Trading with the Enemy, Enemy Trading List. Washington DC: War Trade Board, 1917.

The United States Naval Medical Bulletin, 1915 v.9. Washington DC: U.S. Government Printing Office, 1915.

United States Navy Cruise Book 1941–1945, Ship BB-43 USS Tennessee. Publisher unknown.

van der Vat, Dan. *Gentlemen of War: The Amazing Story of Karl von Muller and the SMS Emden*. New York: William Morrow, 1983.

Von Menz, Brigida, Verena Radkau, Beatriz Scharrer, and Guillermo Turner. *Los Pioneros del Imperialismo Aleman en Mexico*. Tlalpan, Mexico: Ediciones de la casa chata, 1982.

War Trade Board Journal, No. 21—May 1919. Washington DC: Government Printing Office, 1919.